TENTH EDITION

OFF THE BEATEN PATH® WISCONSIN

A GUIDE TO UNIQUE PLACES

MARTIN HINTZ with **PAM PERCY**

gpp®

travel

Guilford, Connecticut

All the information in this guidebook is subject to change. We recommend that you call ahead to obtain current information before traveling.

To buy books in quantity for corporate use or incentives, call **(800) 962-0973** or e-mail **premiums@GlobePequot.com.**

Editor: Kevin Sirois
Project Editor: Heather Santiago
Layout: Joanna Beyer
Text design: Linda R. Loiewski
Maps: Equator Graphics © Morris Book Publishing, LLC

ISSN 1540-2134
ISBN 978-0-7627-7959-8

Printed in the United States of America
10 9 8 7 6 5 4 3 2 1

OFF THE BEATEN PATH®
WISCONSIN ➔

Help Us Keep This Guide Up to Date

We would love to hear from you concerning your experiences with this guide and how you feel it could be improved and kept up to date. Please send your comments and suggestions to:

editorial@GlobePequot.com

Thanks for your input, and happy travels!

To the family, travelers all

Contents

Introduction xi

Western Wisconsin 1

Central Wisconsin 45

Northern Wisconsin 79

Eastern Wisconsin 119

Milwaukee & Environs 169

Index 191

About the Authors

Martin Hintz, a past president of the Society of American Travel Writers and former chairman of its Freelance Council, has been a travel writer for more than three decades. Hintz has some 100 books to his credit, some of which are other travel-related volumes published by Globe Pequot Press. He has written hundreds of magazine and newspaper articles and also publishes *The Irish American Post,* an international online news magazine (www.irishameri-canpost.com), and is director of the Mountjoy Writers Group, an international news syndicate. In addition to his wife, Pam Percy, sons Daniel and Stephen and daughter Kate have collaborated with him on writing projects.

Pam Percy has written *The Complete Chicken,* a coffee table art book about chickens, and *The Field Guide to Chickens.* In addition to working on *Wisconsin Off the Beaten Path,* Percy collaborated with Hintz on *Wisconsin Cheese: A Cookbook and Guide to the Cheeses of Wisconsin* (Globe Pequot, 2008), which contains more than one hundred recipes utilizing award-winning Wisconsin cheese, along with information about serving cheese and the Dairy State's cheese plants, festivals, and related attractions.

Percy and Hintz raise chickens and vegetables on their farmette north of Milwaukee, selling to area restaurants, at markets, and to a lucky group of select customers.

Acknowledgments

Special gratitude to all our friends throughout Wisconsin who helped with this book, especially Andy Larsen and Gary Knowles, plus Lisa Marshall and the staff of the Wisconsin Division of Tourism. Visitor bureaus, historical societies, and local information offices around the state were particularly helpful as well. The people of Wisconsin themselves also deserve rousing applause, from the guy who told us where to find the best pie in his hometown to the volunteer at the local historical site.

Introduction

Wisconsin is a state of imagery: cows, woods, beer, fish.

Sure enough.

But the state has a lot more to offer. For instance, think of Wisconsin in superlatives: It has the world's largest four-sided clock, the biggest penny, and most massive loon. It offers a giant, 5-story leaping muskie in whose massive mouth avid fisherfolk can even be married. The state cradles the nation's most comprehensive collection of works by beloved artist Norman Rockwell and the world's largest carousel. The country's only whooping crane preserve is in Wisconsin, and so is a record-size black bear. The cranes are alive and flopping. The bear is stuffed.

Wisconsin is a place for doing and seeing. It hosts regattas, ice fishing competitions, one-act play festivals, and Civil War reenactments.

There are lead mines, cornfields, and superconductors. There are ship manufacturers, goats on top of restaurants, and milk-carton raft races. One city boasts of its own submarine; another hosts the world's busiest airstrip during a summertime fly-in of experimental and private aircraft.

Wisconsin is a state tailor-made for off-the-beaten-path adventures. You can discover some of the secrets in a corridor of Madison's stately Capitol Building, on the rocky tip of foggy Door County, in a pine-scented North Woods glade, on a narrow Milwaukee side street.

Wisconsin Off the Beaten Path ranges from urban to rural and back again. Pam and I hope that this book will lighten your travel planning, heighten your sensibilities, and increase your fun.

The enthusiastic explorer can use this poke-along guide to uncover secluded hideaways as well as to discover hints about getting around the more well-known tourist attractions.

Care has been taken to ensure accuracy as much as possible. Over time, however, ticket prices, phone numbers, and hours of operation may change; establishments may close for one reason or another; and personnel may move on. Subsequently, there may be a few discrepancies in this edition that will have to wait for the next update. So please be patient and let the publisher know of any necessary adjustments, because you, as reader, can also be a great scout. Who knows what neat new Wisconsin discoveries you will find to share with other readers!

On your journeys, always, *always* remember to verify lodging arrangements before arrival. It pays to call ahead. Even that most off-the-beaten-path bed-and-breakfast could be booked the night you wish to register.

Resident admission stickers for Wisconsin state parks cost $25 annually, $7 daily, and $5 for 1 hour. For resident senior citizens (65 and older), stickers are $10 annually and $3 daily. For nonresidents the cost is $35 annually, $10 daily, and $5 for 1 hour. Stickers are required on all motor vehicles entering and stopping in state parks. They can be purchased at the parks, at local Department of Natural Resources (DNR) offices, or by writing the DNR, Bureau of Parks and Recreation, Box 7921, Madison 53707-7921 (608-266-2181 or 888-947-2757; www.dnr.state.wi.us). Half-price annual tickets are available for additional vehicles in a resident family.

One thing you'll notice as you journey through the state is that Wisconsinites have a way with slogans and nicknames. Almost every city, town, and hamlet has a booster phrase posted along the roads leading to Main Street. Abbotsford brags about being "Wisconsin's First City." Albany is the "Sweetest Village on the Sugar River." You can pedal like crazy in Brodhead, "the Bicycle Gateway to Wisconsin" or in Sparta, which is the "Bicycling Capital of America." Be sure to shake hands in Cumberland, "Famous for Friendliness," and in Middleton because it's the "Good Neighbor City." Don't stop now, because Marion is "Where Strangers Are Friends We'd Like to Meet," and "You're Always Welcome" in Holmen. You'll never get away from Monroe because "We Bring You Back." Yet don't forget that Frederic is "A Beautiful Place to Visit, A Great Place to Live."

You'll have to come to the state to find who is "Tops in Wisconsin," "the Gem City," and "Home of the World's Largest Sauerkraut Plant."

Wisconsin is also the capital of self-proclaimed "capitals." Almost every community worth its civic salt has given itself some municipal distinction. Onalaska is the Sunfish Capital. Birchwood is the Bluegill Capital. Algoma is the Trout and Salmon Capital. Bayfield is the Lake Trout Capital. And a fierce battle to retain the Walleye Capital tag is constantly being waged by Presque Isle, Stone Lake, and Long Lake (depends on the size and amount of the annual sportfishing catch, and, by the way, it takes an average of 100 hours to catch a 33.4-inch muskie). With all these titles, don't think that there's something fishy about Wisconsin. After all, Sheboygan is the Bratwurst Capital. Racine is the Kringle Capital. Green Bay is the Toilet Paper Capital (because of its paper products industry). Bloomer is the Rope Jumping Capital. Monroe is the Swiss Cheese Capital. Elmwood and Belleville each claim to be the UFO Capital of the World.

Consequently, it's quite obvious that visiting Wisconsin is a capital idea, whether we're on or off the beaten path. But much of the fun in Wisconsin comes in discovery, in finding the little known and the really unexpected. You can find that out for yourself.

Restaurant cost categories refer to the price of entrees without beverages, desserts, taxes, and tips. Those listed as inexpensive are $10 or less; moderate, between $10 and $15; and expensive, $20 and over. Places to stay listed as inexpensive are up to $100 per night; moderate, $100 to $200 per night; and expensive, $200 and up per night.

For More Information

There's a lot of help available for planning an off-the-beaten-path expedition After all, any state that hosts the US Watermelon Seed Spitting Championships has to have a lot of affable neighborliness going for it and a lot of fun and interesting events and attractions for you to enjoy. Plus Wisconsin offers plenty of helping finding all this fun.

INFORMATION CENTERS

Wisconsin has seven year-round centers at its borders with Illinois, Iowa, and Minnesota. You may wish to pull into any one of them for a driving break and to browse through brochure racks, check on maps, and discover what's going on in nearby communities. Bathrooms are readily accessible.

Open all year are facilities at Beloit (I-39/90, Rest Area 22); Kenosha (I-94, Rest Area 26); La Crosse (I-90, Rest Area 31); Marinette (on Bridge Street at the Menominee River crossing); Platteville (275 W. Business Hwy. 151); Prairie du Chien (at the Highway 18 bridge) and Superior (Highway 53 and Harborview Parkway). Hours vary by season and can be found on www .travelwisconsin.com.

For the convenience of travelers, the state has 32 year-round, heated toilet stops along major highways and 163 primitive sites. The latter are closed in the off-season, so plan to accommodate your carload of kids accordingly. Look for the red triangle on state road maps for locations.

Aside from being functional, most of the sites offer the bonus of exceptional views of the countryside. One of the best is about 5 miles west of Fennimore on Highway 18. On both sides of the road, deep valleys roll toward the horizon. Currier & Ives farmsteads dot the oak-shrouded hills, their red barns and white houses dappling the scenery. A tired traveler can lie on a sun-drenched summer hillside there and count clouds before meandering eastward toward Madison or west toward the Mississippi River. Unfortunately, area bathrooms are among those locked in the winter, although the access road is plowed. I've always wanted to stop there on our holiday trips to see Iowa relatives, but for one reason or another, we've always had to forgo the thrill of swooshing down the steep hillsides.

HISTORICAL MARKERS & RUSTIC ROADS

Historical sites abound in Wisconsin. There's the usual selection of baronial mansions, rough-hewn pioneer settlements, and George-Washington-slept-here sorts of places—not that the famous Founding Father ever actually visited Wisconsin according to anyone's tall tale, but many other presidents and other notables have stopped by since then, either simply to say hello or to do some fishing.

Don't whiz past the numerous historical markers scattered along Wisconsin's highways. Nobody has ever kept an accurate total of the state, county, and local signposts, but 3,000 is a conservative estimate. They'll tell you of famous personalities, famous fires, famous floods, famous Native American battles, and famous industries. Roadway signs about 0.5 mile before each marker alert motorists that such a monument is just down the pike.

One prime way to wander Wisconsin is to follow any of the 50 officially designated paved or gravel Rustic Roads at key points around the state. The program started in 1973, with the first designation made in 1975. The roadways range from 2.5 to 37 miles long and are marked by easily identifiable brown-and-yellow signs that are highlighted by an outline of the state's boundaries to indicate the appropriate routes.

For a free map and brochure telling about these "less-traveled roads," write to the **Wisconsin Department of Tourism,** 201 W. Washington Ave., PO Box 8690, Madison 53708-8690, or call (800) 432-8747 or (608) 266-2161, or visit www.travelwisconsin.com.

The Department of Transportation, which puts together the Rustic Roads guides, has added several online. They are available at www.dot.wisconsin .gov/travel/scenic/rusticroads.htm.

To have one of its byways so designated, a community or county submits an application to the board, which reviews the proposal and determines if it fits the following criteria: The road should have outstanding natural attributes, such as native vegetation, scenic vistas, or historical significance; it should be lightly traveled; no widening or other improvement can be scheduled to detract from the original condition of the road upon application; and the road should be at least 2 miles long.

TRAVEL INFORMATION BUREAUS & CONTACTS

For the latest general information on the state's travel scene, contact the **Wisconsin Department of Tourism,** 201 W. Washington Ave., PO Box 8690, Madison 53708-8690 (608-266-2161 or 800-432-8747; www.travelwisconsin.com).

Bureaus for the state's primary tourism regions can provide details about specific areas, so write or call:

- **_Visit Milwaukee,_** 648 N. Plankinton Ave., Suite 425, Milwaukee 53203-2917 (414-273-3950 or 800-231-0903; www.visitmilwaukee.org).

- **_Wisconsin Indian Head Country,_** Box 628, Chetek 54728 (715-924-2970 or 800-472-6654; www.wisconsinindianhead.org).

For information about specific lodgings, attractions, or parks, contact:

- **_Wisconsin Association of Campground Owners (WACO),_** Box 130, Galesville 54630 (608-582-2092 or 800-843-1821; www.wisconsincamp grounds.com). To receive a directory of the 154 WACO members, send $2 to cover postage. Otherwise, directions are free at tourist information centers, travel shows, chambers of commerce, and campgrounds.

- **_Wisconsin Department of Natural Resources,_** Bureau of Parks & Recreation, Box 7921, Madison 53707-7921 (608-266-2181 or 888-947-2757; www.dnr.state.wi.us).

- **_Wisconsin Historical Society,_** 816 State St., Madison 53706-1417 (608-264-6400 or 608-264-6535; www.wisconsinhistory.org).

- **_Wisconsin Innkeepers Association,_** 1025 S. Moorland Rd., Suite 200, Brookfield 53005 (262-782-2851 or 800-589-3211; www.lodging-wi.com).

- **_Wisconsin Restaurant Association,_** 2801 Fish Hatchery Rd., Madison 53713 (608-270-9950; www.wirestaurant.org).

- **_Wisconsin Society of Ornithology,_** 2022 Sherryl Ln., Waukesha 53188-3142 (262-844-8187; www.uwgb.edu/birds/wso).

- **_Wisconsin State Horse Council,_** 132A S. Ludington St., Columbus 53925 (920-623-0393; www.wisconsinstatehorsecouncil.org).

Remember that most communities have a chamber of commerce or tourist office eager to help with drop-in requests. They'll load you down with printed material or describe the best place in town for pecan pie. Or simply stop in at the corner pub, ask at the local gas station, or inquire of a passerby. Most likely, you'll get some friendly suggestions and lots of advice on what to see and do locally.

WISCONSIN TRAVEL PUBLICATIONS

For a look at what Wisconsin has to offer, especially in the nooks and crannies of the state, subscribe to _Wisconsin Trails._ The glossy, comprehensive magazine is published bimonthly ($24.95 a year for six issues or $4.95 per issue on the newsstand). Articles range from folksy pieces on how to bake onion-dill bread to reports on the latest bed-and-breakfast facility. I've written features for the magazine on subjects such as kringle bakers in Racine and Milwaukee's best ethnic eateries. My subsequent paunch proclaims proudly that "somebody has to do it." (For a list of other Wisconsin publications, see page xix.)

For a selection of excellent maps of the state, secure a copy of the *Wisconsin Atlas & Gazetteer* ($19.95), published by the DeLorme Mapping Company (2 DeLorme Dr., PO Box 298, Yarmouth, ME 04096; 800-561-5105; www.delorme .com). The state is broken into 81 quadrangular topographical sections, which show every bump and less-traveled path in the Badger State. There are also listings of bike routes, canoe trips, lighthouses, waterfalls, and a ton of other handy information for anyone into hard-core meandering.

Wisconsin Fast Facts

WISCONSIN TRIVIA

Although half the fun is in getting here, you may need some time fillers for the tykes in the backseat. So here are some background statistics and little details to use when, for the umpteenth time, the youngsters ask, "Are we there yet?" Have them guess these facts:

- **Population:** 5,686,986 (2010)
- **State tree:** maple
- **State bird:** robin
- **State animal:** badger
- **State fish:** muskie
- **State capital:** Madison
- **State cheese:** Colby
- **Length of Wisconsin:** 302 miles
- **Width of Wisconsin:** 291 miles
- **Annual average snowfall:** 45 inches
- **Forest area:** 14,487,000 acres

- **Lakes:** 14,927 (the largest is Lake Winnebago, at 137,708 acres)
- **Golf courses:** 463
- **Bike trails:** 10,000 miles
- **Off-road bike trails:** 155 miles
- **Camping sites:** 51,748
- **Cross-country skiing:** 20,835 miles
- **Snowmobile trails:** 22,000 miles
- **State parks:** 59
- **State trails:** 17

Had enough? Aw, how about a few more for the record? Wisconsin has 500 different types of soils; 108,000 miles of roads; 2,444 fantastic trout streams and a couple that aren't so good (those are the ones where we don't bag our limit); the Fox River flows north (one of the few in the country to do so); and Beatles recording luminary Paul McCartney owns the rights to the rousing state song, "On, Wisconsin."

CLIMATE OVERVIEW

- **Average July temperature:** 70 degrees F (21 degrees C)

- **Average January temperature:** 14 degrees F (-10 degrees C)

- **Record high temperature:** 114 degrees F (146 degrees C) at Wisconsin Dells on July 13, 1936

- **Record low temperature:** -54 degrees F (-48 degrees C) at Danbury on January 24, 1922

- **Average yearly precipitation:** 31 inches

POPULATION FIGURES

- **Population:** 5,686,986 (2010)

- **Population in 1840:** 30,945

- **Density:** 104.7 persons per square mile; the US average is 80 persons per square mile

- **Distribution:** 66 percent urban, 34 percent rural

- **Rank among states:** 18th

WISCONSIN CITIES WITH THE LARGEST POPULATIONS (2010 CENSUS)

- **Milwaukee:** 594,833

- **Madison:** 233,209

- **Green Bay:** 104,057

- **Kenosha:** 99,218

- **Racine:** 82,196

- **Appleton:** 78,0861

FAMOUS WISCONSINITES

- **Don Ameche** (1908–1993), actor

- **John Barden** (1908–1991), winner of two Nobel Prizes in physics

- **August Derleth** (1909–1971), author of more than 150 books

- **Edna Ferber** (1887–1968), best-selling novelist, Pulitzer prize winner

- **Robert M. LaFollette** (1855–1921), US senator and progressive political leader

- **Zona Gale** (1874–1938), Pulitzer prize–winning author of *Miss Lulu Bett*

- **Hamlin Garland** (1860–1938), Pulitzer prize–winning author of *Main Traveled Roads* and numerous novels

- **Eric Heiden** (1958–), five-time Olympic gold-medal winner in skating

- **Woody Herman** (1913–1987), band leader

- **Harry Houdini** (1874–1926), escape artist, magician

- **Tom Hulce** (1953–), actor

- **George F. Kennan** (1904–2005), diplomat

- **Aldo Leopold** (1886–1948), conservationist, ecologist, author

- **Liberace** (1919–1987), born Wlaziv Valentino Liberace, noted pianist and flashy showman

- **Joseph McCarthy** (1909–1957), conservative Republican US senator

- **Golda Meir** (1898–1978), Israel's first female prime minister

- **Agnes Moorehead** (1906–1974), actress

- **John Muir** (1838–1914), geologist, naturalist, author

- **John Norquist** (1949–), world's tallest (6'7") singing mayor of Swedish heritage, mayor of Milwaukee (1988–2003)

- **Patrick O'Brien** (1899–1983), actor

- **Georgia O'Keeffe** (1887–1981), noted painter

- **Les Paul** (1915–2009), musician whose guitar modifications made him world famous

- **William Rehnquist** (1924–2005), Chief Justice, US Supreme Court

- **John Ringling** (1866–1936), circus owner

- **Carl Sandburg** (1878–1967), poet, essayist, Pulitzer prize–winning author of *Abraham Lincoln: The War Years*

- **Justin Vernon** (1981–), musician, founder of the band Bon Iver

- **Gene Wilder** (1934–), actor

- **Laura Ingalls Wilder** (1867–1957), author of Little House books

- **Thornton Wilder** (1897–1975), Pulitzer prize–winning author of *Our Town*

- **Frank Lloyd Wright** (1869–1959), architect

- **Frank Zeidler** (1912–2006), historian, political activist, Socialist mayor of Milwaukee (1948–1960), Socialist candidate for president in 1976

- **David Zucker** (1947–) and **Jerry Zucker** (1950–), film producers

Wisconsin Newspapers & Other Publications

MAJOR DAILIES

Green Bay Press Gazette
435 E. Walnut
Green Bay 54307
(920) 435-4411
www.greenbaypressgazette.com

Janesville Gazette
1 S. Parker Dr.
Janesville 53547-5001
(608) 754-3311
http://gazettextra.com

Marshfield News-Herald
111 W. 3rd St.
Marshfield 54449
(715) 384-3131
www.marshfieldnewsherald.com

Milwaukee Journal-Sentinel
333 W. State St.
Milwaukee 53203
(414) 224-2000
www.jsonline.com

Oshkosh Northwestern
224 E. State St.
Oshkosh 54901
(920) 235-7700
www.thenorthwestern.com

Rhinelander Daily News
314 Courtney St.
Rhinelander 54501
(715) 365-6397
www.rhinelanderdailynews.com

Shawano Leader
1464 E. Green Bay St.
Shawano 54166
(715) 526-2121
www.shawanoleader.com

Sheboygan Press
632 Center Ave.
Sheboygan 53081
(920) 457-7711
www.sheboyganpress.com

Watertown Daily Times
113–115 W. Main St.
Watertown 53094
(920) 261-4949
www.wdtimes.com

Waukesha Freeman
801 N. Barstow
Waukesha 53187
(262) 542-2501
www.gmtoday.com/waukesha-freeman
.htm

Wausau Daily Herald
800 Scott St.
Wausau 54402
(715) 842-2101
www.wausaudailyherald.com

West Bend Daily News
100 S. 6th Ave.
West Bend 53095
(262) 306-5000
www.gmtoday.com/promotions/cust_
service/dailynews.asp

Wisconsin Rapids Daily Tribune
200 1st Ave. South
Wisconsin Rapids 54494
(715) 423-7200
www.wisconsinrapidstribune.com/

Wisconsin State Journal
1901 Fish Hatchery Rd.
Madison 53713
(608) 252-6200
http://host.madison.com/wsj

MAJOR WEEKLIES

CNI Newspapers
15700 W. Cleveland Ave.
New Berlin 53131
(262) 938-5000
www.mycommunitynow.com

ALTERNATIVE PUBLICATIONS

Madison Isthmus
101 King St.
Madison 53703
(608) 251-5627
(published on Friday)
www.thedailypage.com

Shepherd Express
207 E. Buffalo St.
Milwaukee 53202
(414) 276-2222
(published on Wednesday)
www.expressmilwaukee.com

CITY MAGAZINES

These monthlies are available at news-stands, online, and by subscription:

Key Magazine
(262) 242-2077
www.keymilwaukee.com

M Magazine/Conley Publications
W61 N306 Washington Ave.
Cedarburg 53012
(262) 375-5100
www.mmagazinemilwaukee.com

Madison Magazine
PO Box 44965-53744
7025 W. Raymond Rd.
Madison 53719
(608) 270-3600
www.madisonmagazine.com

Milwaukee Magazine
126 N. Jefferson St., Suite 100
Milwaukee 53202
(414) 273-1101
www.insidemilwaukee.com

DAILY ONLINE MAGAZINES (FREE)

Onmilwaukee.com
1930 E. North Ave., 2nd Floor
Milwaukee 53202
(414) 272-0557
http://onmilwaukee.com

Helpful Wisconsin Websites

- **Maps of Wisconsin:** www.northwoodmap.com; www.delorme.com

- **Wisconsin Department of Tourism:** www.travelwisconsin.com

- **Wisconsin Innkeepers Association:** www.wisconsinlodging.org

- **Wisconsin Restaurant Association:** www.wirestaurant.org

WESTERN WISCONSIN

The rolling, muddy waters of the Mississippi form most of the western boundary of Wisconsin. The river edges a slow way from where it first touches the state at Prescott, meandering 200 miles south to the rural southwestern corner of the state near Dubuque, Iowa. The Great River Road, Highway 35, skirts the rim of the river, crawling through sloughs, up over the ridgebacks, and along short straightaways that end much too soon in a sweeping curve. The road has consistently been voted one of the country's most scenic routes by everyone from motorcycle clubs to travel editors. The route is well marked by white signs with a green riverboat pilot's wheel.

For a map of the entire Great River Road, covering the 3,000 miles from Canada to the Gulf of Mexico, contact the Mississippi River Parkway Commission, 222 State St., Madison 53703; (866) 763-8310; www.experiencemississippiriver.com.

Muscular tugboats, with their roaring diesel engines, shove blocks of barges loaded with coal, oil, lumber, and other goods. They make these runs almost year-round between Minnesota's Twin Cities, Minneapolis and St. Paul, to the Gulf of Mexico. Only the freezing cold of midwinter forces closing of

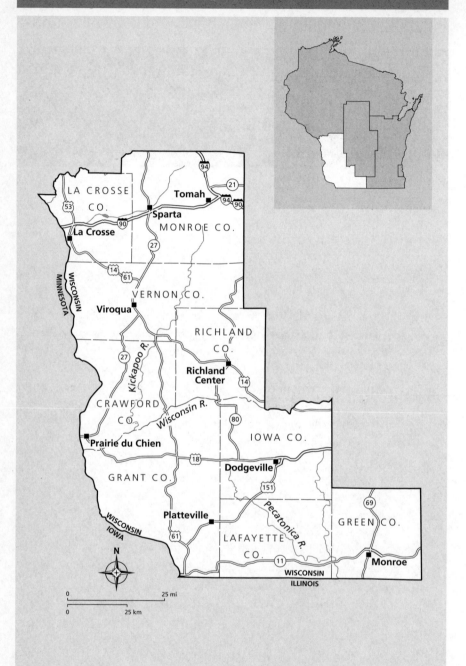

LA CROSSE CO.

Tomah

94

21

Sparta

94 90

53

La Crosse

90

MONROE CO.

27

14
61

VERNON CO.

Viroqua

RICHLAND CO.

27

Richland Center

14

CRAWFORD CO.

Wisconsin R.

80

Prairie du Chien

IOWA CO.

18

Dodgeville

GRANT CO.

151

Platteville

Pecatonica R.

69

GREEN CO.

61

LAFAYETTE CO.

11

Monroe

WISCONSIN
ILLINOIS

WISCONSIN
IOWA

WISCONSIN
MINNESOTA

Kickapoo R.

N

0   25 mi
0   25 km

the river traffic. The river is then turned over to hardy anglers who brave the blustery winds in search of the Midwest's best-tasting bluegills and catfish. The hapless fish are plucked through holes chopped in ice that can be 2 or more feet thick.

Trappers range along the riverbanks, bringing in dozens of muskrat, beaver, and fox pelts each year to satisfy the demands of the national and international markets.

The river is straight out of Mark Twain, with memories of the steam-spitting *Delta Queen* that called at quays in Prairie du Chien and La Crosse. I remember camping on a riverfront sandbar one summer and being awakened in the predawn hours to the crash of paddle wheels storming downriver. A quick glance out the tent flap revealed what seemed to be a sky-high bank of lights surging south on the blackness of the river. Waltz music wafted through the humid night air, just audible over the roar of machinery. Then it was gone, like a 19th-century dream. Or was it? These days, the *La Crosse Queen* paddle wheeler offers daily sightseeing tours, plus pizza. Sunday brunch and lunch cruises along with weekend dinner jaunts

The river itself is dotted with islands, fringed with marshlands, and speckled with drowned trees, which are the reminders of the Mississippi's many spring runoff tantrums. But on decent days, canoeists can paddle along the

WESTERN WISCONSIN'S TOP HITS

American Players Theater

Badger Mine Museum

Elroy-Sparta Trail

Fennimore Doll & Toy Museum

First Capitol State Park and Museum

Grand Army of the Republic Hall

Grant County Courthouse

House on the Rock Resort

Joseph Huber Brewing Company

Mount La Crosse

Nelson Dewey State Park

Norskedalen

Pendarvis

Prairie du Chien Museum at Fort Crawford

Prairie Villa Rendezvous

Spurgeon Vineyards and Winery

Stonefield Village

Sugar River Trail

Swiss historical village

Villa Louis

Wisconsin High School Rodeo Association Championships

backwater sloughs in search of great, flapping herons and slithery muskrats. Houseboaters can drift along in tune with seasons.

Crawford County

This is a county of rivers. The Wisconsin bisects the landscape, meandering downstream from the state's Northland. Its importance in history is marked by a sign in Portage (Columbia County) that reads:

ON JUNE 14, 1673, JACQUES MARQUETTE AND LOUIS JOLIET STARTED THE

1.28 MILE PORTAGE FROM HERE TO THE WISCONSIN RIVER, WHICH LED TO THEIR

DISCOVERY OF THE UPPER MISSISSIPPI, JUNE 17, 1673, AT PRAIRIE DU CHIEN.

Other markers in the county should be perused as well. While you are in Gays Mills for the annual **Blossom Day Festival** in May or the annual **Apple Festival** in September, read the marker on Highway 171 east of town. It tells of the early lives of the pioneers who developed the apple industry there. A marker commemorating early governor James Davidson is on Highway 61 near the village of Soldiers Grove. A marker on Highway 35 south of Lynxville describes the log rafts that used to float down the Mississippi in the 1800s. The Prairie du Chien marker is at the tourist information center on the Mississippi River, memorializing the building of the third frontier fort in the Wisconsin Territory. Another marker in Prairie du Chien, located at Villa Louis, outlines the importance of Fort Crawford in protecting the American frontier during the War of 1812. A Marquette-Joliet marker at the state's tourism information center where Highway 18 crosses the Mississippi honors the two French explorers and their five French-Canadian *voyageur* companions as being the first whites to travel the Upper Mississippi.

After the Mississippi and the Wisconsin, Crawford County's third major waterway is the Kickapoo, a name derived from the Winnebago Indian term *kwigapawa,* which means "moves about from here to there." The Winnebago knew what they were talking about. The Kickapoo offers more twists and turns than a dish of spaghetti on its crooked north and south route, joining the Wisconsin River at Wauzeka.

Lovely as it is, the Kickapoo can be nasty. A flood in late August 2007 inundated much of Gays Mills, and the angry waters overflowed the banks so often that the town of **Soldiers Grove** moved from its base in the river valley to higher ground in 1978. The community now brags that it is America's First Solar Village. Originally called Pine Grove, the town of 680 was an encampment for troops during the Black Hawk War in 1832 and subsequently changed its name in honor of the soldiers who bivouacked there. All buildings in the rebuilt community, now high above the floodline, receive 50 percent or more of their power supply from the sun. The solar panels over the bank, super-markets, clinic, stores, and homes give the town a futuristic look. The site of the former village has been turned into a riverside park with a ball diamond, a campground, tennis courts, and a picnic spot. Tourist information is available at the **Solar Town Pharmacy,** 100 Passive Sun Dr., (608) 624-3344. Just outside of town is the **Inn at Lonesome Hollow** (15415 Vance Rd.; 608-624-3429 for reservations; http://lonesome hollow.com), lovingly situated on 160 picturesque acres. The Main Inn has 3 bed-and-breakfast rooms, the Cedar Cabin is a snug little 2-bedroom place with a deck and screened-in porch for lolling away the those wonderful vaca-tion hours, and the Homestead has two 2-bedroom suites. Many of the rooms are complete with two-person whirlpool tubs. Rates vary with numerous packages and specials. For any stay of 5 nights or longer, guests receive a discount of 20 percent.

oldabe

The "Eagle Regiment," the 8th Wisconsin, took its name from Old Abe, a tamed bald eagle that the unit carried into battle during the Civil War. During the fighting, the bird would perch on a cannon or fly overhead, taking part in 22 battles and 60 skirmishes. After the war he lived in the basement and yard of the state capitol.

Nearby is the **Country Garden Restaurant,** which offers, as the counter girl says, "great home cookin'." The Country Garden is usually just open for weekday lunches from 11 a.m. to 1 p.m., but it does have an all-you-can-eat fish fry on Friday evenings.

There are two explanations of how **Prairie du Chien** was named. One legend says the place was called "Field of the Dogs" by French trappers who gathered here and saw acres of prairie dog mounds. Another version says the town was named after "Big Dog," a local tribal leader. Whatever the true story, the city that evolved from the early frontier encampments has been a major Wisconsin trading center and river port for generations. Wisconsin's first mil-lionaire, fur dealer Hercules Dousman, put the place on the map when he built his mansion, **Villa Louis,** in 1843. That original house was razed in 1870, and the current Italianate building was constructed. The richly appointed building and its grounds are now owned by the State Historical Society of Wisconsin.

There's a bit of personal history attached to the Villa Louis. My maternal great-grandmother, Bridget O'Malley, was a linen maid there when she came from Ireland to the United States around the time of the Civil War.

Her beau, Louie Larson, was a young Norwegian shopkeeper who lived in Marquette, on the Iowa side of the Mississippi. In the winter Louie would ice-skate across the river to court Bridget.

AUTHORS' FAVORITES

Badger Mine Museum, Shullsburg

Dickeyville Grotto

Fennimore Doll & Toy Museum

Pendarvis, Mineral Point

Spurgeon Vineyards and Winery, Highland

St. John Mine, Potosi

Swiss Historical Village Museum, New Glarus

Yellowstone Lake State Park, Blanchardville

In the summer he would take his sailboat, *The Bluebird,* across the river to pitch woo to his lady love. Naturally Bridget was quite smitten with all this attention, and the couple eventually married and moved to Iowa. Violà! Without them, *Wisconsin Off the Beaten Path* might never have been written—at least not by yours truly.

Great-grandma Bridget was always hospitable, according to reliable family memories, so she probably wouldn't mind the guests who come to the Villa each June to try their hand at preparing breakfast in a Victorian kitchen. Up to 16 adults can sign up for a hands-on cooking class in the mansion's kitchen. Reservations are required; call the historic site. But as Bridget would have admonished, "Just clean up after yourselves and put everything back in the proper drawer."

The Villa Louis, 900 W. Bolvin St. (608-326-2721; http://villalouis.wisconsin history.org), is open from 9:30 a.m. to 5 p.m. daily May 10 to October 31. Admission is $10 for adults, $8.50 for seniors age 66 and older, and $5 for children ages 5 to 17. Family rates are $27. To get to the Villa from downtown Prairie, take Main Street north to Washington Street West.

Prairie du Chien annually hosts the ***Prairie Villa Rendezvous*** on St. Feriole Island near the Villa Louis on the third weekend in June. Grizzled mountain men, Native American trappers, and appropriately garbed military men from the era fill the grounds with their tents and tepees. This is the place to pick up skins, beads, blankets, tomahawks, flintlock rifles, traps, and similar frontier accoutrements for the suburban homestead. As I've always said, "You never know when you might need a bolt of cloth or a kettle." The participants lay out trade goods, talk shop, cook over open fires, scratch, and look at us 21st-century types with bemusement. But when the weekend is over, they all go back to being bank presidents, mechanics, nurses, shop owners, and lawyers. For details contact the Prairie du Chien Chamber of Commerce and

Tourism Council, 211 S. Main St., Prairie du Chien (800-732-1673; www.prairie duchien.org).

Prairie du Chien also played another part in our family history. Great-uncle Charlie (one of the sons of the aforementioned Louie and Bridget) and a couple of his friends sneaked across the old railroad pontoon bridge that linked Iowa and Wisconsin at the turn of the 20th century. They had hitched an all-night ride on an eastbound freight train from their hometown to see the *Buffalo Bill's Wild West* show in Prairie du Chien. They got more than their money's worth in that hot summer of 1901.

The show folk and the townspeople began brawling in the streets, a brouhaha that resulted in calling out the Wisconsin militia. Uncle Charlie and his frightened young pals hid in an old boiler next to a tavern as they watched the boisterous fight. Buffalo Bill managed to round up his crew before the militia arrived and scurried westward across the river to the safety of Iowa.

It's a lot quieter now in Prairie du Chien. Down the street from the Villa Louis is the **Depot Bar & Grill**, a tavern at the old train station that claims to serve the best Bloody Marys on the Mississippi River. Judge for yourself at 220 Water St. (608-326-8548).

St. Feriole Island is actually a spit of land jutting into the Mississippi on the west side of the city. The cars parked south of the quay in **Lawler Park.** The site is at the end of Blackhawk Avenue, where the railroad pontoon bridge used to link Wisconsin to Iowa.

Each Father's Day, a rendezvous that brings alive memories of the fur-trapper days is held on St. Feriole Island. Hundreds of reenactors portray traders, voyageurs, soldiers, and Native Americans in a large encampment of tents and huts. Interested in a skunk pelt? Tomahawk? Flintlock? Everything a frontier family could use is for sale. Even a contemporary suburban home can probably do with an iron kettle or two. There are black-powder musket firings, dances, fiddling, tall tales, and plenty of rough-and-ready types to photograph. In mid-July a War of 1812 military reenactment is held featuring British-Canadian and US troops. The pageant is held on the lawn of the Villa Louis.

While in Prairie du Chien, stop at the **Prairie du Chien Museum at Fort Crawford,** 717 S. Beaumont Rd. (608-326-6960; www.fortcrawfordmuseum .com) and view its extensive collection of frontier surgical instruments and medical devices. Seen in today's light, they look more like inquisitor's tools than anything else. Dr. William Beaumont, whose studies on the digestive system revolutionized the medical world, was once stationed at Fort Crawford. While there he conducted some of his experiments on a French-Canadian trapper who had been wounded in the stomach. Beaumont would put food, tied onto a string, into the man's stomach and withdraw it for study. The doctor published a book about his experiences in 1853.

The fort, built by Zachary Taylor and Jefferson Davis, was one of the most important outposts in the young United States, especially during the Black Hawk War. Hours are 9 a.m. to 4 p.m., May through Oct; Admission is $5 for adults, $4 for seniors, $3 for children under 12, and $15 for families.

Grant County

Grant County is tucked into the far southwestern corner of Wisconsin, where the Mississippi joins the state with Iowa and Illinois. The county has some 49 miles of prime river frontage on its western border and 42 miles of Wisconsin River on its northern rim. To capitalize on this watery connection, the county operates 10 boat landings on the rivers, augmenting the dozens of private put-in sites.

The landscape consists of rolling ridges and deep valleys, with thick stands of oak and maple overlooking the waterways. **Nelson Dewey State Park** and **Wyalusing State Park** offer the best scenic overviews. Each perches some 400 to 500 feet on the limestone crests towering above the valley floors. Excellent views of the confluence of the Wisconsin and the Mississippi can be had at Wyalusing on Highway X near Bagley.

Native American mounds dot both sides of the **Sentinel Ridge Trail** in Wyalusing State Park along the Mississippi River. The park is only 2 miles south of Prairie du Chien off US 18. After studying the mounds, many are the times we perched on the rocks high above the river and looked over the sprawling river valley below. This vista is especially great during October, when the oaks and maples are in full glory. Daughter Kate and elder Hintz even did an early spring look-see, at a time when ice still coated the shaded trails. But it was time for spring's new life to peek through the snow patches. And it did: Skunk cabbage, morel mushrooms, jack-in-the-pulpit, and trillium were everywhere. You also can take this trail from the top of the bluffs at Point Lookout to a boat landing on the Mississippi. The area here is part of the **Upper Mississippi Wildlife and Fish Refuge.** Stay on the trail because the adjoining ground is marshy. Yet despite the mushiness, the bird-watching opportunities make this side trip worthwhile.

In addition to bird-watching possibilities, Nelson Dewey State Park (named after Wisconsin's first governor) near Cassville offers a good view of the **Stone-field Village** historic site (608-725-5210; www.cassville.org/stonefield.html). Take County Trunk Road VV north of town to the village (across the highway from the entrance to the state park), operated by the state historical society.

TOP ANNUAL EVENTS

JANUARY

Bald Eagle Days
Cassville
(608) 725-5855
www.cassville.org

Ice Rally Cross (auto racing on ice)
West Salem
(608) 785-1773
www.westsalemwi.com

JUNE

Cheese Curd Festival
Ellsworth
(715) 273-6442
www.ellsworthchamber.com/
cheesecurd.htm

Town & Country Jamboree
St. Feriole Island, Prairie du Chien
(800) 732-1673
www.prairieduchien.org

SEPTEMBER

Cranberry Festival
Warrens
(608) 378-4200
www.cranfest.com

Driftless Area Art Festival
Soldiers Grove
(608) 624-3264
www.driftlesswisconsin.com

Horse & Colt Show
Viola
(608) 627-1831
www.horseandcoltshow.com

OCTOBER

Center Color Festival
Richland Center
(608) 647-6205
www.richlandchamber.com

Hmong New Year Festival
La Crosse
(608) 781-5744
www.lacrossehmaa.org/HMAA/
newYearInfo.aspx

Oktoberfest
La Crosse
(608) 784-3378
www.oktoberfestusa.com

Oktoberfest Car Races
West Salem
(608) 786-1525
www.westsalemwi.com

Shihata Orchard Fest
Prairie du Chien
(608) 326-2785
www.shihataorchard.com

Sledfest Grass Drag Racing
Friendship
(608) 548-3308
www.vintagesleds.com/events

The community is a re-creation of an 1890s village, complete with railroad station, shops, firehouse, and school. The facility is open Memorial Day to Labor day, 10 a.m. to 4 p.m., and then open weekends only until mid-October, 10 a.m. to 4 p.m. Stonefield is a good place to bring kids, who can talk with costumed interpreters portraying characters of the period. Admission is $8 for

Picnic, Parks & Mounds

Wyalusing State Park, on Grant County Highway VV along the Mississippi, is a prime location for camping sites, hiking trails, and picnic areas. Native American mounds dating back 1,000 years can be found on the bluff overlooking the river. From the vantage point on the Sentinel Ridge Walk, you can see where the Mississippi and Wisconsin Rivers converge. The park, sprawling over 2,700 acres, is a wildlife haven. I've spotted white-tailed deer, bald eagles, Canada geese, muskrats, raccoons, wild turkeys, turkey vultures, and possums.

Here are some of the best hiking trails in the park:

Bluff, Indian, and Flint Ledge Trails. Take the 2-mile walk down the bluff side for great views of the Mississippi. These paths are not recommended for toddlers.

Mississippi Ridge Trail. Hikers do not have any difficulty getting across the 3.5-mile trail overlooking the river.

Old Immigrant, Old Wagon Road, and Sand Cave Trails. The trails run for more than 3 miles through heavy oak and maple groves and have some steep slopes, so watch your step. As the names imply, early settlers moving overland into the river valley used these tracks.

Sentinel Ridge Trail. The 1.6-mile trail runs south from the park's main campground along the high ridge. It offers some of the best views of the river.

Walnut Springs Trail. This 2.6-mile grassy pathway is a 2-hour-long walk.

---

adults, $4 for children ages 5 to 7, and $7 for seniors and college students. There are also group rates.

A moody color photo of Stonefield, taken from the Nelson Dewey bluffs just as the oaks shredded the morning fog, captured the grand prize in a Wisconsin tourism division photo contest. Needless to say, the place is photogenic . . . with or without the mist. So bring cameras and plenty of color and black-and-white film.

After visiting Stonefield, head into **Cassville,** the "doorway to nature's wonders and historic past." The Cassville Historical Society has drawn out a map that guides you on a walking tour of buildings constructed by early Cassville residents. The sites and buildings that are included were chosen for their architectural and/or historical significance to the development of Cassville.

The first stop on the map is the **Denniston House,** which was built in 1836. It was first constructed by a New York company, Daniels-Denniston Co., and later was purchased by Nelson Dewey, who converted the building into a hotel. This beautiful brick building has been standing tall for more than 160 years and is worth admiring. Feel free to pack a lunch and stop at Riverside Park for a picnic if you wish. It has been a village park since the 1890s. The 1889 *St. Charles Borromeo Church,* a Victorian Gothic structure built of solid brick laid upon a limestone foundation, has a steeple that soars 137 feet in the air. Open doors welcome you to enter and see the Gothic decor.

Take the tour on foot, hop on your bicycle, or cruise in your automobile.

Continue east on Highway 60 to *Boscobel* and the yellow limestone *Boscobel Hotel,* where the Gideon Bible Society was founded in 1898. A group of local businessmen formed the Christian Commercial Men's Association of America, more commonly known as the Gideons International. They thought it would be important to place Bibles in hotel rooms to keep traveling salesmen on the straight and narrow. Since that time, the society has distributed more than 10 million Bibles to lodgings around the country.

The hotel is a funky, comfortable old place that was remodeled with period antiques. The owners, however, decided to move back home to California and put the place up for sale. But you can still drive past the hotel with its high arched windows and plain facade at 1005 Wisconsin Ave. And, yes, there are—or were—Gideon Bibles in each room. If you wish to stop, the hotel now houses only a tavern, and most of the rest of the building is closed. Room 19, where the Gideon idea was launched, can be visited if one of the bartenders is able to take a break from serving patrons.

Immediately off Wisconsin Avenue in Boscobel is the last remaining *Grand Army of the Republic (GAR) Hall* in the state. Built in the 1880s, the building has been left as it was when Civil War veterans met there to reminisce about their salad days in uniform. Plenty of memorabilia and regimental documents pack the display cases.

The hall is open at irregular hours, so it's a hit-or-miss proposition. Yet for any Civil War fan, an attempt is worth it. You'll probably be lucky.

OTHER ATTRACTIONS WORTH SEEING

A. D. German Warehouse, Richland Center

Cassville Car Ferry

Hamlin Garland Homestead, West Salem

La Crosse River State Trail

Painted Forest Folk Art Museum, Valton

Palmer-Bullickson Octagon House, West Salem

Pump House Regional Center for the Arts, La Crosse

Farm Fun

Looking for a good getaway with the clan? Spend a few days at the *Life O'Riley Farm & Guesthouse,* where Jean Murphy and her family run an operating farm. Visiting parents and kids can feed chickens, pet the pig, and generally see how crops are raised and harvested. Guests stay in a renovated 100-plus-year-old schoolhouse that has its own kitchen, with a fridge well stocked with homemade goodies and farm-raised eggs.

Life O'Riley has a great picnic spot on a rise overlooking the farm, where everyone can commune with nature. Little signage marks the place. "That way, people think they are the only ones who've discovered us," laughs Jean. "It's nothing fancy, but quiet and fun." It isn't really that hard to reach. Just take Riley Road south 6 miles out of Boscobel. The farm is located at 15706 Riley Rd., Boscobel (608-375-5798 or e-mail at mjmurphy@mwt.net).

From Boscobel, take off to Highland, driving southeast via County Roads S to T to M to Q. From Highland, go west 4 miles on County Highway Q to Pine Tree Road, then north to the *Spurgeon Vineyards and Winery* for a sample of its various vintages (608-929-7692; www.spurgeonvineyards.com). The vineyards host an annual Harvest Festival on the Sat and Sun of Columbus Day weekend in October. They also have a wine and cheese extravaganza in June and a children's open house in December with hayrides, live music, and free tours. The vineyards are open 10 a.m. to 5 p.m. daily year-round except for Christmas and Easter.

Spurgeon grows such American grape varieties as the Concord and Delaware, in addition to French hybrids such as Rosette and Aurora. Prices of the distinctively labeled wines range from $7.15 to $9.95, a dollar less per bottle if you purchase by the case. Tours are $3, and tasting is free.

From the vineyards, return to Highland and drive south on Highway 80 to the tiny community of Cobb. Go west from Cobb to *Fennimore* (www .fennimore.com). Drive through town, heading west on Highway 18 to the *Fennimore Railroad Historical Society Museum.* You can't miss the little park that features, of course, a little train. The locomotive, made by the late Vern Wilkinson, a local train buff, took several years to build. Kids love riding along the operational 15-inch gauge rail line with its 700 feet of track at the facility. An appropriately small-scale depot and water tower finish off the layout. A ticket booth has old-time telegraph equipment and a potbellied stove. Plenty of memorabilia and photos from Fennimore's railroad past can also be perused. A real narrow-gauge engine on display is appropriately known as the Dinky, which operated between Fennimore and Woodman from 1878 to 1926, meandering through the scenic Green River Valley. The museum is open daily from Memorial Day weekend through Labor Day from 10 a.m. to 4 p.m. and weekends only through Sept and Oct. The facility is located at 610 Lincoln Ave. (608-822-6144; railmuseum@fennimore.com).

The *Fennimore Doll & Toy Museum* (608-822-4100; www.dollandtoy museum.com) has more than 5,000 dolls representing a span of generations. The dolls are made of wood, cloth, plastic, ceramic, and even stone, collected over the years by a local farm woman who wanted them to be available for viewing in her hometown, rather than in some big-city museum. Anyone who thinks dolls are too feminine will get a kick out of the display of *Star Wars* figurines and John Wayne and Roy Rogers action characters. But the biggest attraction is probably the Barbie collection, which covers the 50-plus years from the first leggy, buxom doll to the most contemporary. All her friends and accoutrements are shown as well.

The *Fenmore Hills Motel*, 2 miles west of town on Old Highway 18, has 24 uniquely themed rooms. If you want to try out the circular waterbed, give the place a call at (608) 822-3281, or visit www.fenmorehillsmotel.com. That room costs weekend guests $125, but the rate is a mere $100 Sunday through Thursday. A regular room, with steam bath, runs $60. Add a bathroom with a whirlpool for $64. Take some cheese along, and don't forget the Spurgeon wine.

After lolling on the waterbed, continue south out of Fennimore on Highway 61 to *Lancaster* for a peek at the *Grant County Courthouse.* The

NATIONALLY KNOWN BLUES & ROCK BANDS FROM WISCONSIN

The Blifftones	Killdozer
BoDeans	Laarks
Bon Iver	Larry Lynne Group
The Chevelles	Little Blue Crunchy Things
Cimmeron Show Review	The Nomads
Die Kreuzen	Reverend Raven and the Chain Smoking Altar Boys
5 Card Studs	
The Gufs	Short Stuff
I'm Not a Pilot	Violent Femmes

imposing structure, in the middle of the town square, has a copper and glass double dome modeled after St. Peter's Basilica in Rome. The building was constructed in 1905, following a design by architect Armand Koch. Inside the dome are four beautiful murals painted by Franz Edward Rohrbeck. Another town landmark is the City Hall, which now includes a movie theater. Built in 1922, the building was designed by architects Claude and Starck, emphasizing a fashionable, prairie-style look. The Lancaster Chamber of Commerce (608-723-2820; www.lancasterwisconsin.com) can help tell of building tours and other activities around town.

The square is also the site of the first Civil War monument erected in the United States, according to local lore. The statue was dedicated on July 4, 1867, after a private and county fund drive.

The "great, big, tall" monument (as proudly described by Lancaster citizens) is on the northeast side of the square and consists of a central marble pillar surrounded by eight smaller pillars. The memorial is inscribed with the names of 755 Grant County soldiers who either died or were injured during the Civil War. Don't confuse that monument with the one erected in 1906 by the ladies' auxiliary of the Grand Army of the Republic, a soldier atop a pedestal on the northwest side of the courthouse.

On the southeast corner is a statue of Grant County resident Nelson Dewey, who was the county's first clerk of courts in 1836 and Wisconsin's first governor in 1848. Dewey is perched importantly in a chair, looking appropriately governor-like. Dewey's Lancaster home is located at 147 W. Hickory St., now occupied by an insurance agency. I've been told the folks there will probably let you peek around a bit, if you come during business hours.

Look at the display on the first floor of the courthouse featuring the county's collection of Civil War memorabilia. Much of it was donated by the family of Gen. John Clark, the town's resident Civil War general—long deceased, of course. Among the artifacts is a captured Confederate battle flag.

After spending an hour or two wandering around Lancaster and admiring the older homes and commercial buildings, follow Highway 61 south to 133, which leads to Potosi, an old lead-mining boomtown tucked into a deep, skinny valley.

Around the War of 1812 most of the lead mined in the country came from this region. Several of the villages were larger than Chicago and Milwaukee at the time. Today all you see are the remains of pits and furnaces where the mostly Welsh and Cornish miners set up camp. The state's nickname, "the Badger State," came from these early miners. Let me explain: When the men first moved to the vicinity, prior to building barracks they dug shallow trenches in the hillsides to get away from the rain. The holes served as protection from

RECOMMENDED READING FOR FAMILIES

Alden, Sharyn. *Historical Wisconsin Getaways: Touring the Badger State's Past.* Black Earth, WI: Trails Books, 2001. 168 pp.

Bergin, Mary. *Hungry for Wisconsin.* Blue Mounds, WI: Itchy Cat Press, 2008. 254 pp.

Bergin, Mary. *Sidetracked in Wisconsin.* Blue Mounds, WI: Itchy Cat Press, 2007. 242 pp.

Bie, Michael. *Classic Wisconsin Weekends.* Black Earth, WI: Trails Books, 2003. 240 pp.

Brown, Harriet. *Madison Walks.* Madison: Jones Press, 2003. 124 pp.

Davenport, Don. *Natural Wonders of Wisconsin.* Castine, ME: Country Roads Press, 1995. 158 pp.

Hintz, Martin. *Hiking Wisconsin.* Champaign, IL: Human Kinetics, 1997. 212 pp.

Hintz, Martin, and Daniel Hintz. *Day Trips from Milwaukee.* Guilford, CT: Globe Pequot Press, 2002. 288 pp.

Hintz, Martin, and Stephen Hintz. *Fun with the Family Wisconsin.* Guilford, CT: Globe Pequot Press, 2004. 272 pp.

Hintz, Martin, and Pam Percy. *Wisconsin Cheese: A Cookbook and Guide to the Cheeses of Wisconsin.* Guilford, CT: Globe Pequot Press, 2008. 272 pp.

Hintz, Martin, and Bob Rashid. *Backroads of Wisconsin: Your Guide to Wisconsin's Most Scenic Backroad Adventures.* Stillwater, MN: Voyageur Books, 2002. 160 pp.

Johnson, Steve. *Biking Wisconsin: 50 Great Road and Trail Rides.* Black Earth, WI: Trails Books, 2004. 120 pp.

Knowles, Gary. *The Great Wisconsin Touring Book.* Black Earth, WI: Trails Books, 2000. 162 pp.

McGrath, Chad. *Great Cross-Country Ski Trails.* Black Earth, WI: Trails Books, 2001. 240 pp.

Smith, Susan Lampert. *Wisconsin Family Weekends.* Black Earth, WI: Trails Books, 2000. 160 pp.

Stuttgen, Joanne Raetz. *Cafe Wisconsin: A Guide to Wisconsin's Down-Home Cafes.* Madison: University of Wisconsin Press, 2004. 392 pp.

marauding Native Americans as well, since they were always dug near another miner's hideaway for musket crossfire. In calmer days visitors saw these holes in the slopes and likened them to badger burrows, hence the state's nickname. Some of these pits, framed by low stone barricades, can be seen on the hillsides around ***Potosi.***

The workmen who went south in the winter, when some of the mines closed for the season, were called "suckers," after a type of Mississippi River fish.

There are about 40 crumbled old buildings, open pit mines, smelters, and huts scattered around the vicinity of the one-street town, once the leading port on the northern Mississippi. By 1833, more than 237 steamboats were making regular stops at Potosi. River towns along this stretch of the Mississippi all the way to Fort Snelling in St. Paul, Minnesota, used the town as a storage facility for whiskey, flour, trade goods, bacon, and munitions. The boats would leave the docks laden with lead, heading for New Orleans and ocean-bound freighters. Hard-swearing teamsters picked up the supplies the paddle wheelers dropped off and hauled them inland, using huge carts pulled by 10 oxen at a time over muddy trails.

Years ago, a "Ripley's Believe It or Not" column said that Potosi's main street was the longest in the world without an intersection. It extended some 5 miles through the valley, linking the scattered mining sites and ethnic enclaves such as British Hollow (built by the English) and Van Buren (home for Dutch settlers). There's not much there now, except for scattered gas stations and several antiques stores. Developers have considered refurbishing the battered but still serviceable Potosi Brewery building into a complex of crafts shops or even reopening it as a brewery. Several local residents established a foundation in 1999 to attempt preserving what is left of the dilapidated old facility and reconnect the town with its brewing heritage. To accomplish this, they sponsor dinners and raffles to raise funds for a restoration. To help, contact the Potosi Brewery Foundation, Inc., Box 177, 209 S. Main, Potosi 53820 (www .potosibrewery.com).

The **St. John Mine** (608-763-2121) in Potosi is open for summer touring, after a succession of owners attempted to make it a tourist attraction. Stories about the mine date from 1640, when French explorers found Winnebago living there and mining lead for trade (*Ho-Chunk* is the nation's own name for its tribal members). After a peace treaty was signed with local Winnebago tribes in 1827, miners poured into southwestern Wisconsin. One intrepid soul who became rich during those rough-and-tumble lead-mining days was Willis St. John, after whom the largest mine was named. Mining in the vicinity died out during the Gold Rush of 1849, but there was a resurgence throughout the Civil War. In that conflict, Wisconsin's mines provided most of the lead for the Northern armies. The lead deposits eventually petered out, and the St. John Mine officially closed in 1870 until reopening as a tourist destination generations later.

Today, watch your step in walking up the steep slope to the cavern, and be sure to wear comfortable walking shoes if you plan to enter the mine. Once inside, look for pockmarks and cuts on the walls, gouged out by the picks and chisels in those early days. It's an eerie feeling, knowing that long-ago miners once worked here, often on their hands and knees or crawling along on their bellies. The museum is open daily from 9 a.m. to 5 p.m., May through Oct.

There's fantastic canoeing on the slow but powerful Grant, Big Platte, and Little Platte Rivers near Potosi. It's best to bring your own equipment because of the difficulty in finding an outfitter that stays in business from year to year. Among the better put-in spots along the Grant is one at Klondike Springs on the left bank of County Trunk K, which can give you a 19-hour run downstream to the Potosi boat landing on the Mississippi if your muscles are so inclined.

Louthain Bridge on the right bank of County Trunk B is a fine set-off on the Big Platte. For the Little Platte, try the Church Road Bridge (right bank on Church Road), Shinoe Bridge (where Highways 61 and 35 intersect—use the right bank), or the Banfield Bridge public boat landing.

If you need a break from all that pad-dling, make a stop at a funky museum. Rollo Jamison, a Beetown farmer/repair-shop owner/tavernkeeper/janitor, had a fever for collecting just about anything. He filled sheds with "valuables," orga-nizing his finds into categories: stoves, vending machines, farm machinery, and so on. When the 93-year-old Jamison died in 1981, the city of Platteville took over the assemblage of oddities and moved everything to the old high school, where it can currently be viewed.

Now called the ***Rollo Jamison Museum,*** the school building at 405 E. Main St. is open daily May through Oct from 9 a.m. to 5 p.m. A self-guided gallery is open Nov through Apr from 9 a.m. to 4 p.m., Mon through Fri.

Next door to the Jamison place is the ***Mining Museum,*** where visitors can descend 90, count 'em, 90 steps down into a shaft of the ***Bevans Lead Mine,*** reopened in 1976. Above ground, rides are given on a train of ore cars pulled by a restored 1931 locomotive. For those with phobias about knocking their heads on the ceiling, hard hats are standard issue at the entrance. The museums are open daily 9 a.m. to 5 p.m., May through Oct. Call (608) 348-3301 or visit http://mining.jamison.museum.

The mine was discovered in 1845 by Lorenzo Bevans, who had used his life's resources and was in debt up to his highbrow nose while searching for lead. On a mid-July day of that year, he could afford to pay his hired hand only until noon. But the fellow agreed to stay on until the end of the day. At 2 that afternoon, the two men broke into one of the richest veins of lead ever discovered in southwestern Wisconsin.

Before leaving Grant County, check out the ***Dickeyville Grotto,*** built by parish priest Father Mathias Wernerus. The dedicated clergyman assembled bottles, stone, glass, and other cast-off artifacts to make his shrine, spending the years 1925 to 1929 collecting, hauling, and cementing the whole thing together. "We built better than we knew" was his motto. About seven carloads of rock were taken from quarries around the Midwest, with other stones coming from every state and from the Holy Land. Some Chippewa Indians from northern Wisconsin even donated arrowheads and axes for inclusion in one section. The grotto, on the east and south sides of Holy Cross Church, is located at 305 Main St. (608-568-3119). Hours are 9 a.m. to 5 p.m. daily, April 15 through October. From November up until mid-December, the grotto is open on weekends with limited hours. Donations are accepted. Father Wernerus's grave is in the rear of the church.

In addition to Father Wernerus's glittering, ponderous masterpiece, Dickeyville is noted for its more secular May and September motorcycle and four-wheel-drive hill climbs and tractor pulls.

Not that all roads lead to Dickeyville, but most do in this corner of Wisconsin. To get to this old German farming community, take either Highways 61, 35, or 151.

Green County

Folks in Green County brag that their landscape is a Little Switzerland. They certainly are correct when it comes to driving over hills and dales that could easily pass for alpine meadows. For this reason, thousands of Swiss émigrés settled here in the 1800s. Their tidy homesteads dot the countryside, where cows outnumber people five to three.

In 1986 Green County celebrated its 150th anniversary, a fete topped off by the opening of the refurbished courthouse in **Monroe,** the county seat. The town's fund-raisers, "the Steeple People," collected nearly $50,000 for the restoration of the building's ornate tower and its four-sided clock.

But Monroe isn't just a place to sit on your hands in the town square and watch the time pass. The community hosts the annual county fair, something it has been doing since 1853. In late July the exposition of giant vegetables, nose-wriggling rabbits, beefy cattle, rounds of delicious cheese, grandma's pickles, and 4-H crafts creates a lot of hoopla for celebrating farm life.

A must-see attraction in Monroe is the **Minhas Craft Brewery,** which has been around since 1845 under varying names, most recently the Joseph Huber Brewing Company. Tours are available every day of the week at $10 per person. Children under 12 are free, and they'll have to stick to the root beer. The brewery is located at 1208 14th Ave. (608-329-4244; minhas brewery.com).

Say *Lactobacillus bulgaricus* in Monroe, and nobody's eyebrows will go up. The bacteria are among the ingredients in manufacturing swiss cheese, an economic mainstay in the Monroe area with its 20 factories (a total of 36 are in the county).

The limestone subsoil makes this heart of Wisconsin's dairy land rich in the right kind of milk for muenster, limburger, and other cheese varieties, as well as swiss. The county's Holsteins and Brown Swiss are truly contented cows.

Many of the plants in the county allow visitors, but you have to be on hand by noon or most of the day's work will be over. The factories kick into gear around 5 a.m. For a list of licensed outlets, check the Cheese Days website at www.cheesedays.com. The plants, all members of the Foreign Type Cheese-makers Association (FTCA), are headquartered in town. The members sponsor the Monroe Cheese Days, held in September every even-numbered year. These Big Cheeses of the county's agricultural community offer an average of 11 tons of the stuff for nibbling at these events. When they say "cheese," they mean it! The festival features a Cheesemaker's Kickoff Ball, Cheese Day Chase marathon run, cheesemaking demonstrations, factory tours, and, of course, lots of cheese sandwiches.

After the festivities, go on a cheese hunt throughout Green County, concentrating on the Monroe area. But first, cheese-seekers need a bit of history, so stop at the **Historic Cheesemaking Center,** 2108 7th Ave., Monroe. The center is in a restored depot, with exhibits on cheesemaking and its impact on Green County. The building is open daily from March to mid-November, 9 a.m. to 4 p.m. Group tours are available by appointment only during Dec; and is closed Jan and Feb. Contact Jim Glessner at (608) 325-4636 for more information. Once you've had your fill of history, you're ready to begin your tour.

Green County Tours

Green County is an antiques lovers' paradise, with nooks and crannies in several towns offering "the stuff o' grannies" that make for charming home decorating. Dedicated treasure hunters claim they can spend upward of a week scouring the area's shops for that "perfect find." As always, call ahead to confirm times and to see if the proprietors have any specialties, whether furniture, jewelry, farm equipment, photos, or related items. Here are several places from which to start that search: *The Recovery,* 1204 19th St. (608-325-5916), in Monroe; *Glarnerladen Antiques & Collectibles,* 101 6th Ave., New Glarus (608-527-6325); *Ott To Recover,* 203 N. Main St., *Monticello* (608-938-4124); and *Center Avenue Antique Mall,* 1027 1st Center Ave., Brodhead (608-897-2696). Happy hunting. For more area listings, check the "Antiquing" section of www.greencounty.org/attractions.iml.

There are many production plants in the area that offer fun tours or a place to pick up a wheel of Edam. For more information, contact Green County Tourism (414-455-0523; www.greencounty.org).

One of the top bike jaunts in Wisconsin is along the 23.5-mile *Sugar River Trail,* which meanders through the county along an abandoned railroad right-of-way. Even though the route opened in 1986, it has yet to "be discovered" by hordes of outsiders.

Cyclists need a $4 trail permit, however, which can be obtained at Sugar River headquarters at the New Glarus Woods State Park, Box 781, New Glarus 53574 (608-527-2335 or 888-222-9111). Bikes can be rented at the park, but car shuttle service is not available.

The gently rolling grade is barely 1 percent, making it a great trip for short-legged kids. For puffing oldsters there are plenty of pit stops along the way in *New Glarus,* Monticello, Albany, and Brodhead. Better than Epsom salts is a foot soak in the Sugar River, where the restored 19th-century Clarence Covered Bridge spans the stream near Brodhead. It's also a good place to hunker down while waiting out a rainstorm. The ford is one of 14 along the route as the trail zigzags back and forth across the river and its tributaries. The route is also excellent for fervid cross-country skiers during Wisconsin's blustery winters. Midway between connecting points of New Glarus on the north and Brodhead on the south is the *Albany Wildlife Refuge.* Look for the herons and other birdlife that inhabit the reeds and woodlands. The Sugar River Trail is also part of the 1,000-mile-long *Ice Age National Scenic Trail* that connects routes throughout Wisconsin.

Pause while biking and take in the *New Glarus Woods*—with its 350 acres of woods, farmland, and prairie—a favorite picnic spot for area families. Check

Biking & Cheese

Located in the heart of dairy country, the **Cheese Country Trail** links Monroe, Browntown, South Wayne Gratiot, and Mineral Point. The relatively easy trail is around 40 miles south of Madison, with the southern trailhead in Monroe at the intersection of 21st Street and 4th Avenue West. The north end is in Mineral Point at Old Darlington Road. Mountain bikes make for the most comfortable ride. The trail system accommodates horseback riders, hikers, snowmobilers, bikers, all-terrain vehicles, and skiers. There are at least 30 cheese factories in the three counties—Green, Lafayette, and Iowa—that incorporate the trail system. Some sections of the Cheese Country Trail have included elements of the Pecatonica Trail. Links are marked for the appropriate use: ATVs, for example, aren't allowed where horses can be ridden, so be alert for signage. A $15 trail-user fee is required and can be purchased at most gas stations near the trail and at other businesses in towns along the way.

Fishing Fun

We like to fish at the ***Browntown–Cadiz Springs State Recreation Area,*** where the living is easy and the crappies are jumping. The placid waters of Lakes Beckman and Zander—both within the recreation area boundaries—are divided by an earthen dike. Zander, the smallest of the two bodies of water, was used for raising bullfrogs commercially in the 1930s. Kids can catch largemouth bass and bluegills from several fishing piers overlooking the water.

Browntown-Cadiz sprawls over 723 acres of marsh and grassland. When I've walked quietly down to the end of the dike, I could get close enough to watch the Canada geese feeding in the sloughs. Be aware that hunting is allowed in the area during autumn, so don't go wandering off into the woods without brightly colored clothing. Better yet, stick to the picnic and fishing areas.

The recreation area is 7 miles west of Monroe on Highway 11. Get to the Allen Road exit, then go south a hilly 0.7 mile to Cadiz Springs Road, turn west, and drive 1.5 miles to the recreation area entrance. For details on the site, call the Department of Natural Resources in Monroe at (608) 966-3777 in the summer and (608) 325-4844 in the winter.

out the following park trails: The ***Basswood Nature Trail*** is less than 0.5 mile long, running from the picnic area near the park office to the north of County Highway NN. ***Chattermark Trail*** loops from the campgrounds through an oak and maple grove. Pick up the ***Great Oak Trail*** for a short stroll around the north end of the park, departing from the edge of the primitive camping area. The ***Walnut Trail*** proceeds south from the west end of the campground and links with the ***Havenridge Nature Trail.*** The latter is the most extensive system in the park, with loops north and south of County NN. It leads through heavy groves of oak and maple and past extensive prairie plantings. Redwing blackbirds, turkey vultures, sparrows, wrens, and other birds swoop and soar overhead as you trek along trails framed by the tall bluestem and swaying buffalo grass. It makes for a special time, especially on a hot August afternoon. A cool drink back in the shade of oak groves will be truly appreciated.

For information on the park, contact the Park Superintendent, c/o Wisconsin Department of Natural Resources, Pleasant View Annex, Monroe 53593. In the summer, call (608) 328-9393; in winter, (608) 325-4844. You can also log on to www.dnr.state.wi. To find the site, take Highway 69, 4 miles south of New Glarus.

New Glarus probably epitomizes all those Green County place-mat images of Switzerland. Settled by pioneers from the Swiss canton of Glarus in 1845, the town remains small. Only about 2,100 citizens live here, so it's not hard to find your way around. In the summer, downtown shops and many homes feature window boxes exploding with crimson geraniums.

Many of the houses in the community date from the turn of the 20th century, and a **Swiss historical village** on the west side of town shows how life was on the Wisconsin frontier prior to the Civil War. The cluster of buildings at 612 7th Ave. (608-527-2317) is open daily 10 a.m. to 4 p.m., May through Oct. No designated time for last tour. Admission is $9 for adults, $3 for ages 6 through 13, and free for ages 5 and under.

The townspeople hearken back to their heritage with locally staged summertime productions of *Heidi,* the famed folktale of the Swiss mountain girl, and *Wilhelm Tell,* of apple-shooting fame. Women from New Glarus made all the costumes for the shows, staged in the town's outdoor amphitheater. Don't despair in case of rain—with inclement weather, the shows are readily moved to the air-conditioned high school auditorium. Look for the live goats on stage. Call (608) 527-2095.

Need a rest? Outgoing Swiss-born hosteller Hans Lenzlinger owns and manages the New Glarus Hotel (608-527-5244; www.newglarushotel.com), a chalet-style hostelry bedecked with flowers hanging from heavy wooden balconies.

For a varied New Glarus/Green County munch other than cheese, try Flannery's **Wilhelm Tell Supper Club,** featuring a respectably extensive Swiss menu. The club is located at 114 2nd St. You will need to call or log on to the website for weekend reservations (608-527-2618; www.flannerysnewglarus.com).

Iowa County

Nope, you aren't in the wrong state when you come to Iowa. The county is in the heart of the Hidden Valleys tourism area of southwestern Wisconsin. **Mineral Point,** a prime jumping-off spot for an off-the-beaten-path adventure, is one of the oldest communities in the state. It was founded in 1827 by lead miners who easily scooped up the precious metal from surface pits near the town. Evidence of their digging can be spotted from any backcountry road in the vicinity.

Peek into the miners' past at Mineral Point's **Pendarvis,** a complex of restored cabins built by settlers from Cornwall more than 150 years ago, when the streets of southwestern Wisconsin were paved with zinc and lead, not gold. The new arrivals immediately began quarrying Galena limestone for use in their cottages.

Walking along Tamblyn's Row, a stretch of rowhouses, you'd think you were back in England. Shake Rag Alley is typical of the street names. Its moniker is derived from the practice of the miners' wives waving their aprons or dish towels from the house windows when lunch was ready. The Pendarvis property was acquired by the state historical society in 1971. It is open daily 10 a.m. to 5 p.m., May through Oct. Guided tours are offered as well (608-987-2122; www.wisconsinhistory.org/sites/pend). The last tour leaves at 4 p.m. The State Historical Society of Wisconsin administers the facility.

Admission is $9 for adults, $7.75 for seniors, and $4.50 for youngsters ages 5 to 12. Discount rates are offered for children's groups. Families (two adults and two or more dependent children) can pay $24.

While in the neighborhood, try a Cornish pasty (pronounced PAST-ee), a meat pie with a thin crust that a worker would take with him to the mine facing. Most of the town's bakeries and restaurants offer these ethnic delicacies. Try one at the **Red Rooster Cafe,** 158 High St., in Mineral Point (608-987-9936). The cafe has been a local favorite for more than 30 years. Prices are moderate.

Take Highway 151 from Mineral Point to **Dodgeville,** seat of Iowa County and home of the state's oldest courthouse, which dates from 1859. South of Dodgeville about 2 miles, just off Highway 18, is the **Folklore Village** (608-924-4000; www.folklorevillage.org), which offers regular Saturday-night folk dancing and singing programs in the old Wakefield Schoolhouse. The place is the brainchild of Jane Farwell, who usually is on hand wearing Tyrolean peasant clothing. Since the 1940s Jane has set up folk-dance camps and seminars around the country, bringing that expertise with her to Wisconsin in the mid-1960s. Throughout the week, craft demonstrations, programs for youngsters, and music lessons are held. Holiday time has ongoing fun. Scandinavian midsummer feasts, Ukrainian and Greek Easters, Israeli Purim, husking bees, and other events fill the calendar.

Drive north of Dodgeville on Highway 23 to the **Don Q Inn.** You'll know that you've arrived after spotting the grounded Boeing prop C-97 parked alongside the highway. The 90-ton beast was flown to the site, parked there, and left as is by the resort's flamboyant former owner, Ron Dentinger.

The Don Q is one of the kinds of places that make a weekend away a something-else eyebrow-raising treat. One of the rooms is in a spire from an old Methodist church adjacent to the main complex. On the bottom floor of the steeple are the bathroom facilities; on the second level is a queen-size bed; on the third is a stereo complex, a pile of pillows, and windows for the best view (if you're looking) of the countryside around Dodgeville. It's a great place to try an inspired "let down your long hair" routine on your significant other. Several of the Don Q's 24 suites have hanging beds, baths made from copper cheese vats, and assorted similar, delightfully quirky wonders. Try the Float Room, with a queen-size bed set in a Viking ship, a heart-shaped hydrotherapy tub, and mirrors on the wall ($105 Sun through Thurs and $125 Fri and Sat). Or how about Tranquility Base, featuring a re-creation of a Gemini space capsule and a 10-sided waterbed? The rates differ for each type of suite. The FantaSuite suites range from $149 during the week to $199 on weekends. The Original Theme suites are $105 Sun through Thurs and $125 on Fri and Sat. Deluxe suites are $149 during the week, $224 on weekends. Call (800) 666-7848, or visit www .donqinn.net. Sam & Maddie's Restaurant and bar is connected to the main building by a 300-foot tunnel.

Immediately to the north of the Don Q is the entrance to ***Governor Dodge State Park,*** a hilly, sprawling preserve of 5,270 acres with 2 lakes, camping sites, hiking trails, and fishing spots. The park provides marvelous habitat for muskrats, deer, fox, and coyote. For bird lovers there are wild turkeys, numerous species of waterfowl, soaring vultures, red-tailed hawks, and the always-busy pileated woodpeckers. When camping, put all food away in a safe place, such as a car trunk, to safeguard it from hungry raccoons, Houdini-like critters that can open almost anything. The park's forest is made up primarily of oak and hickory, with some red pines. In the spring, wildflowers burst from every patch of ground. Even in the shaded areas, ferns can be found in abundance.

Nearby is Spring Green's ***House on the Rock,*** a home perched on a pinnacle of stone called Deershelter Rock, 450 feet above the floor of Wyoming Valley near the Baraboo Range. The home was built in the 1940s by Alex Jordan, a noted Wisconsin sculptor and art collector. It was opened to the public in 1961.

A musical museum and the world's largest carousel (weighing in at 35 tons and standing 80 feet high) are located at the base of the rock. Most of the home is open for touring, with passageways cut through the rock and neat nooks and crannies set aside for reading, loafing, or peering out over the countryside far below.

Jordan had a penchant for doing big things. The central fire pit is large enough to roast a woolly mammoth (critters that actually roamed the valley a few millennia before the House on the Rock was built).

The buildings are now open year-round. The main season, between April 28 and November 5, offers 3 different tour packages, while only 2 tours are offered from early January through April. Get into the Christmas spirit from mid-November through early January, when more than 6,000 St. Nick collectibles are displayed. Tickets go on sale at 9 a.m., with the last tickets being sold about 1 hour prior to early evening closing, due to the time it takes to tour the complex. Hours vary from spring to summer; call (608) 935-3639 or log on to www.thehouseontherock.com for more information. Admission is $28.50

for adults, $26.50 for those intrepid explorers aged 65 or older, and $15.50 for children between the age of 4 and 17; ages 4 and younger are free. A group of 20 or more can get a discounted tour rate. Sales tax will be added to the admission price.

The Spring Green area (Iowa and Sauk Counties along the Wisconsin River) was called home by famed architect *Frank Lloyd Wright,* who worked there on his uncle's farm as a kid. The crusty, eccentric, and brilliant Wright built his home, *Taliesin,* into the brow of a hill near the Wisconsin River (Iowa County). The building is not open to the public, but other Wright structures in the area are.

Before the junction of Highway 23 and County Road C is the Wright-designed *Hillside Home School* (Iowa County), which includes a drafting studio and galleries displaying some of the builder's notable designs. The school is

The Right Place at the Wright Time

Famed architect *Frank Lloyd Wright* made central Wisconsin his home base during the peak of his career. A visitor center (open 9 a.m. to 6 p.m.; 608-588-7900; www .taliesinpreservation.org) and restaurant at the corner of Highway 23 and County Road C is the starting point for tours. Many Wright-connected buildings are in Jones Valley, 3 miles south of Spring Green on Highway 23. Hillside tours are held daily Apr through Oct every hour on the half hour between 10:30 a.m. and 4:30 p.m. Tours start at $16 per person. A handy tip: Reservations are recommended for all tours; walk-ins are accepted only with space permitting.

This natural getaway was at least one reason why Wright loved this area so much. He established his *Taliesin studio* as a "hope and a haven" for creative thinking; it became a complex of buildings that shaped design for generations. At Taliesin, Wright developed plans for the Imperial Hotel in Japan, the Johnson Wax administration building in Racine, and other marvelous structures. Tours of his former home, now a national landmark, are regular components of the tourist scene in the area. Wright designed the elaborate, 300-foot-long visitor center, as well. Tell the kids that the trusses throughout the center were made from the skeleton of the USS *Ranger,* a World War II aircraft carrier, and they should be impressed.

My book, *Got Murder? The Shocking Story of Wisconsin's Notorious Killers,* looks in detail at the butler-done-it 1914 hatchet massacre of Wright's lover Martha (Mamah) Bothwick Cheney, along with her two children, and several workmen at Taliesin. The crazed murderer, Julian Carlton, swallowed muriatic acid following the attack in an attempted suicide. He was nearly lynched by a mob but was taken to the Dodgeville jail, where he died from starvation 7 weeks later. No one really knew why Carlton snapped. Perhaps it was the hazing he received at the hands of the other workmen, a job dispute with Cheney or whatever. With Carlton's suicide, the real cause was never known.

FRANK LLOYD WRIGHT–DESIGNED BUILDINGS

A. D. German Warehouse, Richland Center

Annunciation Greek Orthodox Church, Milwaukee

S. C. Johnson Wax Administration Building, Racine

Seth Petterson Cottage, Lake Delton (available for vacation rentals)

Unitarian Meeting House, Madison

open for visitors from late June through Labor Day. Tours are at 11:30 a.m. and 3:30 p.m. from Apr through Oct. A 2-hour tour of Taliesin and specialty tours are also available. Admission is charged. For information call (608) 588-7900.

A wide range of tour prices is available, depending on the length of time a guest wishes to spend at the facility, which buildings are toured, the number of visitors in a group, and the ages of the participants. We recommend that you call or check Taliesin's comprehensive website to determine which program is best for you (www.taliesinpreservation.org).

Folks in Spring Green still reminisce about the master architect's strolling about the town as if he owned it. Although Wright died in 1959, the town of Spring Green in Sauk County remains the headquarters for Taliesin Associated Architects and the Frank Lloyd Wright School of Architecture. Buildings designed by the architectural firm include the Valley Bank in downtown Spring Green. To see other Wright buildings, stop at the **Riverview Terrace Cafe** inside the Frank Lloyd Wright Center at Taliesin, which is open daily from 9 a.m. to 9 p.m., except for Mon, when it is open from 9 a.m. to 3 p.m. The building is easily accessible on Highway 23 along the banks of the Wisconsin River (608-588-7937). Or swing past **Wyoming Valley School,** 4 miles south of Taliesin on Highway 23. The last two are in Iowa County.

While in the Spring Green area, turn east on County Road C off Highway 14 to get to the **American Players Theater.** Its resident troupe presents Shakespearean productions and other classics during the summer.

Bring bug repellent and dress for the weather, because seating is under the open sky. There's something fantastic about watching *A Midsummer Night's Dream* under an umbrella of stars. Korean-American actor Randall Duk Kim and his associates constructed the theater in 1980. For a time the company was treading thin financial ice, but a concerted marketing effort and aggressive ticket promotions saved the day. With the crowds, you'll now need to have reservations. Contact the theater at Box 819, Spring Green 53588

(608-588-7401; box office, 608-588-2361; americanplayers.org) for the year's production lineup.

For the best in relaxation, try the **House on the Rock Resort** (800-822-7774; www.thehouseontherock.com), across the country road from the American Players Theater and 7 miles south of the House on the Rock museum complex. It is one of the classiest resorts in western Wisconsin, with a gourmet chef, family health-club programs, and golf, golf, golf. There is a Wright feel to the place, with its rooms and interior furnishings that bespeak comfort without overstating it. And there is space for skis, golf clubs, and other outdoor gear as well, along with a microwave, refrigerator, and kitchen nook in each suite.

La Crosse County

La Crosse County marks the northwestern boundary of the Hidden Valleys tourism region. The city of **La Crosse,** population 51,000, is the largest in the western part of Wisconsin. The French named the site after watching a rough-and-tumble Native American game that utilized long-handled racquets.

The competition reminded the trappers of the aristocratic game of tennis, called *la crosse.* A statue by Elmer Peterson in front of the La Crosse Radisson Hotel depicts several Native Americans swinging into action during a spirited match.

A good place to keep an eye on all the folks in town is from atop the 500-foot **Grandad's Bluff** on the east side of the city. From the sharp drop-off, the flatlands leading to the Mississippi look like a slightly rumpled bedsheet covered with toy houses and crisscrossed by tiny cars.

To get to the bluff, take Main Street through town toward Hixon Forest. It's quite a drive up to the parking lots near the crest, but some tough bikers always seem to be puffing their way upwards.

Not me. I've always preferred to drive and arrive refreshed. Telescopes at the far end of the observation platform can be used to spot La Crosse landmarks, such as the city's meeting center, the G. Heileman Brewery grain elevators, and the playing fields of the University of Wisconsin–La Crosse. As for the last, you'll get better seats for viewing athletic events in the stadium stands. But it's a challenge to try to pick out which football team is which from that distance. Look for the varied colored jerseys. About midway up the roadway in the rear of Grandad's Bluff is a refreshment stand for quick sand-wiches and soda.

From I-90 take Highway 53 south to State Street and go west to Riverside Park, where the La Crosse and Black Rivers join the Mississippi. At the north end of the park is **Riverside USA,** with an animated display focusing on the

Seek & Ye Shall Find Old Stuff

The Wisconsin Department of Tourism has developed **The Wisconsin Heritage Traveler,** a guide to the state's Heritage Sign Program. The project is the nation's first to identify historic sites for the traveling public through uniform directional road signs.

The Wisconsin Heritage Traveler lists 121 historic sites, districts, museums, and heritage areas that offer opportunities to poke around the state's history and culture. The sites are referenced by number so they can be easily found in the book and on the road . . . a great idea.

The free, 100-page publication is available to the public at each of the 11 Wisconsin Travel Information Centers, participating historic sites, or by calling (800) 432-8747 or (800) 372-2737 or visiting www.travelwisconsin.com.

The historical importance of each location, along with the address, phone number, hours of operation, and services available, are provided in the guide. Easy-to-read maps illustrate site locations.

When on the road, look for the brown-and-white signs that feature an outline of the state and the word *Heritage* along with the reference number of the site.

history of the Mississippi River. At the park, kids can try captaining a riverboat, the *Belle of La Crosse*. The pilothouse is a reproduction of what an actual vessel would look and sound like. Riverside USA is open daily during the summer from 10 a.m. to 5 p.m.

From the park take a 90-minute cruise on the real thing, the **La Crosse Queen.** The 300-passenger stern-wheeler departs regularly for cruises along the river. Perching on the upper deck, leaning back in a chair, and admiring the sun's rays dancing across the water are grand ways to laze away a summer afternoon. For information or reservations contact the *La Crosse Queen,* Box 1805, La Crosse 54602-1805 (for lunch, brunch, and dinner cruises, 608-784-2893; for charter and group sales, 608-784-8523; www.lacxrossequeen.com). The riverboat dock is located in Riverside Park, at the west end of State Street in downtown La Crosse

Some years back, a friend and I tried a more rugged approach to the river. We took a small boat, loaded it with camping gear at a La Crosse dock, and aimed downstream for a week's adventure. Cruising past the 25-foot-tall, 25-ton *Hiawatha* statue at the confluence of the La Crosse, Black, and Mississippi Rivers, we waved goodbye to comfort for a week. Of course, it was late autumn. The wind was fierce, the rain crept up under our ponchos, and the fish weren't biting. But that was all still ahead of us as we set off. Now, older and just a bit wiser, I'd still take such a jaunt out of town, but I'd probably do it in the summer aboard a houseboat.

Performing a Huck Finn routine on the Mississippi River is as easy as vacationing aboard a Mississippi River houseboat. *Fun 'n the Sun Houseboat Rentals* of La Crosse has 3-day weekend, 4-day midweek, and weeklong options for a family. Fun 'n the Sun is one of several companies in the area that put fully equipped boats on the river. All you need is the grub. If you get really hungry, go fishing! What we've liked about such river houseboating is the ability to go either upriver or downriver. (We became houseboating fans after a trip to Canada's New Brunswick when the kids were small.) Contact Fun 'n the Sun in Alma, 2221 Highway 35; (888) 343-5670.

The city's nationally known fall festival, *Oktoberfest,* is held at the end of September. Capitalizing on the Germanic heritage of many of its current residents, the 9-day festival offers something for the entire family, including the Grand Maple Leaf Parade, authentic German entertainment, arts and crafts for sale, the Torchlight Parade, plenty of polka parties, beer tents, and grilled bratwurst (608-784-FEST).

Winter is a good time to come to the La Crosse area. There are numerous cross-country ski trails that range from beginner to advanced. Try pathways near the city in Hixon Forest, Blue Bird Springs, Goose Island, and Perrot State Park. For trail guides contact the La Crosse Convention and Visitors Bureau, 410 E. Veterans Memorial Dr., La Crosse 54601 (800-658-9424; www.explorelacrosse.com).

Regardless of the season, however, La Crosse and its surrounding area have activities that are off the beaten path or off the wall, but not off the mark. Pen these suggestions in the old date book, starting with February and *Mardi Gras.* Just before Lent you can party before doing your penance—40 days' worth, according to the Roman Catholic religious calendar. The city's Mardi Gras weekend kicks off at the La Crosse Center, starting with a celebrity auction and masquerade ball. Dates vary from year to year, depending on when Lent falls. In that case, for details contact La Crosse Mardi Gras, Box 1433, La Crosse 54602-1433 (www.lacrossemardigras.com).

Reggae Sunsplash in May brings a bit of the Caribbean to Wisconsin, to dazzle the spring with lively music and Jamaican food at the Trempealeau Hotel. Call (608) 534-6898 or log on to www.trempealeauhotel.com. Sunplash is followed by a *Blues Bash* two weeks later. The local Lions Club *Catfish Days* in mid-July celebrates one of the state's great-tasting fish. Events are held at the Village Park in nearby West Salem. Softball tournaments, a crafts fair, a tractor pull, a parade, and music are on tap.

In July, *Riverfest* brings top-name entertainers to the city's Riverside Park. A Venetian parade on the Mississippi River lends an exotic touch. Call

Milk Anyone?

Southern and southwestern Wisconsin have some of the state's prime dairy-herd acreage. It's a fact obvious to anyone driving past pasture after pasture with grazing Guernseys, Jerseys, and Holsteins. And always remember this advice: "Speak to a cow as you would a lady," said **William D. Hoard,** publisher of *Hoard's Dairyman* magazine and experimental farmer who settled in Fort Atkinson.

Encouraged by Hoard, Wisconsin's dairy industry grew enormously. By 1899, 90 percent of the state's farms had dairy cattle. By the 1930s, the state could boast of having two million dairy cattle, which was 400,000 more than second-place New York. In the 1950s, dairying contributed 53 percent of the state's farm output. Today there are some 1.5 million dairy cows munching contentedly across the Wisconsin landscape.

Dairymen from around the county gathered in 1922 for the dedication of a bronze statue of *Hoard,* which stands outside the Wisconsin College of Agriculture's main building in Madison. "Cow College" or "Moo U" remains internationally known for its studies in dairy science.

(608) 782-6000. August's *Art Fair on the Green* attracts artists from around the country, who exhibit their work on the campus of the University of Wisconsin–La Crosse. Call (608) 788-7439 or (800) 658-9424. *A Holiday Folk Fair* is held in November at the La Crosse Center, with wares showcased by more than 130 vendors. Items are geared specifically to the holidays. Call (608) 789-7410.

There's no need to miss any of those events because you don't know the time. Visit the *La Crosse Clock Company,* 125 S. 2nd St., (608) 782-8200. There are more than 1,000 timepieces on the shelves in the shop, which is across from the Radisson Hotel and the Civic Center in downtown La Crosse. The wide range of cuckoos, grandfather, mantel, and other clocks will keep you on schedule.

Downhill skiing is pretty good at *Mount La Crosse,* 2 miles south of the city on Highway 35. The hill has a 516-foot vertical drop and a run of 5,300 feet. It also offers cross-country skiing, instructions, and rentals. Call (608) 788-7878 (800-426-3665 if you're calling outside of Wisconsin) or log on to www.mtlacrosse.com.

Here are more exceptional locales for winter thrills in the La Crosse area: *Bluebird Springs Recreation Area,* N2833 Smith Valley Rd., (608) 781-2267, has 25 miles of groomed cross-country trails open during daylight hours. They are open April 15 through October 15. *Goose Island Campground,* (608) 788-7018, near downtown La Crosse, also has excellent groomed paths. ***Hixon Forest Nature Center,*** 2702 Quarry Rd., (608) 784-0303, presents about 5 miles of trail through heavy woods and along high ridges. The trails are always open, and the nature center is open 9 a.m. to 4 p.m. Mon through Fri and 1 to 4 p.m. Sat and Sun; closed November 1 to May 1 on Sat and Sun. A butterfly garden there is open 1 to 3 p.m. Mon through Thurs and 1 to 4 p.m. Sat.

How about a winter sleigh ride? Try ***Sunset Riding Stables,*** W4803 Meyer Rd., La Crosse 54601; (608) 788-6629 (by reservation only). The 45-minute ride through the snow is $5 per person with a minimum of 10 people. Dress for the weather. After all, this *is* Wisconsin.

Approximately 100 miles of snowmobile trails crisscross La Crosse County, eventually hooking up with another 650 miles of trails in the surrounding region. Seven local snowmobile clubs ensure that the trails are groomed to what seem to be interstate highway specifications. To receive maps, write or call the La Crosse CVB, 410 E. Veterans Memorial Dr., Riverside Park 54601-1895; (608) 782-2366.

Other outdoor recreation opportunities are plentiful in the La Crosse area. Use the city as a jumping-off point for biking, hiking, canoeing, and other outdoor fun. In the spring we often tied in an excursion of some kind after daughter Kate won medals in her high school state champion track meets. The tourneys were held at the University of Wisconsin–La Crosse.

The ***Black and La Crosse Rivers*** are popular with paddlers, who also have discovered ***Coon Creek,*** the ***Mississippi River,*** and its backwaters. The latter might be difficult for beginning canoeists due to the swift current and underwater obstructions. There are numerous rental and sales outlets throughout the region, supplying everything from anchors to life preservers. Check the La Crosse yellow pages for listings.

The ***La Crosse River Marsh*** on the west side of La Crosse is a marvelous example of a natural wetland, one used by schools and area universities for study. The marsh, which is included in the Mississippi River floodplain, covers 1,077 acres. Knowledgeable hikers can spot at least 100 different kinds of vegetation, including trees such as oak, cottonwood, and basswood, as well as the less obvious algae, moss, and fungi. On the animal side, there are 24 differ-

funfacts

Wisconsin ranks 26th in size among all the states and 10th in size among midwestern states.

ent species of mammals, 139 different species of breeding and migratory birds, 9 species of reptiles, 6 species of amphibians, and 53 species of fish, plus hundreds of varied insects.

The La Crosse area is a cyclist's image of dying and going to heaven. The major state bike trails meander through the region to combine urban and rural rides geared to the interests of all ages. The **Great River State Trail** begins in Onalaska near La Crosse's far north side and rolls about 22 miles along the Mississippi River. Shuttle service is available by contacting the Center for Commerce and Tourism in Onalaska, 800 Oak Forest Dr. (608-781-9570 or 800-873-1901; www.discoveronalaska.com), but 24-hour notice is required. The **A-1 Cab Company** (608-781-6655) and the **Bee Cab Company** (608-784-4233) provide the service. Rentals at $15 per day are available at the **Blue Heron Bicycle Works,** 114 2nd Ave. North in Onalaska (608-783-RIDE [7433]; www.blueheronbikes.com). Kevin Miller's well-stocked cycle shop is about 2 blocks from the trail, and he can make repairs as necessary for visiting bikers. The shop is open from 10 a.m. to 6 p.m. Tues through Sat and 11 a.m. to 4 p.m. Sun, but it is closed Mon. Helmets come with the rental. Miller does not provide shuttle service, but he can arrange for a local cab company to pick up riders who journey to nearby towns along the bike trail. Costs range from $20 to $25 for a vanload of cyclists. The **La Crosse River Bicycle Trail** is a 21.5-mile expedition paralleling the La Crosse River. The route cuts along farm pastures, streams, and maple groves. This trail connects with the Elroy-Sparta Trail and the **Great River State Trail.** There is plenty of camping along the routes, most of which are hard-surface crushed rock along old railroad beds.

West of La Crosse on Highway 16, about a mile or so north of I-94, is **West Salem,** home of pioneer author Hamlin Garland. The bushy-haired, Pulitzer prize–winning novelist was born here in 1860 and returned when he was an adult. He wrote dozens of short stories and novels about the farmers and other people who lived in the "coulee country" of La Crosse County. A *coulee* is a valley, usually with very steep sides. Among his best-known works were *Son of the Middle Border* and *Main-Traveled Roads.*

When Garland moved to Iowa late in his life, my poet father became friends with the old storyteller, who offered many good-humored suggestions on writing styles. Garland's West Salem house is located at 357 W. Garland St. (608-786-1399; www.westsalemwi.com) and is open Memorial Day to Labor Day from 1 to 5 p.m. Admission is charged.

The West Salem Rustic Road, accessible from I-90 at the town's freeway exit, is the only one in the state featuring a residential area within a major stretch of its 2.5-mile route. The road edges past the home of Thomas Leonard, founder of West Salem; the village's main business district; Garland's homestead; the Octagon House (on the National Register of Historic Places) at the corner of Highways C and 16; and Swarthout Lakeside Park.

Lafayette County

The little community of **Belmont,** where today's Highway 126 bisects US 151, can brag about its flirt with history in 1836. At the time, settlers were casting about for a capital of the Wisconsin Territory. Since the population was equally spread through what is now Iowa, the Dakotas, Wisconsin, and Minnesota, there was a lot of disagreement about the best locale. Governor Henry Dodge picked Belmont because of its centralized location and because it wasn't far from his own home. The choice received so much criticism that Dodge retreated and allowed the territorial representatives to suggest alternative locations. Subsequently, the capital was moved to Iowa for a time before coming back to Wisconsin. Madison eventually won the nod and continued as capital when Wisconsin was made a state.

The **First Capitol State Park and Museum** (608-987-2122; www.first capitol.wisconsinhistory.org) recalls that 19th-century controversy. Drive 3 miles north of Belmont on Highway G to the park, operated by the Lafayette County Historical Society (608-776-8340). The emotional air is calmer now, and the long-forgotten debate is far removed from the minds of picnickers and hikers on the trails. The museum is open from 10 a.m. to 4 p.m., Memorial Day through Labor Day, but is closed Mon and Tues.

Take a hike on the **Pecatonica Trail**, which follows a Milwaukee railroad line for almost 10 miles between Belmont and Calamine in Lafayette County. Look for the trail signs. The gravel-and-cinder-surfaced trail travels along the Bonner Branch of the Pecatonica River. Walkers and bikers are welcome during nonwinter months. When the snow flies, snowmobilers and cross-country skiers can utilize the pathway. Bonner Branch is a swift moving little creek that swings back and forth under the trail, making it necessary to have 24 bridges on the stretch between the two towns. That totals 1,306 feet of planking. I've spotted quails, pheasants, squirrels, woodchucks, and the occasional deer on various strolls.

funfacts

Wisconsin covers 56,145 square miles. This figure includes 1,831 square miles of inland water. Add to that figure the 9,355 square miles of water from Lakes Michigan and Superior.

Speaking of capitols, the **Lafayette County Courthouse** in Darlington was built in 1905 through the generosity of local mining magnate Matthew Murphy. Financed through his will, the imposing limestone structure features a central rotunda and an elaborately painted dome. Marble walls and fancy woodwork round off the building.

Guests are free to wander the halls and study the graceful architectural style at their leisure. The county clerk requests, however, that visitors come during the week's regular working hours.

Lafayette County is geared for outdoors enthusiasts. ***Blackhawk Memorial County Park*** in Woodford annually hosts a black-powder shoot and Indian encampment in May, sponsored by the Yellowstone Flint and Cap Blackpowder Club. Adding variety to the program are tomahawk throwing and a candle shoot. Although we're black-powder shooters ourselves, using a smoothbore Brown Bess musket patterned after the regulation British army piece of the Revolutionary War, I've never participated in the Blackhawk rendezvous. But the event is highly recommended by buckskinning friends who have enjoyed the reenactment.

Tell the kids the story behind the park, which is seemingly calm today when its hook-shaped Bloody Lake is smooth as glass in the afternoons. But this is the site of an 1832 battle in which outnumbered Sac and Fox Indians under Chief Blackhawk fought frontier militia and regular army troops. Later that year the Sac were slaughtered while trying to surrender to US cavalry at Bad Axe in Vernon County along the Mississippi River. In 1990, Governor Tommy Thompson formally apologized to the descendants of the Sac Nation for what had happened those many years ago. It was the first time that any government representative tried to make amends to Native Americans for war crimes committed against their ancestors.

The oak- and willow-shaded park is hushed, except for the whoops of fishing fans pulling in whoppers. A boat ramp leads into the slow-moving east branch of the Pecatonica River, where bass, catfish, and trout are reported to lurk. Primitive camping is allowed, but there are no sewer, water, or electric hookups available. If you don't mind roughing it a bit, this park is great. It's not hard to find, tucked as it is along Sand Road and Lafayette County Highway Y near Woodford.

Just to the north, along Highway 78, is ***Yellowstone Lake State Park*** near Blanchardville (608-523-4427; www.dnr.wi.gov/org/land/parks/specific/yellowstone). The 445-acre lake is the focus of the park's activities. In the winter a 12-mile public snowmobile trail connects the park to Darlington. Each June, the city hosts a Canoe Fest, which includes a 10-mile race along the Pecatonica River with 20 categories for its hundreds of contestants. With odds like that, even landlubbing duffers like me who spend more time bumping into riverbanks than cruising merrily along have a chance to snare a trophy.

To help in this regard, Lafayette County's historic churches stand ready. In 1844, missionary Father Samuel Mazzuchelli built a neat wooden church in

Start at the Beginning

The *Point of Beginnings Heritage Area* has been designated by the state to preserve and promote history in Grant, Iowa, and Lafayette Counties. The name comes from the Point of Beginnings marker, a benchmark where government surveyor Lucius Lyon began the state's official survey in 1831.

For you geography buffs, the Point of Beginnings is where the fourth principal meridian crosses the Illinois/Wisconsin border, south of Hazel Green. Lucius's crew built a mound 6 feet tall and 6 feet square, hammering an oak post deep into its center. Every inch of the state has been surveyed from this mark. In the 1970s state surveyors dug up the original post and replaced it with a modern marker. The numbers in the center of the monument correspond to the land sections that come together at the Point of Beginnings.

For more information on Point of Beginnings, contact the trail offices at Box 608, Platteville 53818; (608) 723-4170.

New Diggings, a lead mining town in the western section of the county. Serving the "badgers" in the neighborhood, hearty Mazzuchelli tromped through the woods to encourage his rough-and-tumble frontier flock to attend mass.

At the other end of the county, Lutheran pastors founded the East Wiota Lutheran Church in 1844. Descendants of Norwegian settlers who lived here in those days are still using the church. The tidy, trim building is the oldest Norwegian Lutheran church in North America.

Like its neighboring counties, Lafayette County was born and weaned during those heady lead-rush days that extended from the late 1820s to the 1840s. The hub of the county's mining and commercial world was Shullsburg.

The county lies at the southern edge of the glacial movement that pancaked most of Wisconsin eons ago. Geologists call the vicinity west of town a "driftless area" because it was never smoothed under the towering plates of ice. The deep, dark valleys and moody ridgetops that were untouched by the ice are obvious while driving along Highway 11. Since the glaciers never dispersed or buried the lead deposits, early miners found fairly easy pickings.

The *Badger Mine and Museum,* 279 Estey St. (608-965-4860; www.shullsburgwisconsin.org/BadgerMineMuseum.htm), takes visitors into that era with an extensive display of old-time mining gear. The museum, on the site of the Badger Lot Diggings that began operations in 1827, is open daily Memorial Day through Labor Day Wed and Thurs from noon to 4 p.m.; Fri through Sun, 11 a.m. to 4 p.m. The facility is closed Mon and Tues, excluding holidays. Admission is $5 for adults; children under 10, $3; senior citizens, $4.

The men who worked in the diggings labored 12 hours a day for the princely sum of $1. They were lowered by windlass 40 to 50 feet underground, where they crawled on hands and knees to the lead facings in the rock. Working by candlelight, these stocky Cornishmen could seldom stand completely upright, even though most of them were barely over 5-feet tall. Visitors have it easier now, although they are still 47 feet under the surface. You can stand up straight in parts of the mine traversed during the 0.25-mile tour.

The miners believed that a form of goblin, the Cornish Knockers, had followed them from tin mines in the Old Country and lived in the darkest recesses of the New World caverns. Generally the Knockers would make their appropriate tap-tap sound to indicate a rich mineral vein. In exchange the miners had to leave a bit of their luncheon pasty as a thank you. If they didn't receive such a gift, the angry Knockers could cause mine roofs to collapse. Don't worry about that today—there haven't been any reports of Cornish Knockers in the Shullsburg vicinity since the Badger Lot Diggings closed in 1856.

Shullsburg itself is a community designed for strolling. Park anywhere and amble along winding streets with such lilting names as Hope, Charity, Friendship, and Justice. Originally the roads were mere paths followed by miners from their homes to the shafts and were named by the good Dominican friar, Father Mazzuchelli, on one of his Bible-thumping jaunts through town.

Monroe County

The earliest of the state's major bike paths, the famed *Elroy-Sparta Trail*, opened in 1966 and annually hosts more than 55,000 riders. Since the trail is on an old railroad bed, you'll even travel through three-century-old tunnels that save you the legwork you would have needed for steeper grades. The trail wanders for 32.5 miles across Monroe County into Juneau County. During the summer, all-you-can-eat pancake breakfasts are served in the Wilton Municipal Park. The Lions Club serves the breakfasts, which cost $5, from 7 to 10:30 a.m., running from Memorial Day weekend until Labor Day. Wilton is about the midway point on the ride. For information on bike rentals, auto shuttles, campgrounds, and other lodging and restaurant listings, contact the Elroy-Sparta State Trail, Box 297, Kendall 54638 (608-463-7109; www.elroy-sparta-trail.org). Highway 71 parallels the trail for almost the entire route, which makes it convenient for tired riders who need to be picked up.

Don't be surprised if you are driving through Angelo, just a hop and a jump

funfacts

Wisconsin became the 30th state on May 29, 1848.

north of Sparta, and a giant eagle appears to be taking wing from a parking lot. Look twice and you might see an elephant, a monster gorilla, a huge beaver, or some other bigger-than-life creature. There's no cause to worry, however, since the pack of critters is nothing more than completed products, made by F.A.S.T. Corp., headquartered in Sparta (www.fastkorp.com).

The acronym stands for *Fiberglass Animals, Shapes & Trademarks,* which makes the animals for displays around the world. They're often kept outside the plant until ready for shipping. As a result, former F.A.S.T. president Jerry Vettrus is used to cars screeching to a halt in front of his place.

If you're so inclined, you can purchase something big for the backyard pool. How about a spouting whale or a leaping muskie? It'll probably cost about $2,000 for something under 20 feet tall. But wouldn't it be worth it?

Richland County

Richland Center hosts the *Wisconsin High School Rodeo Association Championships* (www.cowboycalendar.com/wihsra) each June at the Richland County fairgrounds on County Road AA on the city's north side. Kids from around the state compete in calf roping, bulldogging, bronc riding, barrel racing, and other bone-jarring events. Some of the youngsters eventually go on to college rodeo teams and then to the pro circuit. In addition to June Dairy Days, a Rodeo Parade also takes place the weekend of the Rodeo Championships. Call or stop by the chamber of commerce downtown office (608-647-6205), located adjacent to the caboose. They'll also be able to tell you about the tractor pulls held at the county fairgrounds each July. Some of the heavy-equipment operators can haul 12,000 pounds or more over a set course on the dirt track.

Take Highway 40 north about 7 miles to *Rockbridge* and *Pier Natural Bridge Park,* site of one of the first white settlements in Richland County. There are scenic rock formations all along Highways 80, 60, 58, and 56, which spin around Rockbridge like spokes. The park's main feature is a long bridge of rock, at least 60 feet high and 80 feet wide.

If spelunking is your thing, the county's *Eagle Cave* is another of the state's larger underground caverns. The cave is just off Highway 60, west of Eagle Corners. But if claustrophobia hits and subsurface roaming is not to your liking, there are 26.5 miles of hiking trails above the cave site. Eagle Cave is open to the public Memorial Day to Labor Day, but the cave and grounds are used in the off-season by scout troops. For more details contact Eagle Cave, 16320 Cavern Ln., Blue River 53518 (608-537-2988; www.eaglecave.net). To keep the crowds coming, the Wisconsin Skyrocket Coon Dog Field Trials are held here each June.

Vernon County

About 38 miles north of Prairie du Chien on Highway 35, which is nicknamed the Great River Road, the Bad Axe River empties into the Mississippi. Here Black Hawk attempted to surrender his Sac and Fox followers to the white militia and Sioux warriors who had encamped at Fort Crawford. The troops, including Abraham Lincoln, ignored Black Hawk's white flag and chased the Native Americans into the river, where many drowned. The few survivors who made it across to the Iowa side were captured by the whites' Sioux allies on the far bank and sent back to the fort, where they were imprisoned.

The site is the saddest along this stretch of the Mississippi, especially when autumn mists rise slowly out of the hollows along the roadway. You can feel the heaviness in the air before the harsh sun drives the fog away.

This is Vernon County, which was originally called Bad Axe County, but in 1861 image-conscious residents asked the state legislature to change the name to the less negative "Vernon," a loose Anglicizing of *verdant,* meaning "green." The legislators obliged, recalling the incident with Black Hawk, no doubt.

The **Genoa National Fish Hatchery** (608-689-2605; www.fws.gov/midwest/genoa) raises both cold- and warm-water species of finny critters. The hatchery hosts an Annual Kids' Fishing Day in May where eager young anglers learn about fishing ethics and conservation, jig making, fish anatomy, fish cleaning, and fish behavior and habitats. Being avid fisherfolk, the Hintz clan likes to check out these kinds of places . . . just to be sure there will be plenty of stock for Wisconsin's lakes and streams hungry for our bait. Bass, walleye, trout, and sauger are among the two million fish produced annually and shipped to state and federal release points around the country. Now that's talking fish! The hatchery is 5 miles south of La Crosse. Visitors can tour the facility between 8 a.m. and 2 p.m., Mon through Fri. For a free look-see, call ahead to arrange.

While in the area, we also like to park near **Lock and Dam No. 8** on Highway 35 (the Great River Road) and watch barges and boats navigate up and down the Mississippi River.

The eastern portion of Vernon County has a large population of Amish, some of whom work in a furniture factory on County Road D northeast of Westby. Their creations of bent hickory rockers and other pieces are excellent. With the slow-moving Amish wagons on the county's back roads, motorists must be very careful. The highways through the area are notorious for curves and loops. Of course, the scenery compensates for the required slower-paced driving.

Trillium, in La Farge, a bed-and-breakfast in the heart of the Amish community, is on an 85-acre farm where visitors can really get away from it all by strolling through the hills around the Kickapoo Valley and Driftless Region, not flattened by glaciers eons ago. Trillium has 2 private cottages available for rental. For fresh-baked, homemade bread, owner Rosanne Boyett's touch is superb. Her breakfasts have been showcased in many books. Call (608) 625-4492 or visit www.trilliumcottage.com.

The *Westby House Inn and Restaurant* is another interesting bed-and-breakfast, located at 200 W. State St. in *Westby* (608-634-4112; www .westbyhouse.com). The house is at the corner of Ramsland and State, only a block off Highway 14. The Victorian-style 1890s home has 10 suites and rooms and even a guesthouse, all done up with antiques and crafts made throughout the area. Rates range from $79 to $299 for the guesthouse. Rooms (2 with private bath) have queen-size beds. Kids are welcome. If you can't stay for the night, the public dining room offers a wide-ranging menu and is open for lunch and dinner throughout the week. Reservations are always recommended.

Westby is also an outdoors town, with the *Snowflake Annual Ski Jumping Tournament* (www.explorewisconsin.com/communitypages/westby.html) in February. The event is held at the *Snowflake Ski Club* (north of town off Highway 27 on Vernon County Highway P). The 65-meter run's landing zone converts to a 9-hole, par 3 golf course in the summer. I've never let the kids practice these dives off the roof of the house into a snowbank, but they got a thrill out of watching the airborne pros.

Wildcat Mountain State Park (608-337-4775) seems to appear out of nowhere, a mere 20-minute ride west of Hillsboro on Highway 33. All of a sudden there it is, with deep gorges, pines, limestone cliffs, and racing waterways that show a dramatically rugged side of Wisconsin.

Hillsboro itself is a quaint village that boasts its own museum, an 1860s log cabin on the northeast side of town. The little house, part of the Hillsboro Historical Society, is open on Sun from 1 to 4 p.m. early June to Labor Day. By calling the city clerk at (608) 489-2521 or (608) 489-3192, you can probably get inside on other days. Half the building looks like an old post office, and the other half contains typical pioneer furnishings.

If fishing is one of your favorite pastimes, be sure to travel in western Vernon County, for it borders the great Mississippi River. Stoddard is located in the northwest corner of the county, where ice fishing is a popular sport for those who don't mind braving the freezing temperatures and howling winds of Wisconsin winters. The village of Genoa draws people from more than 200 miles away, offering some of the best Mississippi catfish, bullheads, and other creatures of the Old Maid. De Soto Harbors, in the southwest corner of the county, is the historic area of the final defeat of the famed Indian chief Black

Hawk. Blackhawk Memorial Park, where you can find your fill of camping and fishing, is just north of the village.

The Czechs and Bohemians celebrate their heritage in mid-June with an annual town festival in June at the **Czech-Slovak Community Festival** in Phillips (http://czech-slovak.tripod.com). Polka-dancing fans come from miles around to flit around the dance pavilions. The active exercise is a requirement to get rid of pounds gained from nibbling rich Bohemian foods at the concession stands.

County seat Viroqua annually hosts the Vernon County Fair on the grounds at the north edge of town. Some of the best harness racing in the state can be seen at the September event. Drivers and breeders don't mind bragging when inquisitive visitors come around to see the stables and the animals. This is of one of the oldest fairs in Wisconsin, the first being held in 1856. The 5-day event is held in September and features a demo derby, tractor pull, and harness racing. For details, contact the fair office at (608) 637-3165 or on the fair site: www.vernoncountyfair.com

There's a lot of competition in dairy classes as well. Watching the judging will help you learn the difference between a Holstein and a Guernsey. There's a lot to know between one breed and an-udder.

Later in the month, usually on the last Saturday in September, nearby Viola (just 13 miles east of Viroqua on Highway 56) features a free, yearly **Viola Horse and Colt Show** (www.horseandcoltshow.com). Get there by 9:30 a.m. to watch the pony- and horse-pulling contests. No, the spectators don't pull the horses. The teams are hitched to weighted sleds that are to be pulled a certain distance. The horse show usually begins at 9 a.m. and runs throughout the day. There's an afternoon parade, a dance at night, a tractor pull, midway rides, and exhibits by the Future Farmers of America and the 4-H. It's all real down-home.

Good Old Days

For an old-time July 4, swing through Viroqua for the community's traditional Ice Cream Social on the lawn of the historic *Sherry-Bett Historic Civil War Museum*, 795 N. Main St. (608-637-7336). An impressive 19th-century mansion, this fully restored home of a Civil War colonel and his family is furnished as it was in the late 1800s. The building is open from 1 to 5 p.m. Sat and Sun or by appointment from Memorial Day through mid-September. Devouring a heaping plate of strawberry shortcake is an integral part of the fun. Check out the activities through the Vernon County Historical Society, 410 S. Center Ave. (608-637-7396; www.frontiernet .net/~vcmuseum).

The descendants of Norwegians, Czechs, and Bohemians make up a strong percentage of the Vernon County population. In fact, one of the largest clusters of Norwegians outside the Old Country lives in the stretch along Highway 14 between La Crosse and Westby. *Norskedalen* (translated as "Norwegian Valley"), on County Road P at Coon Valley, is a refurbished pioneer homesite and a 350-acre arboretum along with nature trails (http://norskedalen.org).

The center is open year-round with loads of exciting family events, such as an old time threshing bee and "Always on Sunday" programs at the Thrune Visitor Center, where authors and history experts give lectures. A Civil War Heritage Weekend in October always packs in crowds eager to see the musket firing. Classes are offered in rosemaling, wood carving, Hardanger fiddling, and weaving. Tours take in the Bekkum Homestead, a recreated turn-of-the-last-century farm and the 112-acre Gundersen Arboretum, and guests can even spend the night at the 130-year-old Paulsen Cabin. For nonmembers, rates Monday through Thursday are $95 a day and $215 on Fri and Sat. For Sun, add on $65; or book an entire week (6 nights) for $500; with more than six persons, it's an extra $10 a day. Be aware that the cabin has steep stairs to the sleeping loft and stairs to the bathroom in the basement.

Places to Stay in Western Wisconsin

BAGLEY

Bagley Hotel
175 S. Bagley Ave.
(608) 996-2300
Inexpensive
Only 6 bedrooms for a comfortable, intimate getaway; common sitting room; no televisions, which allows for a perfect vacation.

LA CROSSE

Best Western Riverfront Hotel
1835 Rose St.
(877) 688-9260
www.bestwestern.com
Moderate
Good river views, spotless rooms; close to major highways and attractions.

Radisson Hotel
200 Harborview Plaza
(608) 784-6680
www.radisson.com/LaCrosse
Moderate
Convenient downtown location overlooking the Mississippi River, short stroll to La Crosse Center and Riverside Park; great for corporate, as well as families.

Wilson Schoolhouse Inn
W5718 Highway 14-61
(608) 787-1982
www.wilsonschoolhouseinn.com
Moderate
Historic 1917 getaway, all restored and elegantly furnished; in rural surroundings but minutes from downtown La Crosse.

NEW GLARUS

Chalet Landhaus Inn
801 Highway 69
(608) 527-5234
(800) 944-1716
www.chaletlandhaus.com
Moderate

WISCONSIN INFO

For Wisconsin travel information, contact the **Wisconsin Department of Tourism,** 201 W. Washington St., Madison 53707 (608-266-7621 or 800-372-2737; www.travelwisconsin.com).

For information on the state's economy, history, or government, contact the **Office of the Governor,** State Capitol, Box 7863, Madison 53707.

Hot tub, steam room, high-speed DSL available in hotel lobby; great summer getaway packages.

New Glarus Hotel
100 6th Ave.
(608) 527-5244
(800) 727-9477
www.newglarushotel.com
Moderate
Whirlpool suites, Alpine restaurant serving Swiss and American foods; "Barefoot Becky" regularly performs.

Swiss Aire Motel
1200 Highway 69
(608) 527-2138
(800) 798-4391
Inexpensive
All rooms nonsmoking, truck parking for RV rigs and over-the-road types, free Wi-Fi, barbecue grill picnic area.

WESTBY

Old Towne Motel
102 E. Old Town Rd. (US 14/61 and Highway 27 South)
(608) 634-2111
(800) 605-0276
www.oldtownemotel.com
Moderate

If a regular guest, they'll know your name; hospitable, small town feel.

Westby House Victorian Inn & Restaurant
200 W. State St.
(608) 634-4112
(800) 434-7439
http://westbyhouse.com
Moderate
Wrap-around porch for seasonal sitting, 2 Jacuzzi suites with gas fireplaces, tearoom open to the public.

Places to Eat in Western Wisconsin

DARLINGTON

Darlington Golf and Country Club Bar & Grill
17098 Country Club Rd.
(608) 776-3377
www.darlingtoncc.com
Inexpensive to moderate
Best overview of any 9th hole this side of the Mississippi River; open grill is available 7 days a week from for sandwiches and appetizers.

Towne House Restaurant
322 Main St.
(608) 776-3373
Inexpensive to moderate
Home-style cooking reminiscent of great-grandma's, generous portions for the hungry; meet the locals.

DESOTO

Great River Roadhouse
9660 Highway 35
(608) 648-2045
www.mississippiriver
adventures.com/greatriver
roadhouse.htm
Inexpensive
Homemade pizza, ribs, chicken, and carryouts available for Friday fish fry; good river view; really casual setting.

FENNIMORE

The Cottage Baker
1030 Lincoln Ave.
(608) 822-3646
Inexpensive
Espresso bar, fresh bagels, no trans fats or corn syrup, soup-and-sourdough lunch Wed and Fri.

Canterbury Garden Cafe, Fennimore Rose Garden Florist & Chocolate Shoppe Ice Cream
1080 9th St.
(608) 822-4438
www.canterburycafe
androsegardenflorist.com
Inexpensive
Breakfast and lunch in the parlor, classical background music, decadently sinful chocolates, plus flowers.

Friederick's Family Restaurant
430 Lincoln Ave.
(608) 822-7070
Inexpensive
Casual, old-school cafe, kid-friendly; no credit cards nor alcohol; right in the middle of town.

LA CROSSE

The Freight House
107 Vine St.
(608) 784-6211
www.freighthouserestaurant
.com
Moderate to expensive
Premier steak and seafood; a *Wine Spectator* winner; blazing fireplace for winter lounging.

Three Rivers Lodge, Radisson Hotel
111 Front St.
(608) 793-5018
www.threeriverslodge.com/
home/contact/contact.asp
Moderate to expensive
Contemporary, upscale feel with lots of stone and hardwoods; breakfast banana-almond french toast to die for;

reservations suggested for nighttime dining.

LANCASTER

Doolittle's Pub & Eatery
(608) 723-7676
Inexpensive
Wild, wild, live band in a happening evening place, so put on your dancing clogs.

Zippy's Brass Rail
120 E. Maple St.
(608) 723-2356
Inexpensive
Hefty burgers galore, can even call ahead; husky pours of refreshing beverages.

MONROE

Gillett's Golden Oldies Restaurant
1713 11th St.
(608) 328-4373
Inexpensive to moderate
Known for its breakfast starting at 6 a.m., try the cinna-ring doughnuts and Southern-style biscuits and gravy.

NEW GLARUS

Flannery's Wilhelm Tell Bar & Restaurant
14 2nd St.
(608) 527-2618
www.flannerysnewglarus
.com
Moderate
Go ahead and yodel over succulent prime rib, hefty steaks, and seafood, plus other nightly specials; it's popular so be sure to call ahead.

New Glarus Hotel Restaurant
100 6th Ave.
(608) 527-5244
(800) 727-9477
www.newglarushotel.com
Moderate to expensive
Wiener schnitzel and sauerbraten, polka bands, local New Glarus beers, plus imported Swiss wines.

ONALASKA

Lakeview Restaurant
N5135 Highway 35
(608) 781-0150
Inexpensive to moderate
Perfect for a relaxing meal after biking on the Great River State Trail and canoeing nearby Perrot State Park; buffalo burgers; cozy lounge.

PLATTEVILLE

Owl Cafe
80 N. 2nd St.
(608) 348-4416
Inexpensive
Simple grub, kickback feel makes for a fab eating place, no pretensions; cash only.

Steve's Pizza Palace
15 S. 4th St.
(608) 348-3136
www.stevespizzapalace
.com
Inexpensive
Opened in 1963, pizza is king, sniff the aroma of pasta sauce and hot peppers; takeout, too.

SELECTED CHAMBERS OF COMMERCE

**La Crosse Convention and Visitors
Bureau**
410 Veterans Memorial Dr.
La Crosse 54601
(800) 658-9424
http://explorelacrosse.com

**New Glarus Tourism Bureau and
Chamber of Commerce**
418 Railroad St.
New Glarus 53574-0713
(608) 527-2095
www.swisstown.com

Platteville Chamber of Commerce
275 Highway 151 West
Platteville 53818
(608) 348-8888
www.platteville.com

**Prairie du Chien Chamber of
Commerce and Tourism Council**
211 S. Main St.
Prairie du Chien 53821-0326
(608) 326-8555
(800) 732-1673
www.prairieduchien.org

Windsor Food & Spirits
75 N. 2nd St.
(608) 348-3373
Moderate
Lots of UW–Platteville
students and visiting
parents, really hip place,
wide a range of Wisconsin-
brewed products.

PRAIRIE DU CHIEN

Culver's
1915 S. Marquette Rd.
(608) 320-5360
www.culvers.com
Inexpensive
Perfect roadside drive-
through pit stop for hot
fudge malt, then hit the
road again.

Jeffer's Black Angus
37640 Highway 18
(608) 326-2222
Moderate to expensive
Think meat or chicken
livers sautéed with bacon
and onions, plus plenty o'
pasta; great for kids.

Main Entrance
215 W. Blackhawk Ave.
(608) 326-4030
Inexpensive
Open mic acoustic jam
sessions and appearances
by top bands, along with
gallons of beer and a
kazoo-playing bartender;
no televisions on the walls
(hurray!).

SPRING GREEN

**Round Barn Restaurant
& Lodge**
E4830 Highways 14
and 60
(608) 588-7512 (restaurant)
(608) 588-2568 (lodge)
www.theroundbarnlodge
.com
Moderate
Actually was a barn before
becoming an Italian-
menued restaurant, plenty
of pizza options plus
breakfast and lunch.

**Spring Green General
Store & Cafe**
137 S. Albany St.
(608) 588-7070
Inexpensive
http://springgreengeneral
store.com
Short plays and readings,
microbrews, breakfast five-
grain cereal, vegetarian
chili, and sweet chicken
salad.

**The Kitchen at Arcadia
Books**
102 E. Jefferson St.
(608) 588-7638 (bookstore)
(608) 588-3923 (kitchen)
Inexpensive
Coffee, sweets, carryout
or lunch and dinner, plus
books for a what-more-
could-you-want experience.

CENTRAL WISCONSIN

Central Wisconsin is a rare mixture of tourism fun, urban bustle, political muscle, and natural beauty. It seems as if the best of what the state has to offer has come together here in a potpourri of sights and color.

There's the hustle and bustle of Dane County and Madison, the state capital, combined with the rural "outcountry" of Wisconsin's river heartland.

Columbia County

About 4 miles south of Arlington on Highway 51 is the *Arlington University of Wisconsin Agricultural Research Station,* an outdoor lab run by the University of Wisconsin. Researchers work on crop, livestock, and soil studies, and no one minds if you stop by for a quick visit. The farm at N695 Hopkins Rd. (608-846-3761) is open all year from 8 a.m. to 4:30 p.m. Mon through Fri. If you need a goose to get you to Arlington, there are plenty to be had at the Goose Pond, so take Highway 51 north from Madison to Country Route K. Go west on K to Hopkins, and then turn south to find the station.

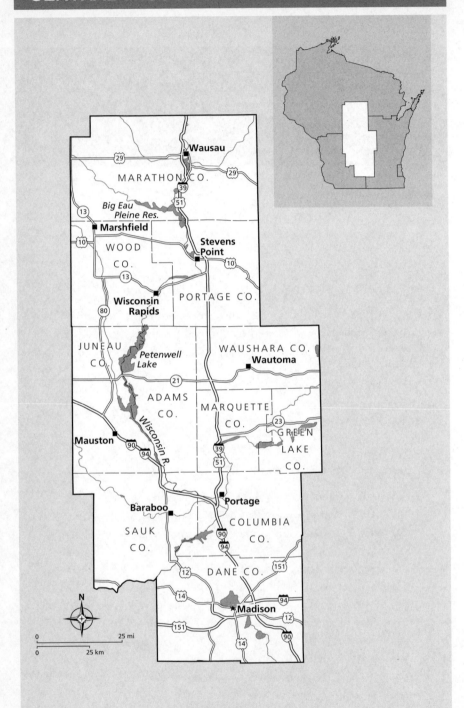

Spring and fall migrations cover the marshland and nearby cornfields with great gaggles of geese. I've always wondered about how many pillows and quilts we could fill with all those fluttering feathers.

Four miles north of Arlington is the *MacKenzie Environmental Center* at Poynette, 1 mile east of town on Highway CS. The state Department of Natural Resources manages the center, which offers displays of native Wisconsin animals and has an interlocking network of excellent hiking trails. The center is open daily from 8 a.m. to 4 p.m. (the grounds are open until dark) and is closed on winter holidays and weekends November 1 through April 15. Call (608) 635-8105 or log on to www.mackenziecenter.com if you need more specifics.

Folks in *Portage,* the Columbia County seat, say this is where "the North begins." A trading post was established here in 1792, and entrepreneurs formed transport companies to aid commercial travel between the Fox and Wisconsin Rivers. Oxen would tow empty barges across the connecting mudflats for $10; 50 cents per 100 pounds of merchandise was the going price for loaded vessels. A canal eventually was dug, linking the rivers and opening with much fanfare in 1851.

Portage is home of the *Historic Indian Agency House,* built in 1832 for agent John Kinzie and his wife, Juliet, a prolific writer. One of her works, *Waubun,* was a detailed account of her family's trip to Fort Winnebago that

CENTRAL WISCONSIN'S TOP HITS

Art Fair off the Square	MacKenzie Environmental Center
Capital Brewery and Beer Garden	Merrimac ferryboat
Cave of the Mounds	Mid-Continent Railway Museum
Christopher Columbus Museum	Mission Coffee House/Supreme Bean
Circus World Museum	National Watermelon Seed Spitting Contest
Devil's Lake State Park	
Geology Museum	Rib Mountain
Historic Indian Agency House	Song of Norway Festival
Hoofbeat Ridge	Wisconsin Historical Museum
Law Park	Wisconsin Veterans Museum
Leopold Memorial Reserve	Wollersheim Winery

told as well about general pioneer life and their frontier home. Their granddaughter, Juliette Gordon Low, founded the Girl Scouts of the United States of America.

The Kinzie house was restored by *The National Society of the Colonial Dames of America* in the state of Wisconsin in 1932; it was placed on the National Register of Historic Places in 1972. The venerable structure is open from May 15 through October 15, with guided tours available for a nominal fee. There are picnic tables on the grounds.

The house is opposite the site of the old fort, facing the canal built near the portage between the two rivers. The Fort Winnebago Surgeon's Quarters is the only remaining building in what was once an expansive complex of barracks, offices, and stores. Several well-known military men served at Fort Winnebago during its heyday. Their ranks included Jefferson Davis, then a young lieutenant, who went on to become president of the Confederacy during the Civil War.

The quarters overlook the site where French explorers Louis Joliet and Father Jacques Marquette beached their canoes in 1673 on the Fox River banks. Displays in the rough-looking building include period medical books, desks built by soldiers, an operating table, and the fort's records.

Anyone interested in building restorations should study the design of the place. Shaved pine logs squared off by axes form the outer walls. Tamarack poles make up the floor and ceiling joists. Much of the original plank flooring is still in place. The interior was plastered over handmade lathwork. The restorers left a portion uncovered so visitors can see the skill that went into making the building inhabitable. For hours and fees, call (608) 742-2949 or e-mail surgeons quarters@frontier.com. This site is maintained by the Wisconsin Society Daughters of the American Revolution.

Pardeeville, about 8 miles east of Portage on Highway 33 and 2 miles south on Highway 22, has hosted the *Pardeeville Watermelon Festival* since 1968. The event features the *US Watermelon Speed-Eating and Seed-Spitting Championships,* one of the country's largest, and even a watermelon-carving contest. The program kicks off on the second Sunday in September. Admission is free, but come early. Competition in 12 different categories is always tough. Hope for a strong wind.

Across the river from Portage is the *Leopold Memorial Reserve* (608-393-7352), covering 1,300 acres of "sand country" loved by the famed naturalist Aldo Leopold. If you plan on visiting, read an excellent book on the outdoorsman's life by Curt Meine, entitled *Aldo Leopold: His Life and Work* (University of Wisconsin Press, 1988). In the 1930s and 1940s, Leopold wrote much of his famous *Sand County Almanac* in "the Shack," a converted chicken coop that he used to get away from the rush and bustle of urban life. The spartan retreat

AUTHORS' FAVORITES

Breweries, distilleries, and brewpubs, Madison	**Mid-Continent Railway Museum,** North Freedom
Circus World Museum, Baraboo	**Museum at the Portage (Zona Gale home),** Portage
Devil's Lake State Park, Baraboo	
International Crane Foundation, Baraboo	**Wisconsin Chamber Orchestra Concerts on the Square,** Madison
Madison museums	**Wisconsin Dells water slides**
Madison's lakes	**Wisconsin State Capitol,** Madison

is still on the reserve property, the nucleus of 80 acres that had been part of Leopold's river-bottom farm. Tours are by appointment only. A donation is requested from nonmembers. A "legacy" interpretive and education center was constructed in 2007.

Columbus is proud to be named after the great Italian explorer, and it celebrated in grand style the 1992 anniversary of Columbus's landing in the New World. A sprawling *Christopher Columbus Museum* is packed with artifacts and memorabilia from the 1893 World's Columbian Exposition, which marked the 400th anniversary of the navigator's arrival in America.

The museum is on the top floor of the Columbus Antique Mall. The mall's 82,000 square feet, featuring 200 dealers and 400 booths, make it the largest antiques sales outlet in Wisconsin. "You name it, we have it. If it isn't here, you won't find it anywhere," claim the sales clerks. Owner Dan Amato purchased the 3-story, tan-brick former canning plant and opened the mall in 1983. Collecting the Columbus material started out as a hobby and then grew out of control. The mall and museum are open 8:15 a.m. to 4 p.m. daily except Thanksgiving, Christmas, and Easter. There's a $2 admission charge (ages 18 and older) to the museum.

The building, at 239 Whitney St. (920-623-1992), is on the west side of the Crawfish River adjacent to the Columbus Water & Light Company.

Dane County

The Greater *Madison* area has been making a hit with visitors since noted 19th-century newspaper publisher Horace Greeley wrote, "Madison has the most magnificent site of any inland town I ever saw." That was in 1855, 10 years after the community received the nod as capital of the state. Several generations later, the magic was still there. The old *Life* magazine took a closer look and proclaimed that the city's image best represented the "good life in America."

In 1978, the National Municipal League tagged Madison as an All-American City. In 2010, it was named among the top-50 bicycle-friendly cities in the country, as well as earning a number-two nod on the "Healthiest US Cities for Men" list. A chain of business newspapers named Madison as the smartest city in the country back up 2008, while a study based on US Census Bureau data pointed out in 2011 that more than half the community has a college degree. Other studies have said that Madison is one of the most livable cities in the country, as well as being among the most "green," a great walking town, one of America's best vegetarian cities, and among the "50 Fabulous Gay-Friendly Places to Live." Of course, all the tourist and chamber of commerce promotions proudly toot their collective horns over the praise. But is it true? We think so. Besides, Madison's beaten paths are really a bit offbeat anyway, which makes experiencing everything in this town a delightful lark. Mad City is fine-tuned to the needs of citizens.

We like to think **Madison's lakes** make the city something special. Mendota, Monona, Wingra, and Waubesa are within the city limits, comprising some 18,000 acres of watery surface on which to splash, puddle, paddle, or fish. Two sections of town are linked by an isthmus between Monona on the south and Mendota on the north, with the Capitol complex smack in the center. You can get a free map of the lakes at bait shops in town.

Speaking of free, the **Mad-City Ski Team** presents delightfully nerve-racking waterskiing shows most Sundays, Memorial Day through Labor Day, at **Law Park** on Lake Monona, 0.5 mile southeast of Capitol Concourse. The Junior Team show starts at 5:30 p.m., and the main show follows it starting about 6 p.m. Get there early, because the regulars stake out their grassy patch well before showtime, bringing well-stocked coolers, Frisbees, and blankets. Don't forget mosquito repellent for July nights. The buzzers aren't as big as their North Woods cousins, but they can be as aggravating as lobbyists outside the assembly chambers at state budget time.

How can you beat a town that has 150 parks within the city limits, comprising some 3,600 acres of recreation land? In addition, Madison has one of the best places in the world to view a sunset: on the Memorial Union Terrace of the University of Wisconsin, overlooking Lake Mendota.

We have totaled up some other statistics for you, thanks to friends at *Isthmus/The Daily Page,* who put out an "annual manual," as well as other knowledgeable Madison insiders: The city has 6,000 acres of parkland, 89

Helpful Madison Contacts

Greater Madison Convention & Visitors Bureau, 615 E. Washington Ave., Madison 53703 (608-255-2537 or 25-LAKES; www.visitmadison.com). A 24-hour answering service can take messages or record a request for an information packet. Just leave a name and address.

The Isthmus newspaper is free on newsstands ($50 annual 12-month subscription), 101 King St., Madison 53703 (608-251-5627). The publication does the best job reporting on entertainment and events on a weekly basis, coming out on Thursday, or get it daily online at www.thedailypage.com/theguide. **Madison Magazine** is also a good source for the latest scoop on shopping, the arts, dining, events, and business (608-270-3600; www.madisonmagazine.com). Yearly subscriptions are $17.50. The offices are located at 7025 W. Raymond Rd. Also helpful is the city's *Parks Department,* located in the Madison Municipal Building, Suite 120, 215 Martin Luther King Jr. Blvd., Madison 53701-2987 (608-266-4711; www.cityofmadison .com/parks).

tennis courts, 198 basketball teams, 21 baseball teams, 108 volleyball teams, 16 bathing beaches (13 staffed with lifeguards), 6 million volumes in the community's various libraries, 451 summer softball teams (86 in the autumn), 27 fine arts and performing theaters in addition to the 2,200-seat complex in the downtown Civic Center, 9 boat-launching sites (a lake access permit is $8 a day), and 5,519 parking spaces. The excellent bus system is one of the best in the state for ease of transportation.

Biking is a relaxed way to see the city. According to confirmed pedalers who work for the Madison police department, there are three bikes to every car in the city, with some 98 miles of posted bike trails—perhaps that's because of the city's youthful makeup. Out of the total population of about 233,209 residents, about with two-thirds of the city's population are students—when school is in session—35 years of age or younger.

Bring your own bike to town or rent one at the many bicycle shops, such as *Budget Bicycle Center & Bicycle Rental,* 1230 Regent St. (608-251-8413); *Machinery Row Bicycles,* 601 Williamson St. (608- 442-5974; www.machinery rowbicycles.com); or at *Cronometro,* 1402 Williamson St. (608-243-7760; http://cronometro.com). Or get a group together and pedal throughout the town on the Capitol Pedaler. It holds up to 14 passengers and a leader who manages stops at coffee shops, restaurants, parks, and bars. Contact the folks there at (608) 513-3882 or www.capitolpedaler.com. One of the better trails is the loop around Lake Monona through Law Park, B. B. Clarke Park, and the 51 acres of the Olbrich Botanical Gardens. Give yourself at least a half day for that

Bike Touring

Bike Wisconsin (608-843-8412 or 888-575-3640; www.bikewisconsin.com) offers two major tours in the summer pedaling season. One of the most popular tours is the weeklong *Great Annual Bike Adventure Along the Wisconsin River* (GRABAAWR; www.grabaawr.com). Usually more than 1,000 riders puff, pant, and pedal in early June on a 490-mile run from Eagle River near the Wisconsin-Michigan border to Prairie du Chien, where the Wisconsin and Mississippi Rivers link. In early July, up to 400 bikers take part in the *Bike Northwoods Tour* through some of the state's best forestlands (www.bikewisconsin.com/BNT). Then, in early August, the *Schramm's Annual Great Bicycle Ride Across Wisconsin* (SAGBRAW; www.bikewisconsin .com/Sagbraw) is another weeklong ride over mostly flat terrain. Between 1,000 and 1,200 dedicated intermediate-level cyclists participate. The event covers 6 days of cycling heaven with an average of 50 to 60 miles per day.

jaunt. Other good trails cover the scenic lakeshore from the university's Helen C. White Library to the apple trees at Picnic Point, Madison's best-known locale for smooching, proposing marriage, and munching Oscar Mayer ring bologna on Ritz crackers (not necessarily in that order).

Walking is a good way to see Madison up close, too. Start in *Capitol Square,* more popularly called the Concourse. The *Wisconsin Chamber Orchestra* puts on free classical concerts there the last Wed of each June, every Wed in July, and the first Wed in Aug. On the first Sat in June, kicking off the state's Dairy Month, you can milk a Holstein or a Guernsey cow on the Concourse. The bovines belong to the university, brought to the Capitol steps from the school farms on Campus Drive, a mile west of the Concourse. (Madison has the honor of being the country's only major city with a working farm almost downtown.)

Another agricultural tie is the *Dane County Farmers' Market,* touted to be the largest producer-only farmers' market in the country. About 150 vendors set up camp on the Concourse from 6 a.m. to 2 p.m. each Sat and Wed, May through autumn. You can squeeze melons to your heart's content. (In November and December, the market moves indoors to the Civic Center.)

We make a practice out of hitting the *Madison Art Fair* on the weekend after July 4, a show that fills the Concourse with really respectable fine arts. On the same weekend, the *Art Fair off the Square* in Olin Terrace Park, 2 blocks southeast of the Concourse, features tons of items in the crafts vein. This alternative art fair also leans toward unconventional art, the more unusual the better, so turn your mind loose. What's most fun is watching the numerous buskers and street entertainers rambling through the crowds.

The *Taste of Madison,* on the Sunday of Labor Day weekend, brings 50 of the city's best restaurants to the Capitol Concourse. It's always fun to watch the waiters' race, an institution at the event. Dignitaries "love" the Gelatin Jump, into which they can leap for charity fund-raising. Over the past few years, more eateries have begun to provide varieties of food, getting away from the ordinary brat and hot dog review. Yet the venerable *Essen Haus un Trinken Halle,* 514 E. Wilson St. (608-255-4674; http://essen-haus.com), still presents a German beer garden complete with polka bands. Since this is Wisconsin, look for cheese at such well-stocked outlets as Fromagination; Carr Valley Cheese Store (Middleton); Steve's Wine, Beer, Spirits; the Willy Street Co-op, Hy-Vee Grocery Store; Brennan's Markets; Whole Foods; and Metcalfe's Market.

Speaking of racing, enter the *Mad City Marathon* at the end of May. Whether crawling, walking, or running, the leg-stretching event is fun and great exercise for families and folks of any age. The loop extends around the city, starting on the south side of Lake Monona, then winds through downtown and neighborhoods to the north, through Maple Grove (wave to the governor, who comes out to stand on the front porch of the executive mansion), and back down to Lake Wingra.

Take advantage of the free tours in the imposing *Wisconsin Capitol building* itself, built between 1907 and 1917. Kids like to find as many carved badgers as possible hidden in cornices, over stairwells, and elsewhere.

The outside dome is topped by a gold-leafed statue officially known as *Wisconsin,* artist Daniel Chester French's rendition of what he thought the image of the state should be. No, it isn't a dairy cow, but a toga-draped woman of indeterminate age who has a badger on her head! The best place to view this dauntless lady, other than by helicopter, is from the 8th-floor Top of the Park banquet hall at the Inn on the Park Hotel, 22 S. Carroll St. (608-257-8811). The restaurant windows are across the street from the Capitol Concourse to the west.

But let's get back to the Capitol, an occasional old haunt when I was a reporter with the old *Milwaukee Sentinel.* In those days, I was dedicated to chasing politicians and bureaucrats through the labyrinth of hallways in pursuit of truth, justice, and a front-page byline. I learned that some of the byways in the building were more interesting than the politicos. A favorite place was, and still is, the *Grand Army of the Republic Memorial Hall* (608-267-1799), honoring the 83,400 Wisconsinites who served in the Union army during the Civil War.

The state sent 53 infantry regiments, 4cavalry units, and a battalion of heavy artillery into the conflict's smoke and fire, as part of the famed Iron Brigade. Of the total, 11,000 of the men never returned, dying of wounds or disease. Their regimental battle flags are on display in the fourth-floor hall, along with other memorabilia.

The displays are open to the public 9 a.m. to 4:30 p.m. Mon through Sat and also noon to 4 p.m. Sun from Memorial Day to Labor Day.

After strolling around the Concourse, hit State Street. In Madison, that's the avenue to see and be seen on. It's lined with oddball shops where you can purchase 1930s ball gowns or mountaineering gear, scuba equipment, fish sandwiches, books, and crystals. The street is home to the **Madison Civic Center and Gallery,** a couple of theaters, hot singles bars, and the city's trendier restaurants. We won't discuss the last because they tend to come and go. But you'll generally do all right at any of them. Don't simply look at ground level, either. Many of the eateries are on second floors, with banks of windows overlooking the parade below. The eclectic crowd on the street is a mixture of bustling government workers, intent university students, high school kids trying to look cool, bearded street musicians, tourists, and middle-class shoppers.

Williamson Street, better known as Willy Street, is Madison's hip avenue running along the Lake Monona shoreline, with its range of services from a tattoo parlor to a community health clinic. At the mouth of Willy Street is the Gateway building, a strip mall of 10 stores making a neat welcome to the street.

TOP ANNUAL EVENTS

MARCH
Wollersheim Winery Open House
Prairie du -Sac

APRIL
Midwest Horse Fair
Madison

JUNE
Taste of the Dells
Wisconsin Dells

JULY
Art Fair off the Square
Madison

SEPTEMBER
Henry Vilas Zoo Run Run
Madison

WI Futurity Saddlebred Horse Festival
Madison

OCTOBER
World Dairy Expo
Madison

NOVEMBER
Fall Polka Fest
Wisconsin Dells

DECEMBER
Capitol Christmas Pageant
Madison

The merchants and residents in the neighborhood sponsor a great street fair in mid-September.

Nearby is **Willy Street Co-op** (1221 Williamson; 608-251-6776; www.willy street.coop), for getting last-minute coffee in bulk, fresh avocados, or health foods. **The Pink Poodle,** 6017 Odana Rd. (608-276-7467; www.thepinkpoodle online.net), is a shop of another type. The upscale designer shop offers resale fashions, antiques, and collectibles, as well as jewelry and handbags.

For pampering of another sort, the **Mansion Hill Inn** is Madison's ultimate in style. The building at 424 N. Pinckney St. was constructed in 1858 by the tradesman who built Madison's second capitol building. It went through a succession of owners and housed students during its declining years. The place was purchased by Randy Alexander, a young rehabilitation specialist who had resurrected other fading Madison homes and buildings. He returned the mansion to its former elegance, a veritable posh palace. Alexander brought in his army of craftworkers, who spent a year patching, plastering, and painting the place. The antiques-filled rooms are comfortable and cozy, especially when you're coming in from a fog-bound, late-winter day. Each bathroom has been snazzed up by Kohler Corporation (Wisconsin-made!) bath devices that bubble, whirl, and refresh the most battered bodies.

funfacts

The state flag was adopted in 1913 and bears the state seal. The name, *Wisconsin,* and year it became a state, 1848, were added to the design in 1981. The state seal, which was adopted in 1881, includes a sailor and miner supporting a shield with symbols of agriculture, mining, navigation, and manufacturing. The US coat of arms, signifying Wisconsin's allegiance to the Union, also is included. The badger above the shield represents Wisconsin's nickname: the Badger State.

Other pluses: A valet parks your car; another serves coffee by the downstairs fireplace. Mansion Hill has become the "in place" for executives and visiting government types who appreciate such little touches.

Honeymooners enjoy the Mansion as well. They probably don't pay much attention, but the telephones have computer modem hookups and teleconference connections. Call (800) 798-9070 for reservations or log on to www .mansionhillinn.com.

Other must-see places in Madison:

The **Chazen Museum of Art** (formerly the **Elvehjem**), 800 University Ave. (608-263-2246; www.chazen.wisc.edu), is one of the better places in town. But you have to check the traveling exhibits as well as the 10,000 pieces in the permanent collection. The gallery is open 9 a.m. to 5 p.m. Tues through Fri and 11 a.m. to 5 p.m. Sat and Sun. Closed Mon.

Visiting the **Wisconsin Historical Museum** is like exploring my grand-mother's attic; I never know what I'll find. Consequently, the place is one of my favorites in Mad City. Even as it has grown familiar, I've always learned something new on each visit. Three floors of permanent exhibits hold objects of state interest (and mine, too) from the prehistoric past to contemporary times. Two galleries have regularly changing displays. One past exhibit focused on Wisconsin during the dawn of the atomic age. The museum has a lot of quirky items, including a button from the vest of Revolutionary War hero John Paul Jones. The museum is located near the State Capitol at 30 N. Carroll St. (608-264-6555; www.wisconsinhistory.org/museum). Open 9 a.m. to 4 p.m. Tues through Sat; closed Sun and Mon.

Another great museum that is a really hard place to get away from—pun intended—is the **Geology Museum,** at 1215 W. Dayton St. This university facility has a walk-through cave that is spooky enough to be fun for kids and educational enough to be satisfying for serious-minded grown-ups. The main eye-opening display in the museum is the towering skeleton of a mastodon, a critter that roamed Wisconsin 10,000 years ago during the last Ice Age. Call (608) 262-2399 for more details. The Geology Museum is open 8:30 a.m. to 4:30 p.m. Mon through Fri and 9 a.m. to 1 p.m. on Sat. Admission is free.

Amid the bustle of grown-up stuff to see and do in Madison, don't for-get the littlest tykes. You might even walk past the **Madison Children's Museum** if you weren't aware of its location on bustling State Street (at 100 State, to be exact). This is definitely a necessary kid-oriented off-the-beaten-path stop. The museum is a hands-on, child-friendly place. Everyone is encouraged to try out a scientific experiment or get involved in some kind of craft. Eye-level exhibits (for those squirts among us) are aimed at toddlers to grade-schoolers. Displays and activities change regularly. The **Jim & Susan Bakke Art Studio** is among the popular areas, where kids can create their own masterpieces. For details on current admission prices, call (608) 256-6445 or check out www.madisonchildrensmuseum.org. The museum is open Tues through Fri from 9 a.m. to 4 p.m., Sat from 9 a.m. to 5 p.m., and Sun from noon to 5 p.m. From Memorial Day through Labor Day, it's also open Mon from 9 a.m. to 4 p.m.

The **Wisconsin Veterans Museum** is part patriotism, part poignancy, and all pride. The museum is located on Madison's Capitol Square at 30 W. Mifflin St. (608-267-1799). Hours are Mon through Sat (year-round) from 9 a.m. to 4:30 p.m. and Sun (Apr through Sept) from noon to 4 p.m. The museum has 10,000 square feet of displays on the state's citizen-soldiers. The exhibits range from

The Gift of Food

The **Wisconsin Restaurant Association** offers a booklet of gift certificates to member restaurants around the state. Contact the organization at 2801 Fish Hatchery Rd., Madison 53713; (800) 589-3211; www.wirestaurant.org/. The certificates can be ordered in any denomination and are valid at any of the restaurants listed. There is a charge for shipping and handling.

the Civil War to contemporary times. Lifelike dioramas depict historic military events in which Wisconsin troops participated. A computerized Wisconsin Civil War database helps visitors track relatives and other persons who were in service during the war. One diorama has Union troops charging through a cornfield. These, as well as all the other lifelike characters, have faces modeled after real people. It's almost disconcerting. On a more contemporary level, suspended from the ceiling in a simulated rescue flight is a full-size Vietnam helicopter gunship. There are also exhibits from Iraq and Afghanistan. Don't pass up a visit to this museum. There's valor here.

The **Madison Museum of Contemporary Art** features modern and contemporary painting, sculpture, photography, works on paper, video, and multimedia work by area, regional, and internationally known artists. It is part of the **Overture Center for the Arts,** with a rooftop cafe and outdoor sculpture terrace with indoor/outdoor eating space included in the design. The facility is located at 227 State St.; (608) 257-0158; www.mmoca.org/information/index .html. It is closed Mon; check its website for hours.

Don't you dare miss **Babcock Hall** at the University of Wisconsin–Madison. "Ice cream, ice cream, we all scream for ice cream" is the anthem at Babcock, the university's dairy science building, on 1605 Linden Dr.

From the Capitol Concourse, drive west on University Avenue and take the campus exit near the university greenhouses (which look like greenhouses) to Linden, the first left at the four-way stop. Babcock will be immediately on the left by the Stock Pavilion, an export center for horse shows and other agricultural events.

The university's own contented cows and friendly Dane County farmers provide the base product for the whole, 2 percent, and skim milk; buttermilk; cheese; and yogurt produced there. Yet ice cream is the best seller in the Babcock Hall retail store, the Memorial Union, and Union South. Cones and sundaes are available in the two union buildings, while quarts and gallons can be purchased in Babcock Hall. The university's dorm food service also offers the dairy goods for the cafeteria lines.

The ice cream is 12 percent butterfat, rather than the industry standard of only 10 percent, according to the plant directors. Pure cane sugar instead of corn sweeteners is used. With Babcock ice cream, you'll never get just a cone full of air, as with some other commercial preparations.

Warner Park is where Madisonites watch baseball like it oughta be played. The park is home of the **Madison Mallards,** the city's summer collegiate baseball team, where eager young players smack base hits and snag flies. The promotion-minded team, made up of college all-stars, plays from June through August against state rivals. There's hardly a better way to spend a hot summer evening. Be aware that promotions change each season, many geared at kids and families. Contact the Mallards at (608) 246-4277 or www.mallardsbaseball .com to get the latest updates on vouchers, fireworks, hot dogs, birthday parties, and players.

Guests often wind up on the radio waves during the *Whadya Know* show hosted by Madisonite storyteller/comic Michael Feldman. This internationally syndicated program on **Wisconsin Public Radio** (608-263-3970) features the irreverently hilarious Feldman, who regularly pulls people into his goofy on-air quizzes. Hiding in the back rows doesn't work for the bashful. Feldman often crawls over rows of seats to get at folks. It's all in good fun, and it's a good way to win a prize. The program is broadcast on Sat morning starting at 10 a.m. from the Monona Terrace Convention Hall, 1 John Nolen Dr. In addition to its airing on stations around the United States, *Whadya Know* can be heard in Berlin, Stockholm, Helsinki, and Geneva. Tickets are $10 for adults and $2.50 for the under-12 set. Give 'em a ring at (800) WHA-KNOW (800-942-5669) or check out www.notmuch.com.

Fun on the Farm

The *Wisconsin Department of Agriculture* can provide details on county fairs and agricultural tourism (farm tours, cheese plant visits, and related industry news). Contact the ag folks at 2811 Agriculture Dr., Madison 53707; (608) 224-5012; http:// datcp.wi.gov. For details on the state's most promotable product, the *Wisconsin Cheese Makers Association* has it all. The organization, at 8030 Excelsior Dr., Madison 53717-2905, can be reached at (608) 828-4550 or through www.wis cheesemakersassn.org. For even more information, read our *Wisconsin Cheese: A Cookbook and Guide to the Cheeses of Wisconsin* (Globe Pequot Press, 2008). We include more than 100 recipes from farmhouse favorites to sophisticated cuisine gleaned from Wisconsin's top chefs such as James Beard winner Adam Siegel of Bartolottas' Restaurants and many more. It has more cheese trivia, profiles of cheesemakers, and cheese tips than ever believed possible.`

Middleton, Madison's closest western suburb, is home of the *Capital Brewery and Beer Garden,* on 7734 Terrace (608-836-7100; www.capital-brewery .com), one of the area's most popular breweries. Weather permitting, the beer garden here is a great place to loll away a summer Saturday afternoon. This microbrewery makes a smooth GartenBrau in light, dark, and seasonal draughts. Tours are Fri at 3:30 p.m. and Sat at 1:30 and 3:30 p.m. Brewmaster Kirby Nelson pours mean brews while he chats about malts and barleys.

Middleton is also home of *Clasen's European Bakery,* 7610 Donna Dr. (608-831-2032), probably one of the state's best bakeries. Ernest and Rolf Clasen, who immigrated from Gerolstein, Germany, in the late 1950s, own the company. Both are *konditors,* officially recognized pastry chefs. They emphatically state they are *not* just bakers. For a time the brothers made only candy. When the price of sugar skyrocketed in the 1960s, they moved into tortes and coffee cakes, although a major portion of their business remains manufacturing chocolate that is shipped out by the semitrailer truckload and in 50-pound wafers. But, oh, those baked items. In the rear self-service room, banks of refrigeration units house towering cream cakes. Trays are laden with breads and cookies. Just remembering a recent stop adds pounds where they shouldn't be. Shop hours are 7 a.m. to 5:30 p.m. Mon through Sat.

The suburb is also the new home of the *National Mustard Museum* at 7477 Hubbard Ave. Even if you're not a mustard lover, this is a must-see. In 1986, owner and ex-Wisconsin assistant attorney general Barry Levenson had a brainstorm to open such a facility while meandering through supermarket aisles. He decided to amass the world's largest collection of mustard. So, in 1991 he quit his job and opened the museum a year later in nearby Mount Horeb. His dream came true. He is now the proud owner of about 4,000 mustards from all over the world, making it the world's largest collection of the condiment. Samples are available before purchasing. The museum hours are daily from 10 a.m. to 5 p.m. Its National Mustard Day is held there the first Sat in Aug. There's no need to pass the mustard, plenty is within reach. Dial up (800) 438-6878 or (608) 831-2222 or visit www.mustardmuseum.com.

The *Old Middleton Centre* offers a variety of gift shops and boutiques. The outdoor gazebo in the center of the complex, located at 750 Hubbard Ave., is a good place to relax and rest your feet after shopping. The Centre is 3 blocks northeast of the Capital Brewery. From Terrace Avenue East, take the first left (Hubbard), then go 2 blocks, and the shops will be on your left. The Centre is considered one of the best places in the Madison area for purchasing smaller imported gift items such as plates and crystal.

For eating in Middleton, try *Captain Bill's,* 2701 Century Harbor Rd. (608-831-7327; www.capbills.com). Captain Bill's offers a casual, rustic, Key West atmosphere and is located on beautiful Lake Mendota. Enjoy fresh seafood, steaks, chicken, pasta, or sandwiches while admiring the brilliant reds and purples of the sunset illuminating the sky. The restaurant opens every evening at 4:30 p.m.

Cave of the Mounds (www.caveofthemounds.com) is only 20 miles west of Madison on Highways 18 and 151 in *Blue Mounds.* The caves have the usual selection of stalagmites, stalactites, and pools that make a great several-hour stopover for anyone with a carful of kids. The history of the place is the most interesting, however. The farm where the caves were discovered dates from 1828 and is one of the oldest in Dane County. In December 1987 Cave of the Mounds was designated a National Natural Landmark by the Department of the Interior. Call ahead for ticket prices. Hours are 9 a.m. to 4 p.m. from November 15 to March 15, and 9 a.m. to 6 p.m. from Memorial Day to Labor Day. Sixty-minute tours leave on the hour. A self-guided nature trail over 7 acres of the farm is also available. Although there's a restaurant on the premises, the cave owners don't mind if guests bring picnic lunches. They've provided a pleasantly shaded grove for snacking. They also have a great rock and mineral gift shop. For more details, contact Cave of the Mounds at (608) 437-3038; http://caveofthemounds.com.

"Velkommen" is the greeting in *Mount Horeb,* one of several Norwegian communities at the western edge of Dane County. Although the town was originally settled by English, Irish, and German settlers in 1861,

Mounds of History

Wisconsin has a wealth of Indian mounds. Among those that are really off the beaten path is a site on land owned by Bryce Tollackson, a retired farmer who lived west of Madison. Tollackson donated the site to the Archaeological Conservancy in the mid-1990s. The elder Hintz, accompanied by son Steve, interviewed Tollackson for a story in *American Archaeology.* The Tollackson site consists of 13 large effigies, one of the most complete clusters of undamaged prehistoric burial units in the state. The largest is 4 feet high and at least 80 feet long. But it's tough to find the eagle, bear, and other shapes. Brush, trees, and winter snow cover and/or obstruct the view today, whereas about 1,000 years ago they were easily seen.

Tollackson wanted to protect his "graves," as he calls them, so he contacted the conservancy. He worked with University of Wisconsin–La Crosse archaeologist Jim Theler to plot the 40-acre site containing the mounds. For an interesting historical twist, more than a century ago a state surveyor had found but mistakenly mapped the locale. Those notes were forgotten until 1993, when a Mississippi Valley Archaeology Center student stumbled across the mounds on a survey tour of the area.

three-quarters of the population was Scandinavian by 1870. Since there is one-quarter Larson in our blood, we occasionally like to stop and find out the latest on the Norskie front. You'll know this is the right town by the giant trolls lurking outside **Open House Imports,** 308 E. Main St. (608-437-5468 or 800-236-8811; www.openhouseimports.com), one of several excellent import and gift shops. The trolls are statues, of course, yet when our kids were younger they were never quite sure. Since trolls turn to stone in the daylight, they had a sneaking suspicion that there might have once been such live creatures.

Other attractions in the Mount Horeb area include the **Tyrol Ski Basin, Blue Mounds State Park,** and **Little Norway,** a Norwegian pioneer home-site and church.

The only Wisconsin winery on the National Register of Historic Places is the **Wollersheim Winery,** on Highway 188, 0.25 mile south of Highway 60. Just across the Wisconsin River is the village of Prairie du Sac. The original vineyards were planted in the 1840s by Count Agoston Haraszthy, a Hungarian whose dreams exceeded the reality of Wisconsin's harsh winters. The noble-man became discouraged after several years of cold, so he eventually sold out, moved to California to help establish the wine industry there, and subsequently made his fortune. The new owner was Peter Kehl, whose family were vintners since 1533 in Germany's Rhineland.

Kehl built most of the complex's existing buildings, operating the winery until a killing frost in 1899 effectively destroyed the crop. After a generation of vacancy, Bob and JoAnn Wollersheim purchased the grounds in 1972. They replanted the slopes with such hearty hybrids as Millot, De Chaunac, and Foch for red wines and Aurora and Seyval Blanc for white wines.

The Wollersheim's winemaker, Phillipe Coquard, whose family is also in the wine business in the Beaujolais region of France, is especially proud of the Ruby Nouveau produced each autumn. This young wine has beaten out competitors from Oregon, California, New York, and other wine-growing states in major competitions.

In 1990 the Wollersheims purchased the old Stone Mill Winery in Cedar-burg (Ozaukee County). Renamed the Cedar Creek Winery, that facility also has started winning its share of awards.

Winery tours are offered every hour from 10:15 a.m. to 4:15 p.m. daily, fol-lowed by a wine tasting, of course. Fees are $5 for adults, and children 11 and under are free when accompanied by an adult. Throughout the year, the Wol-lersheims do more than just show off their kegs and casks of award-winning wine. As great promoters they sponsor numerous programs, ranging from a spring folk festival to grape-growing seminars, winemaking instructions, and an ice wine release party. For specific dates, contact the Wollersheims at their winery (608-643-6515; www.wollersheim.com).

If you come to the area in winter, bald eagles can occasionally be seen swooping high over the snow-covered cornfields. The huge birds dive for fish on the Wisconsin River, with the best opportunities for spotting the eagles being in the vicinity of the Prairie du Sac dam.

Mazomanie is located along Reeve Road off Highway 14. The town name was taken from the Sauk Indian term loosely translated as "iron horse" or "iron that walks," referring to the old-time trains that rumbled through here during the pioneer era. Take Reeve Road on the west end of town to *Hoofbeat Ridge,* an accredited American Camping Association horseback-riding camp that offers numerous weekend and special events in addition to its regular camp and riding-lesson schedules. The camp has been operated by the Bennett family (founders John and Betty Bennett had 11kids!) and assorted in-laws since 1963. It's one of the largest horse camps in Wisconsin, with strict adherence to safety and promoting the understanding of what horses are all about. Both western and English styles of riding are taught. All our kids have attended several years of summer camp at Hoofbeat and subsequently have become competent, careful riders. What makes Hoofbeat special are the adult riding weekends, family campouts, riding shows, dressage presentations, and similar programs beyond the regularly scheduled riding classes and summer camp. Remember, this is a casual place, one for blue jeans and boots, but highly professional in its approach to teaching folks how to ride properly and well. For

funfacts

The greatest north–south distance in Wisconsin is 302 miles. The greatest east–west direction is 291 miles. There are 72 counties in Wisconsin.

details contact director Ted Marthe, Hoofbeat Ridge Camp, 5304 Reeve Rd., Mazomanie 53560 (608-767-2593; www.hoofbeat.org).

To the southeast of Madison on Highway 18 is the small community of Cambridge, home to several pottery works. *Rowe Pottery,* with its factory at 404 England St., has a broad selection of pottery in gray and blue hues. Rowe's company store is located at 217 Main St. (608-423-3935; www.rowe pottery.com). Store hours are 10 a.m. to 5 p.m. Mon through Sat, and 11 a.m. to 4 p.m. Sun.

This farming community is at the western edge of Wisconsin's major tobacco-growing area. Along the highway are farms with their distinctive open-sided barns, used for drying the tobacco leaves. This Wisconsin product is generally used for cigar wrappings.

Famed artist Georgia O'Keeffe is remembered around her home community of **Sun Prairie,** a rural community about 7 miles northeast of Madison. She was born on a farm 3.5 miles southeast of town on November 15, 1887. A red roadside plaque now marks the spot. When she was 14, she moved away with her family to Virginia and went on to pursue her meteoric career in the American Southwest. An autographed copy of one of her catalogs and one of her works are displayed at the **Sun Prairie Library and Museum** on Main Street. A meeting room in the library, where the town council meets, was dedicated to O'Keeffe in 1987, the year after her death.

The dramatic power of the Ice Age is readily evident throughout this part of the state, especially in the Devil's Lake area and the Baraboo Range. This stretch of jagged limestone cliffs, moraine deposits, and deep valleys lies about 3 miles south of Baraboo and 20 miles south of the Wisconsin Dells. Wisconsin Highways 159, 123, 113, and 33 enter the area of gorges, hills, crests, flatlands, and river bottoms. Access to the state roads is easy via I-90/94, with interchanges some 12 miles east and north of Devil's Lake. Highway 12 cuts straight south from the Dells to the Wisconsin River, crossing at Sauk City and on into Madison.

That highway must have more roadhouses per mile than any other stretch in the state. A roadhouse, as you know, might have a wild and woolly history comprised of equal parts bathtub gin, flappers, and who knows what else.

Marathon County

The sprawling paper factories of **Wausau** pale in significance when compared to **Rib Mountain,** the billion-year-old hunk of rock that towers above the city on its west side. The mountain, complete with a state park campground, mountain biking, and ski runs, was not crunched by the glaciers that flattened the rest of Wisconsin 10,000 years ago. The mountain is 1,940 feet high, the second-highest peak in the state, providing plenty of recreational opportunities for the activity-minded. Just to the south of Rib Mountain is the county's **Nine-Mile Recreation Area** on Red Bud Road off County Highway North, a labyrinth of back roads and logging paths that are available for cross-country skiing and more biking.

For a more urbane experience, Wausau's **Artrageous Weekend** in September takes over the downtown pedestrian mall, where artists and craftworkers display their wares. In addition to wandering musicians, jugglers, and other street performers, there is a children's hands-on area where they paint and learn to make pottery.

Just south of Wausau on Highway S is the 20,000-acre **George W. Mead Wildlife Area** (888-936-7463; www.meadwildlife.org), one of the best picnic areas in the state. It's also a good location for deer and duck watching.

Maybe it's because Stevens Point is a college town where folks like to sit around and chat over a brew, but **Emy J's** is the quintessential coffeehouse. Located at 1009 1st. St. (715-345-0471), this kickback hideaway bubbles up fair trade coffee, with ice cream made in Madison by Chocolate Shoppe Ice Cream. Its smoothies are concocted with real fruit, yogurt, and locally-produced honey.

funfacts

Ninety-seven of every one hundred Wisconsinites were born in the United States. More than half the residents are of German descent. About 5 percent are African American. Other major population groups are Polish, Irish, Italian, and English. Hmong and Laotians from Southeast Asia present a sizable new ethnic face to the state, especially in the Stevens Point and Milwaukee areas.

Sauk County

According to archaeologists, the ancient Wisconsin River cut an 800-foot-deep trench through this vicinity in the eons before the Ice Age. When the latest push by glaciers moved southward in several waves (70,000 to 10,000 years ago), ice from the so-called Green Bay glacial lobe spread its cold fingers around the hills that make up today's rocky Baraboo Range. Both ends of the river gorge were plugged with ice, which created the Devil's Lake basin. Eventually, the ice melted and dumped millions of tons of debris into the riverbed, pushing the river itself about 9 miles to the east, where it is today.

Subsequently softened by expansive stands of oak and birch groves, the resulting landscape, with all its bumps and dips, is considered some of the most beautiful scenery in the state. The centerpiece is the 5,100-acre **Devil's Lake State Park,** which attracts more than 1.5 million visitors a year.

The park offers 450 campsites and hiking trails, as well as swimming, fishing, and sailing opportunities. Since the place is so expansive, you can generally rummage around to your heart's content without rubbing shoulders with anyone else.

The busiest days, however, are those bustling June, July, and August weekends, when the campgrounds are generally booked and the lake banks seem knee-deep in kids with plastic fishing rods.

But don't let that keep you away at other times. Midweek and off-season visits leave plenty of room to ramble. Since the state park is central to the tourist attractions in the Dells, the Madison scene, and other getaways in the vicinity, it makes for a good jumping-off point if your family is in the camping mood.

The second major physical feature of central Wisconsin is the mighty Wisconsin River, which bisects the state. It's the longest river in Wisconsin, easily earning the same name. The waterway runs some 430 miles from the lake district in northeastern Wisconsin to the Mississippi River at Prairie du Chien. At Portage, the Wisconsin connects to the Fox River, which eventually links up with Lake Michigan.

mightyflowage

The mighty Wisconsin River rises in the Lac Vieux Desert on the Wisconsin-Michigan border and flows south 430 miles through central Wisconsin. The tannin-colored waters rush past Portage and then turn west. The Wisconsin empties into the Mississippi River about 2 miles below Prairie du Chien. Near the Wisconsin Dells, it forms Lake Delton, while cutting through sandstone rock to a depth of about 150 feet.

These days, the tannin-colored river is a favorite for canoeists and anglers. In early years the river was a major route for the massive lumber rafts floated downstream to the sawmills. Today, sunbathers, looking like bratwurst on a grill as they loll about during hot summer afternoons, enjoy the seclusion of dunes and sandbars along the riverbanks.

Over the past few years, several of the more remote stretches of beach frontage have been taken over by nudists, many of them college students from the University of Wisconsin in nearby Madison. More than one canoeing party has been surprised by tanned (or brightly sunburned pink) folks in the buff who wave friendly greetings. For decorum's sake, we won't tell you the exact

Tragic Land

Hiking the **Black Hawk Unit** of the **Lower Wisconsin State Riverway** is a challenge. You scamper up steep slopes, trudge across sun-drenched meadows, plunge through mosquito-dense forests, carefully avoid deer droppings, and generally have a wonderful time. It wasn't so swell more than 100 years ago, when a small band of Sac and Fox warriors under Black Hawk held off an overwhelmingly superior force of US militia on this site. In 1832 the Native Americans were trying to flee across the nearby Wisconsin River where they hoped the whites would leave them alone. But the troops caught up with the band on the ridges overlooking the river. While Black Hawk's few able-bodied warriors fought back with bows and arrows, their starving women, children, and elders fled down the hill and crossed the river. One soldier and several dozen Native Americans died in the fierce fighting.

sandbars . . . but . . . if you put your canoe in the river at the Highway 14 crossing, across from Helena and Tower Hill campground. . . .

A more staid way to make the river crossing is via the **Merrimac ferryboat.** Best of all, it's free! Since the Wisconsin Department of Transportation gained control of passage over the Wisconsin River in 1933, motorists, hikers, and bikers have been getting a free ride. The first ferry was operating at the same site as early as 1844. Currently, the *Colsac III* runs 24 hours a day between April 15 and December 1, depending on winter ice conditions. *Colsac* stands for Columbia and Sauk Counties, linked by the ferry. The 7-minute ride accommodates 15 cars or trucks each run; the ferry makes some 40,000 trips a season while carrying 195,000 vehicles. The crossing is reached via Highway 113 between Okee on the south shore and Merrimac on the north. The Wisconsin River is 0.5 mile wide at this point, but the crossing saves a 9-mile drive west or a 12-mile drive east to the closest bridges.

Impress your kids by telling them that an underwater cable links the boat to shore, with the vessel's monster diesel engine pulling the boat and its load back and forth. The tykes will think you're a veritable maritime encyclopedia.

Restrooms and privately run refreshment stands are conveniently located on each shore. Yet a warning is necessary. Don't get boxed between other waiting cars if the kids have to make a last-minute panic pit stop prior to boarding. It's difficult to pull out of line to retrieve a pokey youngster still in the facilities. The child may have to pick up the next ride over if you get carried away in the flow of traffic onto the ferry dock.

The centrally located **Wisconsin Dells,** touching Juneau, Adams, Sauk, and Columbia Counties, is the epitome of what outsiders consider summer fun in Wisconsin. Visitors are drawn from around the Midwest to see the fudge shops, arcades, wax museums, shooting galleries, souvenir shops, and hamburger joints that line the streets of the Dells and the adjacent town of Lake Delton. Tourism is nothing new in the Dells neighborhood. Before the turn of the 20th century, thousands of visitors flocked here to cruise the upper and lower sections of the Wisconsin River and marvel at the scenery. That remains the best part of a vacation in the region. There's little that can beat a river ride upstream on a warm summer day, with the chance to put your feet up on a rail and to admire the passing river bluffs. Use your Internet-capable mobile device and check out Dells.com Mobile for all sorts of updates on what's happening and where to go. The site was designed for Internet browsing on mobile devices and formatted for the smaller screen size. Or check out www .dells.com/wisconsin-dells-update/what-is-new-in-wisconsin-dells.htm.

But some things never change. It seems as if every high promontory has a Native American maiden leaping to her death because her lover died in battle

Off-road Getaway

The **Dell Creek Wildlife Area** (www.dnr.wi.gov/org/land/wildlife/wildlife_areas/dell creek.htm) is a favorite hiking spot for getaway strolls far from the madding crowd. The area spreads out over 2,125 acres of state-owned land in Sauk and Juneau Counties. The main entrance is 7 miles northeast of Reedsburg on County Highway H. You can see ruffed grouse, wild turkeys, rabbits, and plenty of deer. This is an adventure because there are no marked trails in the wildlife area, but take the meandering deer paths and old logging roads. Nearby is Tower Hill State Park, (608) 588-2116 (www.dnr.wi.gov/org/land/parks/specific/towerhill), if you need more information.

or some other legend. The Dells also has such a cliff overlooking the Wisconsin River. A cruise is a great way to such scenic landmarks, via **Dells Boat Tours** departing from the Dells landing downtown (608-254-7227, www.dellsboats .com). I've always thought the Upper Dells were more scenic than the section below the town. But you can make that choice for yourself. An exciting way to see the flowage is a ride on the Ducks, surplus World War II amphibious vehicles that bump and leap over set trails, splash through the Wisconsin River, and rumble along pathways near the town streets—much to the delight of riders. Keep your camera bags and purses off the floor because the splashing water often swirls along the base of the vehicle and out the back. Several companies offer rides.

The crown prince of the Wisconsin Dells was probably the late Tommy Bartlett, the impresario of a water, sky, and thrill show that has been a staple of Dells entertainment for three decades. Bartlett, who looked like Santa Claus on vacation, had packaged a great program of divers, splashers, fliers, and clowns for a show that runs several times daily throughout the season. In 1993, Bartlett was inducted into the Water Ski Hall of Fame in Cypress Gardens, Florida. Yet he only ever water-skied once, on his 70th birthday. Bartlett, 84, died in 1998. His show remains a rain-or-shine proposition, so dress accordingly. Ask for the reserved seats, which are actually comfortable lawn chairs.

Attached to the water-show park is **Robot World,** Bartlett's iconic vision of a futuristic home operated by mechanical people. It's a worthwhile stop, with just the right tongue-in-cheek combination of hokeyness and fun. The lower level of the building is a hands-on science hall, where kids and adults can conduct all sorts of interesting physics experiments. This place is a boon on a rainy day if you are traveling with youngsters. They'll have plenty to do. But get there early—other parents often have the same idea.

Some other rewarding stops in the neighborhood are the **Haunted Mansion, Timbavati Wildlife Park,** and the **Wax World of the Stars.** The interior features glitzy Hollywood sets. An excellent attraction for photography fans is Bennett House, which reopened in June 2000 as a Wisconsin state historic site. This was the home of noted photographer Henry Hamilton Bennett, a 19th-century photographer who concentrated on the rocky Dells landscape for his scenes. You can compare his photos of early Dells tourism to today's lifestyles. There isn't that much difference, other than clothing and hair arrangements. Admission is charged.

But its water parks now have secured the Dells on the vacation map. In 1980, the appropriately named Waterman family opened the first slides at its **Noah's Ark** complex (608-254-6351; www.noahsarkwaterpark.com), which remains one of the largest in the country at 70 acres of fun and games. It wasn't long before other properties jumped on the waterwagon. The **Kalahari** touts itself as the largest indoor water park in the country, with its 125,000 square feet of splash areas. Watch out for the FlowRider surfing simulator, which pushes 50,000 gallons of water per minute into ocean-like waves. Call (877) 253-5466 or visit www.kalahariresort.com/waterparks.

At **Great Wolf Lodge,** 1,000 gallons of water roar down from a tipped bucket high on a scaffolding overhead to drench happy kids and adults alike. For details on the Wolf's Howlin' Tornado 53-foot vertical drop into a pool, call (800) 559-WOLF (9653) or log on to www.dells.greatwolflodge .com. The **Wilderness Waterpark Resort** brags of its combined 350,000 square feet of indoor and outdoor pools and slides. The fun here includes water blasters and depth charges on the Surge, the five-person raft ride on the Fantastic Voyage, and the 4-story Ransack Ridge with its water firing cannons. For more on the Wilderness, check in at (800) 867-9453 or www .wildernessresort.com.

For comprehensive listings of prices, accommodations, and attractions, contact the **Wisconsin Dells Visitor & Convention Bureau,** 115 La Crosse St., Wisconsin Dells 53965-0390 (608-254-8088; www.wisdells.com); in Wisconsin call toll-free, (800) 223-3557.

Our favorite place in Sauk County is **Baraboo,** old home of the Ringling Brothers Circus. Wisconsin is known as "the Mother of the Circus" because more than 100 shows were organized here from pre–Civil War days to the 1980s. Baraboo is subsequently "the High Seat of Circusdom" in Wisconsin. The town is gung-ho showbiz all the way, calling itself "the Circus City of the Nation."

August Ringling, father of the famed circus family, operated harness shops in Baraboo after moving there from Prairie du Chien in the mid-1800s. The Ringling boys loved entertainment life and began their Greatest Show on Earth (it wasn't quite that yet) in 1884. They winter-quartered along the Baraboo River (some folks still claim that an elephant or two was buried along the banks). Their cousins, the Gollmars, also operated a circus out of Baraboo, and numerous city residents were employed in wagon and harness making for the shows. Entertainers built homes in town, with practice barns and halls in their backyards. The friezes around the Courthouse Annex depict this delightful history.

The showpiece of Baraboo is the refurbished *Circus World Museum,* site of the old Ringling headquarters. In 1987 the CWM received a Phoenix Award from the Society of American Travel Writers for its preservation efforts. The museum's buildings and tents house the world's largest collection of rebuilt circus wagons and show off an extensive display of memorabilia, in addition to housing a vast research collection of posters, photos, route books, diaries, and similar artifacts. Wagons from the museum are shown each July in the Great Circus Parade in Milwaukee, hauled there by steam train. Being a circus nut myself, I've been coming to the CWM since the early 1960s, when the place opened. A selection of my own circus photos has even been displayed there. They were taken while I was a correspondent for *Amusement Business* magazine, a national entertainment publication.

Driving around town, you'll see the *Al Ringling Theater,* the harness shop owned by the Ringlings' father, and numerous houses in which circus performers lived. Live performances, including loading and unloading a circus train, are part of the show back on the grounds. Kids love getting their photos taken in the gorilla wagon near the front entrance. I've seen more than one teacher or guide glad to "lock up" a few wild tykes, even if only for a few minutes. The museum, operated by the State Historical Society, is located at 550 Water St. (608-356-8341; www.alringling.com).

Five miles north of Baraboo, just off Highway 12 on Shady Lane Road, is the *International Crane Foundation,* where you can see several species of cranes from around the world. The conservation group that runs the center is always happy to have visitors. The center is open from 9 a.m. to 5 p.m. April 15 to October 31. Tours start at 10 a.m.; and 1 and 3 p.m. Memorial Day through Labor Day. Self-guided tours are also available. Call or visit the website first (608-356-9462; www.savingcranes.org) for admission prices and to find out about the mating and hatching season. During that time the curators often have to perform crane mating dances to get the big birds in the appropriate frame of mind. Now *that* makes for quite a sight, although the ritual is closed to the public.

North Freedom is home of the *Mid-Continent Railway Museum* (608-522-4261 or 800-930-1385; www.mcrwy.com), operated by volunteers who

Bridge to the Past

For an out-of-the-way place to hike, the elder Hintz recommends **Natural Bridge State Park,** a 560-acre site 16 miles south of Baraboo on US 12 and 10 miles farther on County Highway C. The most interesting feature of the park is a sandstone arch with an opening 25 feet high and 35 feet wide. Located in the state's "driftless area" not smushed by glaciers, the "natural bridge" was created by weather erosion of the soft sandstone.

It is estimated that 10,000 to 12,000 years ago, humans were living in the area. They used the rock shelters near the bridge as a retreat from storms, enemies, and wild animals. The site has been extensively researched, with remains of ancient fires and rubble showing that people wandered this region at least 500 generations ago. This fact certainly shows that we are nothing more than another tiny blip on history's forward march. Will anyone notice our remains (decayed shopping malls and an abundance of Styrofoam) in another 500 generations?

love oil cans, iron, steam, and old trains. There are some 300 members of the Mid-Continent Railway Historical Society, which has restored dozens of ancient engines and railcars, offering rides on a regular basis in the summer and autumn.

The D&R No. 9, built in 1884, is one of the country's oldest operating locomotives, repaired by society members in a huge car barn on their property. The "clubhouse" is a depot built in 1894, which houses exhibitions of equipment and railroad mementos. I've always enjoyed the autumn color tours that the club sponsors on weekends when the leaves are reaching their maximum rainbow effect. Occasionally, at a particularly scenic curve, the train stops to allow photographers to get off and take pictures from near the tracks. The train will back up and make a steamy, roaring run past the clicking shutters to magnificent effect. And, yes, the train does return to pick everyone up.

The winter snow run during the third week in February is also great for photographs, but dress warmly. The coaches are heated by woodstoves, just as they were in the old days. Those closest to the stove almost bake while the poor riders in the rear can get *preeeettty* frosty by the time the jaunt is completed. When getting off the train for those extra-special winter-weather photos of a steam locomotive in action, be sure to wear appropriate foot coverings, because snow along the tracks can be quite deep.

During the summer the 50-minute tour travels over its own rail bed between the hills and valleys of the Baraboo Range from North Freedom to Quartzite Lake, stopping at the iron-mining town of La Rue. Now a ghost town, the once-bustling community was served by the railroad in 1903.

Trains usually begin rolling toward mid-May, keeping up the action through Labor Day and on some weekends through mid-October. Rides are scheduled for 11 a.m. and 1 and 3 p.m. daily during the season. The museum is open from 9:30 a.m. until 5 p.m. Admission prices for adults are $16, senior citizens pay $15, and children 3 to 12 pay $10.

Every few summers, some historical society members live on the grounds, sleeping in the private rail coaches for the ultimate in luxury. The care that they have put into repairing the venerable gear is worth a stop, since much of the rolling stock has been featured in commercials and movies. It's like watching someone you know appear in a starring role. Equipment from the museum has been featured in the Swedish film *The Emigrants* and in the movie *Gaily, Gaily,* among numerous others.

North Freedom is reached by taking I-90 to the Baraboo exit and going through Baraboo on Highway 33 to Highway 136, where you can then follow the signs on County Road PF to the depot staging area. The complex is 6 miles west of Baraboo and 50 miles northwest of the Wisconsin Dells. For information on the Mid-Continent Railway Historical Society, contact the organization at E8948 Diamond Hill Rd., North Freedom 53951 (608-522-4261; www.mcrwy.com/).

Every traveler needs a bit of history to jump-start such an adventure here. The best place to begin is at Reedsburg's **Pioneer Village,** featuring a number of restored log cabin structures and pioneer homes gathered from a 30-mile radius of town. Pioneer Village sits in a 52-acre park east of Reedsburg on Highway 33. One of the most interesting is the Kruse cabin, with its unusual puncheon floor made of black locust stakes pounded into the earth. At the Willow Creek Church, if ears are attuned properly, a gentle breeze seems to pick up faint strains of 19th-century Lutheran hymns.

The **Norman Rockwell Exhibit** at the **Voyageur Inn,** 200 Viking Dr., showcases about 4,000 postcards, original magazine covers, calendars, and similar items on original paper stock painted by the famed illustrator between 1911 and 1976. The artwork, collected by Darlyn Merath, adorns the hallways around the inn.

Wood County

Wisconsin Rapids has been a papermaking hub since the 1830s. **Stora Enso,** 510 High St. (715-422-1616), offers tours of its plant and self-guided walks in nearby forestland owned by the firm.

Wisconsin's only drive-through dairy store is located in **Marshfield.** The Weber family, and assorted in-laws, has been prominent in Wood

County's dairy industry for more than 90 years. The retail outlet is just west of Marshfield on 9706 Country Route H. The **Weber's Farm Store** produces, processes, and retails its own milk from its 265-head herd, which grazes contentedly on 600 nearby acres. Talk about fresh. The milk is ready for sale within hours after milking. You can get whole milk, reduced-fat milk, low-fat milk, skim milk, and chocolate reduced-fat milk. (How do they get the cows to do that?) Ice cream, eggs, butter, heavy whipping cream, cheese curds, and fresh cheese also are offered. And the family has excellent lean ground beef from its own beef cattle. Store hours are 8:30 a.m. to 7 p.m. Mon through Fri and 8:30 a.m. to 5 p.m. Sat. Call (715) 384-5639 or review www .flannerysnewglarus.com.

The region around Wisconsin Rapids is known as the state's Cranberry Country, with its many bogs filled each autumn with brilliant red berries destined for the holiday table or for juice. There are several bogs open to visitors during the season, with others available for a look-see from adjacent roads.

But first, some details. The state produces around 50 percent of the country's cranberries, with about 240 growers in 20 counties continuing an agricultural tradition that started in the 19th century. In fact, some bogs have been good producers for more than a century. Cranberries need a marshy area with acidic soil, with abundant water and sand. Those requirements fit Wood County's environment to a T—or is it a "C" for "cranberry"?

OTHER ATTRACTIONS WORTH SEEING

Alliant Energy Center, Madison

Ancora Coffee Roasters, Madison

Bavaria Sausage Company, Verona

Dane County Farmers' Market on the Square, Madison

Duluth Trading Company/Wally Keller Tool Museum, Mount Horeb

Fitchburg Farmers' Market

Fort Winnebago Surgeon's Quarters, Portage

Henry Vilas Zoological Society, Madison

Overture Center for the Arts, Madison

Pioneer Log Village and Museum, Reedsburg

Sauk County Historical Museum, Baraboo

University of Wisconsin Arboretum, Madison

Wingra Boat Rentals, Madison

Wisconsin River ferryboat, Merrimac

The cranberry is a low-growing vine that blossoms in late June or early July, with green berries visible by August. After the berries mature, they are floated to the surface of the flooded bogs and dislodged from the plant by mechanical harvesters. The berries are then corralled by booms, lifted into waiting trucks at the edge of the bog via mechanical elevator belts, and then taken to a processing facility.

Now that you know the methodology, you can watch all this taking place along the roads wending their way around "the Rapids." Follow County Z west from the city's south side and south to where it connects with Highway 73. Take 73 west to Nekoosa and pick up 173 to D, then north to 54 and back east to town. If all that sounds confusing, don't worry. Pick up a map that outlines the **Cranberry Highway** tour from the Wisconsin Rapids Area Convention & Visitors Bureau, 2507 8th St. South (715-422-4650 or 800-554-4484; www.visit wisrapids.com).

One of the best places to stop to observe the picking is at **Glacial Lake Cranberries,** 2480 County Road D (www.cranberrylink.com). Minibus tours depart from company offices at 9 and 11 a.m. and at 1 and 3 p.m. Mon through Fri during the harvest. Depending on the year's conditions, the best viewings are in the month of October, from October 1 on, so it is always wise to call ahead. A small store on-site peddles almost anything anybody would ever want with a cranberry theme. Call ahead (715-887-2095) for reservations. Adults $10, children $5 (4 and under free).

The bogs are important environmentally, as well. These expansive water reservoirs are homes to loons, great blue herons, sandhill cranes, black terns, Canada geese, and other waterfowl. The surrounding forests and open fields dotted with lilies, blazing stars, and blue flag iris are perfect for birders seeking a peek at wild turkeys.

While motoring along Wood County's Cranberry Highway, be sure to visit the **Sandhill State Wildlife Area** off County X, just west of **Babcock.** Take the marvelous 14-mile Trumpeter Trail, which loops through the preserve, providing opportunities to see all sorts of wild critters. Bison, red fox, and ruffed grouse are on the list. Three observation towers are accessible off the trail: One is near the bison herd, the second is atop North Bluff, and the third overlooks Gallegher Marsh.

Hiking and cross-country skiing are also allowed within the wildlife area. Unfortunately, many of the popular naturalist programs once held at the skills center at the entrance to Sandhill have been cut back due to Wisconsin's budget crunch. But the remaining rangers there are always glad to answer questions. Call (715) 884-2437.

The Great Outdoors

The *Sandhill Outdoors Skills Center* in Babcock has a range of outdoors activities that are more than different. Starting the year is a winter mammal-tracking clinic, a timber-wolf ecology seminar and tracking adventure, a nature-on-snowshoe jaunt, a turkey hunters' clinic, and many other activities, such as canoe camping, searching for swamp frogs, and bluebird trail bird banding. For details write to the Sandhill DNR, Box 156, Babcock 55413, (888) 936-7463, http://dnr.wi.gov (search for "Sandhill Outdoors Skills Center").

The **Wood County Park System** is also one of the best in the state, offering five major parks (three of which have campgrounds), a 400-acre all-terrain-vehicle area, and 38,000 acres of public forestland. Fishing on the placid Nepco Lake can be serious or simply kickback; just bring plenty of bait. Outing details can be provided at the Wood County Park & Forestry Department, located in the courthouse in Wisconsin Rapids (715-421-8422).

All this outdoor business is sure to work up an appetite, so before jaunting out on the road from Wisconsin Rapids, stop first for breakfast and a cuppa joe at any of these: **Big Apple Bagels** (101 W. Riverview Expressway, Wisconsin Rapids; 715-424-0555, www.babcorp.com), **Cravings Coffee & Ice Cream Co.** (312 8th St. South, 715-423-6500), or **From the Ground Up Coffee House** (250 W. Grand Ave.; 715-421-5161).

Or try **Herschleb's Restaurant and Ice Cream Co.,** an old-time drive-in at 640 N. 16th St., (715) 423-1760. Look for the giant ice cream cone in the parking lot at the corner of Baker and 16th. The place opened as a dairy in 1939 and is still owned by family members who know the value of down-home chicken soup, potato pancakes, and real cherries in the ice cream. Herschleb's annually makes 20,000 gallons of "ice dream" (yes, it's that good!). Getting into the swing of things during the cranberry harvest, folks here produce their ever-popular cranberry supreme, cranberry splash, cranberry truffle, Alice in Cranberryland, and related tasty varieties of the cold, sweet stuff.

Places to Stay in Central Wisconsin

MADISON

Annie's Garden Bed & Breakfast
2117 Sheridan Dr.
(608) 244-2224
www.anniesinmadison.com
Inexpensive
Cedar shake and stucco
home in craftsman style,
beautiful valley view of
Warner Park near eastern
shore of Lake Mendota.

Arbor House, an Environmental Inn
3402 Monroe St.
(608) 238-2981
www.arbor-house.com
Moderate to expensive
Award-winning,
environmentally friendly;
across the street from the
1,280-acre UW Arboretum,
and a mile from Camp
Randall Stadium.

Doubletree by Hilton
525 W. Johnson St.
(608) 251-5511
www.doubletree.hilton
.com/Madison
Moderate to expensive
Heart of downtown
Madison on eastern edge
of UW–Madison campus,
easy walking to area arts
and cultural attractions,
24-hour business center.

The Edgewater Hotel
666 Wisconsin Ave.
(800) 922-5512
www.theedgewater.com
Moderate to expensive
Political heart of Madison,
see and be seen, overlooks
Lake Mendota, Admiralty
Dining Room has one of
best sunset views in the city.

Hilton Madison Monona Terrace
9 E. Wilson St.
(608) 255-5100
www1.hilton.com
Moderate to expensive
Adjacent to convention
center, close to downtown
bars and restaurants, great
city and lake views.

Mansion Hill Inn
424 N. Pinckney St.
(608) 255-3999
(800) 798-9070
www.mansionhillinn.com
Moderate to expensive
Luxury getaway, ornate
interior, Venetian glass
windows, several suites
feature whirlpool baths,
in-room gas fireplaces,
and balconies or verandas
overlooking downtown
Madison and the state
capitol.

STEVENS POINT & AREA

Americinn
1501 American Dr.
Plover
(800) 396-5007
www.americinn.com/hotels/
WI/Plover
Inexpensive to moderate
Free breakfast, heated
pool, easy access to
highways.

Holiday Inn
1001 Amber Ave.
(888) 465-4329
www.holidayinn.com/
hotels/us/en/stevens-point/
steaa/hoteldetail
Inexpensive to moderate
Just off I-39 and Route
51, making easy to get
to Travel Guard, Sentry
Insurance, Delta Dental,
and other area businesses;
24-hour business center;
close to Sentry World Golf
Course.

A Victorian Swan on Water
1716 Water St.
(715) 345-0595
www.victorianswan.com
Moderate
Antiques, lace curtains,
ceiling fans, and fireplaces;
located near Wisconsin
River.

WISCONSIN DELLS

Aloha Beach
1370 E. Hiawatha Dr.
(608) 253-4741
www.alohabeachresort
.com
Moderate
Swimming beach, outdoor/
indoor pools, sauna, kiddy
playground, canoes and
paddleboats for water fun.

Caribbean Club Resort
1093 Canyon Rd.
(608) 254-4777
(800) 800-6981
www.611ccr.com
Moderate
Condominium rental;
Jacuzzi tubs, king-size bed.

SELECTED CHAMBERS OF COMMERCE

**Greater Madison Convention &
Visitors Bureau**
615 E. Washington Ave.
Madison 53703
(608) 255-2537
(800) 373-6376
gmcvb@visitmadison.com
www.visitmadison.com

Sauk-Prairie Chamber of Commerce
421 Water St., Suite 103
Prairie de Sac 53578
(608) 643-4168
(800) 68-EAGLE
www.saukprairie.com

Spring Green Chamber of Commerce
150 E. Jefferson St.
Spring Green 53588
(800) 588-2054
www.springgreen.com

**Stevens Point Area Convention &
Visitors Bureau**
340 Division St. North
Stevens Point 54481
(715) 344-2556
(800) 236-INFO
www.spacvb.com

**Wausau/Central Wisconsin
Convention & Visitors Council**
10204 Park Plaza, Suite B
Rothschild 54474
(715) 355-8788
(888) WI-VISIT
www.wausaucvb.com

**Wisconsin Rapids Convention &
Visitors Bureau**
841 Goodnow Ave., Suite 103
Wisconsin Rapids 54494
(800) 554-4484
www.visitwisrapids.com

Copa Cabana
611 Wisconsin Dells Pkwy.
(800) 364-COPA (2672)
www.copacabanaresort
.com
Moderate
Outdoor waterfall lagoon,
shuttle service to Ho-
Chunk Casino, water
sports rentals.

Polynesian Resort
857 N. Frontage Rd.
(800) 27-ALOHA (272-
5642)
www.dellspolynesian.com
Moderate
Expansive water park,
fitness center on the first
floor adjacent to Kozy Kids
Korner, game center, and
Tahiti Trader Gift Shop.

WISCONSIN RAPIDS

Hotel Mead
451 E. Grand Ave.
(715) 423-1500
(800) 843-6323
www.hotelmead.com
Moderate
Indoor swimming pool,
whirlpool, sauna, and
fitness center. Romantic
getaway with a possible
ghost as chaperone.

Places to Eat in
Central Wisconsin

BARABOO

**Log Cabin Family
Restaurant**
1215 8th St.
(608) 356-8034
Inexpensive
www.logcabin-baraboo
.com
200 to 300 award-winning
pies made each week—
take one home.

EDGERTON

Mario's Pizza

201 W. Fulton St.
(608) 884-9488
Inexpensive
Pizzas, pastas, plus
American-style dishes, so
go for anything with tomato
sauce.

MADISON

Brickhouse BBQ

408 E. Gorham St.
(608) 257-7675
www.thebrickhousebbq
.com
Moderate
Meats smoked in-house;
creative appetizers, salads,
entrees, and vegetarian
options, with special array
of small batch bourbon
and rye.

Chocolate Shoppe Ice Cream Company

466 State St.
(608) 255-5454
www.chocolateshoppe
icecream.com
Inexpensive
Opened in 1962 in Madison
and now distributing quality
products throughout
Wisconsin; award-winning
strawberry ice cream, but
don't forget the espresso
almond fudge, plus real
whipped cream.

Ella's Deli & Ice Cream Parlor

2902 E. Washington Ave.
(608) 241-5291
www.ellasdeli.com
Inexpensive
Best matzo ball soup
this side of heaven and
mmm-good chopped liver;

vegetarian products are
also available. Started as
a kosher grocery in the
early 1960s on Madison's
downtown State Street,
now on the west side
of town. You can't miss
the place—look for the
carousel out front.

Great Dane Pub & Brewing Company

123 E. Doty St.
(608) 284-0000
www.greatdanepub.com
Moderate
Antique look, a can't-miss
Friday-night walleye fry or
Saturday-night prime rib,
late-night menu available,
plus billiards and free live
music.

L'Etoile Restaurant

1 S. Pickney St., Suite 107
(608) 251-0500
www.letoile-restaurant.com
Moderate to expensive
Noted for organic and
locally grown ingredients,
superb service, award-
winning wine list, elegant
surroundings.

Milio's

454 W. Johnson St.
(locations also at 2145
Regent St., 540 University
St., and 6234 University
St.)
(608) 251-8444
www.milios.com
Inexpensive
Super subs such as the
Texas Longhorn (shaved
roast beef) to the Godfather
(ham and Italian cheese);
freshly baked bread,
especially the wheat rolls,
are dangerously delicious.

MAZOMANIE

The Old Feed Mill

114 Cramer St.
(608) 795-4909
http://mazomaniemills.com
Moderate to expensive
Located in a refurbished
mill circa 1857, signature
dinner items include
turkey and broccoli pie
and pot roast served with
vegetables, garlic mashed
potatoes, and pan gravy;
flavorful smoked pork.

PORTAGE

A&W Portage

717 E. Wisconsin Ave.
(608) 742-5759
www.awdrivein.com
Inexpensive
Best root beer in town.
What more can we say
about A&W, except that
its burgers, chili dogs,
and fries are great on a
hot summer night after a
long day of driving. In late
August the facility hosts
its Nostalgic Night, where
poodle-skirted carhops
serve the customers, a
DJ spins classic songs,
and everyone can swing
along with hula hoops
and participate in a root
beer–chugging contest.
Often collectors come in
their 1950s and 1960s hot
rods and customized cars,
and the crowd "oohs" and
"aahs" at the chrome, giant
fins, and paint jobs. Open
daily year-round.

STEVENS POINT & AREA

Belts Soft Serve
2140 Division St.
(715) 344-0049
Inexpensive
Locally famous, but with a winter hiatus and reopening on one of the first Fridays in early May; go for cookie dough flurries, brownies, and apple crisp.

Bernard's Country Inn
701 2nd St. North
(715) 344-3365
www.bernardscountryinn
.com
Moderate to expensive
Old World, award-winning charm where seafood Normandy in a puff pastry shell is prime appetizer, followed by duck a l'orange.

Ella's Restaurant
616 Division St.
(715) 341-1871
Inexpensive
"Hands-down" best place to meet friends and have a great meal; wide variety of soups, sandwiches, and entrees.

Mitchell's Hilltop Pub & Grill
4901 Main St.
(715) 341-3037
http://hilltoppubandgrill
.com
Moderate
Casual, comfortable, great places for beer and buffalo wings, plus chicken fettuccini Alfredo for those special nights out.

WISCONSIN DELLS

The Del-Bar
800 Wisconsin Dells Pkwy.
(608) 253-1861
www.del-bar.com
Moderate to expensive
One of area's top supper clubs, with prime steaks, walleye, chicken, lamb chops, and roast duck, wonderful platters of onion rings; Prairie-style architecture by James Dresser, a student of architect Frank Lloyd Wright.

House of Embers
935 Dells Pkwy.
(608) 253-6411
www.houseofembers.com
Moderate to expensive
Launched in 1957, still with a cozy, old-shoe feel, especially with comfortable fireplace in the dining when the weather turns cool.

Monk's Bar & Grill
220 Broadway
(608) 254-2955
www.monksbarandgrill.com
Inexpensive
Freshly ground hamburger, monster chef's salad, located in building dating back to the 1880s.

Paul Bunyan's Northwoods Cook Shanty
411 Highway 13
(608) 254-8717
Inexpensive to moderate
www.paulbunyans.com
A staple of the Wisconsin Dells since the 1950s, with flapjacks and a special syrup, plus sausage links and ham; look for the towering signage outside with an image of Ol' Paul; loaded with logging artifacts, stuffed animals, and other North Woods memorabilia.

NORTHERN WISCONSIN

There is a hoary joke they tell in the far reaches of Wisconsin whenever an Alberta Hook weather system swings down from Canada across Lake Superior to slam a wintry punch at the state. Amid the hail, frozen rain, and snow, the lament goes up, "I'm gonna put a snow shovel on my shoulder and walk south, stopping when the first person says; 'What's that you're carrying?'"

The northern rim of the state is considered a frosty snow-belt, with snowfall often hitting upward of 100 inches a year, while southern Wisconsin along Lake Michigan often barely reaches 40 inches. As an example of snow conditions on the Wisconsin "tundra," Bayfield County's Iron River recorded 32.75 inches in January 1988, concluding a 3-month fall of 64.5 inches, making it one of the heaviest on record. But such weather delights outdoors enthusiasts who know how to prepare for it.

Some folks do abandon Wisconsin, thinking that less frosty winters will be a panacea to wintertime woes. Most people along the upper rim of the Badger State, however, take their seasons in stride. What are a few nasty February days when considering long summers in the pine woods, the

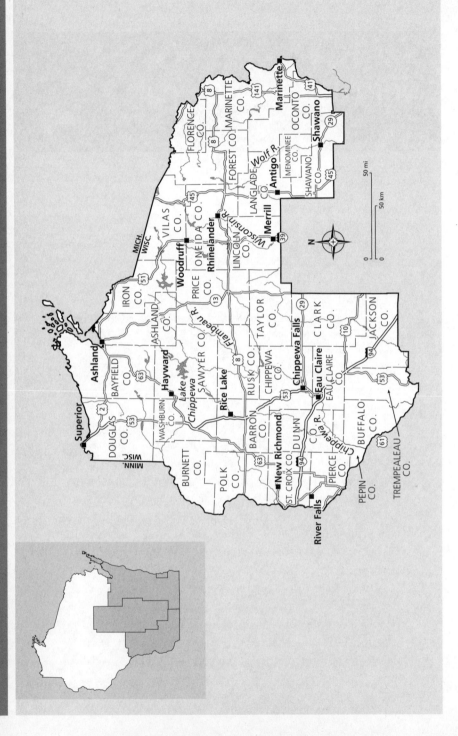

excitement of snowmobiling and skiing in the winter, with the fresh explosion of spring wildflowers and the hazy crimson woods of autumn? These delights of Wisconsin ensure that its residents remain hardy and open to life around them.

And there are plenty of nooks and crannies that need exploring in northern Wisconsin.

Ashland County

The city of **Ashland** calls itself the Garland City of the Inland Seas. That's a pretty hefty title, but since the community celebrated its centennial in 1987, we should allow them some imagery excess. Stepping back further into history, French trappers and traders stopped by here regularly as early as 1659. Where the French used canoes to skirt the shoreline because the timber was so thick on shore, today's travelers can easily drive to **Kreher Park and Beach** or **Prentice Park and Campground** and gaze on the wind-ruffled waters of Chequamegon Bay. Payment is by the honor system.

A century ago, passenger and freight trains made Ashland a major transportation hub in the North Woods. With the demise of passenger trains, Ashland's Soo Line station crumbled. The wreck was a challenge to developer Mike Ryan, a former airline traffic manager who dabbled in refurbishing old buildings. At first, renovating the depot was a task that made him wonder about this

NORTHERN WISCONSIN'S TOP HITS

Amnicon Falls State Park	Ice Age Interpretive Center
Apostle Islands Cruise Service	Lake Superior Big Top Chautauqua
Bad River Chippewa Reservation	Lumberjack World Championships
Chequamegon National Forest	National Fresh Water Fishing Hall of Fame
Copper Culture State Park	
Crex Meadows Wildlife Area	Nicolet National Forest
Dave's Falls	Peshtigo Fire Museum
The Hideout	SS *Meteor*
High Falls Dam	Timm's Hill
HighGround Veterans Memorial Park	Wisconsin Concrete Park

avocation. Then he looked beyond the piles of rubble and the gaping hole in the roof and decided it wasn't so bad after all. After taking about 60 truckloads of trash and wreckage from the shell, Ryan saved the depot from being razed. He turned it into a warren of restaurants, dance floors, and pub rooms with railroad themes. The place opened to the public in 1988, after long hours of hauling debris and rebuilding the interior of the structure.

Ryan kept the best of the old. The carved graffiti in the woodwork along the trackside windows still carries travelers' mute testimony from the turn of the 20th century. Names, dates, and even short poems are etched into the oak.

But alas, on April 1, 2000, the Depot burned down in a spectacular display of flame and smoke. The incident was not much of an April Fool's joke on the staff and management. But they picked up what could be salvaged from the smoking ruins and moved about 7 blocks to the west. There they opened a new restaurant, *L. C. Wilmarth's Deep Water Grille & South Shore Brewery* (808 W. Main St.; 715-682-4200; www.southshorebrewery.com). The restaurant has branched out to offer such exotic items as shrimp jambalaya ($19.99); grilled marinated duck breast served with a sweet cherry sauce ($15.99), and steamed mussels ($9.99). The brewery, which had been located in the late, lamented Depot, was moved lock, stock, and yeast to the upscale property in historic downtown Ashland. It presents 24 types of brews, from ales to lagers to pilsners. And then there's the Alley, offering a more casual fare of pizzas, sandwiches, and hamburgers.

Anchoring the other end of the boardwalk at 101 W. Lake Shore Dr. is the *Hotel Chequamegon* (715-682-9095; www.hotelc.com), modeled after a landmark hotel that was destroyed by fire in 1955. But the modern hotel could have stepped from the pages of history, opening in 1987 about 100 yards from the original site. The hotel's interior decorating scheme is Victorian, with plenty of woodwork, antiques, and ferns. Each of the hotel's suites is named after a local community and decorated with photographs, paintings, and other artifacts donated by residents. Sixty-five rooms are available, which range in price from $115 to $170. There are also special corporate and tour-group rates.

Nice touches include handmade soap in the bathrooms, fresh flowers everywhere, and box lunches that can be prepared for hikers.

The hotel's Sirtoli's Dining Room offers gourmet and regional specialties such as planked whitefish. Its lineup of fresh pasta beats anything this side of the Tiber River. Molly Cooper's Restaurant & Lounge offers a great view of the wild waters of Lake Superior. No one minds casual attire at either establishment.

For standard food, and plenty of it, you can't beat the buffet at the *Breakwater Cafe* (715-682-8388; www.visitashland.com/dining), 1808 Lake Shore Dr. East across Highway 2 from the Lake Superior shore. We've learned to trust where professional eaters such as truckers and mechanics congregate; the Breakwater certainly lives up to that adage. There's plenty of parking around the cozy building, a testimony to accommodating the needs of long-haulers who frequent the restaurant.

Northland College (715-682-1699; www.northland.edu) in Ashland is an independent, coed college that focuses on environmental and Native American studies and outdoor education in addition to other liberal arts. It also led the fight to establish Earth Day, a national remembrance of the need to be respectful of the natural world around us. With this emphasis, the school has an expansive reputation for its conferences and programs on environmental studies. Simply wandering around the campus, perhaps pausing in the ivy-covered Sigurd Olson Environmental Institute, is a respite from the rush of a typical busy day. You'll see more than one canoe mounted atop a car as students head out for a field class.

The **Bad River Chippewa Reservation** (www.badriver-nsn.gov) at the northern tip of the county annually hosts a powwow the third weekend in August, attracting tribes from around the upper Midwest. The reservation also has a furniture-building school, producing everything from picnic tables to desks, and a factory making kits for log homes . . . sort of a giant Lincoln Log set. Both businesses are open to visitors on Tues, Thurs, and Fri and are located on Highway 2, the major roadway between Ashland and Bayfield (Bayfield County).

Across the street from the tribal offices is the headquarters of the Great Lakes Fisheries and Game Commission, which monitors the Chippewas' hunting and fishing activities guaranteed under treaty rights. Ponds to the rear of the building contain walleyes for stocking lakes around Ashland County.

One of the best places to commune with nature in northern Wisconsin is in the pines of the Chequamegon National Forest. The 848,000 acres of woodlands make up one of the 155 national forests in the United States. Chequamegon (pronounced sho-WAH-ma-gon) derives its name from the Chippewa term for

AUTHORS' FAVORITES

Bad River Lodge and Casino, Odanah

Chequamegon National Forest, Glidden District

The HighGround Veterans Memorial Park, Neillsville

Northland College, Ashland

Rhinelander Logging Museum

funfacts

"place of shallow water," a reference to the nearby placid Chequamegon Bay of rugged Lake Superior. This sprawling forest was replanted in 1933 from over-cut and burned land, the result of heavy timber harvesting by private individuals and the government in the 1800s.

Every year, thousands of adventurous types hike, bike, and fish in one of the sections of the forest. The **Glidden District** is located in Ashland County, and other tracts are in Price and Taylor Counties. Son Dan went into the Glidden area on his first deep-woods camping trip when he was about 7 years old, bouncing over the more rugged back trails via a four-wheel-drive vehicle. I was working on features for an adventure driving guide at the time. When we got to our Day Lake campsite, we tested our best rod-and-reel techniques but wound up eating beans and canned stew instead of the walleye that were supposed to go into our skillet that night. But, of course, it must have been the "other guy" who caught the biggie.

So the next day we packed the poles and hit the backwoods roads criss-crossed by numerous rivers, among them the Moose, Torch, and Chippewa. Dingdong Creek, Hell Hole Creek, Dead Horse Slough, and Rocky Run Rapids are the names of smaller streams in the area. Supposedly there was good fishing, according to the locals. But with our already bruised egos, we decided not to embarrass ourselves any more, so we headed out of the woods. It was time, however—already late October with the temperature hovering around 20 to 30 degrees Fahrenheit.

pedalpower

A good day's jaunt through the Chequamegon, one that includes some fishing and hiking, is along the **North Country Trail.** The tour is a 60-mile link that meanders through the Glidden, Hayward, and Washburn districts of the forest. The route begins on FR 390, about 2 miles west of Mellen, and ends up at County Highway A near Ruth Lake, 5 miles south of Iron River. One of the best stops on the trail is off FR 199 at

St. Peter's Dome, a huge outcrop of bald rock from which you can spot Lake Superior about 22 miles to the northeast. It is a steep climb up the back slope of the Dome, fighting your way through the brush. Once on top, you'll find the view worth the struggle. Bring hiking boots if you plan to do much crawling through the underbrush and over the boulders. There is a trail of sorts to the back of the dome, but it is overhung with thorny berry bushes.

The town of **Glidden** is the Black Bear Capital of the World, located just outside the forest entrance on Highway 13. The folks here offer a reward to anyone bringing in a bigger bruin (dead, they expect) than the 665-pounder on exhibit in a glass case on the main street overlooking the rest of the city. The bear was nailed in the nearby woods by a hunter who weighed it on the local mill's truck scale because no one else, not even the local butcher, had a scale big enough to do justice to the brute.

Here's a hint for keeping those walking floor rugs out of your camp at night. If you don't take precautions, you could have a real problem on your hands. *Keep all food hanging high in trees or inside locked car trunks. Be sure everything is out of reach of scratching claws.* Chequamegon's bears have been known to demolish coolers and food lockers in their foraging. And they are not playful teddies on a picnic.

For detailed information about events in Ashland County, call Ashland City Hall, (715) 682-7071. For more information on northern Wisconsin in general, call the **Northern Great Lakes Visitor Center** at (715) 685-9983 or log on to www.northerngreatlakescenter.org.

Barron County

The **Rutabaga Festival** in Cumberland elevates this lowly veggie to unimagined heights. Held the fourth weekend in August, the festival features a 130-unit parade, the Rutabaga Walk & Run, an arts and crafts show, a hot pepper–eating contest, a Rutabaga Queen contest, and the Rutabaga Olympics. In the latter, rutabagas are tossed, turned, and tumbled in a variety of family-themed events guaranteed for a laugh and a lot of fun. Cumberland is easy to find, located as it is on Highway 48, west of Rice Lake. The city chose the rutabaga as its prime image maker because of the numbers of farmers in the area who grow the crop. But when not munching rutabagas, you can hike the Ice Age, Tuscobia, Old Indian, and Old Swamp Trails, which cut through or near the city. The well-marked pathways make Barron County an outdoors lover's paradise.

Hikers also love the **Blue Hills** of eastern Barron County, noted for their rugged, smoky appearance. The scenery is especially delightful in spring and autumn, when the fog hangs heavily around the valleys and deep gullies that

TOP ANNUAL EVENTS

FEBRUARY

Snowshoe Weekend
Bayfield
(715) 779-3335
(800) 447-4094

MARCH

Klondike Days
Eagle River
(715) 891-2679
(800) 359-6315
www.klondikedays.org/index.shtml

MAY

Folk Festival
Ashland
(715) 682-1289

Journeys Marathon
Eagle River
(715) 479-6400
www.journeysmarathon.org

SEPTEMBER

Apostle Islands Lighthouse Celebration
(800) 779-4487
www.lighthousecelebration.com

NOVEMBER

Christmas in Torpy Park
Minocqua
(715) 356-5266
(800) 446-6784
www.minocqua.org

score the region. Some of the ridges there are as high as 20,000 feet. While the area's rough edges were smoothed down by glacial action eons ago, there are still plenty of opportunities for a leg-stretching meander.

Bayfield County

Bayfield County is the largest of all the Wisconsin counties, yet it doesn't have a stoplight. Honest.

Almost 10 percent of the freshwater in the world is around the *Apostle Islands,* according to environmentalists. The picturesque islands dotting Lake Superior here were left by the glaciers.

The ice drifts left behind huge mounds of rubble on their retreat northward eons ago. An early missionary who couldn't quite add gave the archipelago its name. Actually there are 22 islands, ranging in size from the 3-acre Gull Island to the 22 square miles of Madeline Island. Long Island is only 10 feet above the waterline. The entire area is federally protected as part of the Apostle Islands National Lakeshore.

Camping is possible on 17 of the islands. Interpretive programs include lighthouse tours on Raspberry Island; campfire programs at night on South Twin, Rocky, and Stockton Islands; and a tour of a commercial fishing camp on Manitou Island. For cruises around the islands, if you don't own your own sailboat, take the *Apostle Islands Cruise Service* tours (715-779-3925 or 800-323-7619), which operate out of Bayfield. The line offers various excursions, including sunset voyages and a Sunday brunch voyage.

In the winter of 1988, which seems so long ago now, I snowmobiled across the frozen 2.6-mile lake strait to Madeline Island in the predawn hours. It was a time when even the late stars seemed frozen against the sky. The ice bridge linking the island to the mainland is a travel-at-your-own-risk proposition, but generally quite safe in the minus 20 degrees of a January predawn. Cars and trucks even take the route regularly in the winter. When the thaw comes and the summer finally arrives, the *Madeline Island Ferry Line* (800-323-7619) beats swimming.

The island has a nifty museum located 1 block from the ferry dock. The facility is operated by the Wisconsin Historical Society and is packed with artifacts dating from the earliest Native Americans to the white settlers. A Native American burial ground is 0.5 mile from the dock as you drive around the marina. Several of the tombstones date back 200 years. For details about the island, contact the Madeline Island Chamber of Commerce, Box 274, La Point 54850 (888-475-3386; www.madelineisland.com).

The building is open 7 days a week from May through Oct, and Mon through Fri from Nov through Apr. For specific information on the islands, including the interpretive programs, contact the Apostle Islands National Lakeshore, 415 Washington Ave., Bayfield 54814 (715-779-3397; www.nps.gov/apis/).

The area is dotted with wrecks, remains of vessels caught in the headwinds that howl around Bayfield County, a thumb that juts into Lake Superior's belly.

Bayfield is a pleasant resort community, with the usual collection of antiques shops, small restaurants, and motels/hotels. One of the best rainbows

Snowmobiling Adventure

Snowmobiling clubs help maintain the state's winter trail system, which consists of some 25,000 miles of top-quality runs that link every corner of Wisconsin. The Sno-Drifters, Black River Rock Dodgers, Northwoods Riders Snowmobile Club, Medford Stump Jumpers, Jump River Runners, Pine Creek Riders, Moonlite Sno-Kats, Westboro Sno-Dusters, and Interwald Wanderers are among the many organizations that ensure quality riding and safety. In the North Woods the entire family finds snowmobiling a prime winter adventure.

For a free statewide trail map, call the Wisconsin Department of Tourism at (800) 432-8747 or visit www.travelwisconsin.com.

Biking in the Woods

One of the best North Woods bike trails is the *Hiawatha State Park Trail* near Tomahawk. The 6.6-mile stretch of crushed rock was built by Lincoln County and takes riders through dense pine stands and rolling hill country. Watch for deer and other wildlife. A good place to start is on Somo Avenue near Tomahawk's Sara Park, where you can leave your car. Then follow the trail signs. The "Hiawatha" tag is derived from a passenger train that once brought travelers here in the 1940s. For more details call Lincoln County Forestry Land & Parks at (715) 536-0327.

we ever saw arched over the marina there after a brief summer storm a few years ago.

The little park at the corner of Rittenhouse Avenue and Front Street was freshly washed by the rain. The sailboats were bobbing quietly on the smooth water; only the clinking and tinkling of chains on metal masts could be heard. The sun was dipping low behind us, with just enough light to pop that brilliant rainbow out from the dark clouds scudding over the eastern background.

The *Old Rittenhouse Inn* (301 Rittenhouse Ave.; 800-779-2129; www.rit tenhouseinn.com) is a restored Victorian mansion dating from the 1890s with rates ranging from $140 to $325 per night. The dining room is open to the public, offering the most elegant meals in the north country. The Rittenhouse hosts special programs throughout the year, ranging from concerts to Christmas displays. The *C-Side Inn* (715-373-5794) is about 5 miles west of Washburn on Highway C, along the eastern edge of Bayfield County's northern hunk of the Chequamegon. It's a perfect stop for snowmobilers and skiers. A huge pot of homemade chicken soup is always bubbling in the kitchen, to go along with the homemade bread served with slabs of peanut butter and strawberry jam. The food is stick-to-your-ribs fare, just the thing needed when rumbling through the forest's snowbound *Valhalla Recreation Area.* If you prefer fancier fare, have steak, eggs, toast, and hash browns.

The *Bad River Lodge and Casino,* 10 miles west of Ashland along US 2 in the reservation village of Odanah, brings a bit of Las Vegas glitter and Reno glamour to the North Woods. A 50-room lodge adjacent to the casino offers Jacuzzi suites, wheelchair-accessible rooms, and other amenities. If it is your first visit, the management ponies up $5 in casino tokens for stopping by and joining the facility's Casino Club. Call (715) 795-7121 or (800) 795-7121 for lodge reservations, and (715) 682-7121 for casino information, or check www .badriver.com. Slots and blackjack tables keep the action jumping in the main hall. But in case things slow down, drop in at the all-you-can-eat buffet in the casino's restaurant. While gambling may not be everyone's thing, stop anyway to see how it's being done in the forestland.

The *Lake Superior Big Top Chautauqua* in Washburn brings alive the spirit and fun of the old-time traveling tent shows of the 19th century. Performances are held from early July through Labor Day in a breezy park overlooking Lake Superior. For a schedule contact Big Top Chautauqua, Box 455, Washburn 54891 (715-373-5552; www.bigtop.org).

The *Stockyard H&L Cattle Co.* sprawls over 500 acres of undulating hills, pine groves, and fields. If you want horses, this is the place to find them. Within the Stockyard H&L is *Lazy L Tack & Trailers,* one of the best western-themed tack shops in this part of the state, with saddles, bits, cinches, horseshoes, and other accoutrements necessary for any equine-related fun—such as jeans, jackets, hats, and shirts. For serious riders, owners John and Susan Loomis offer team penning, barrel racing, and horse shows. But there are also wagon rides and a Labor Day weekend event for the slower-paced. The farm is adjacent to the Buffalo State Trail for

funfacts

There are 10 metropolitan areas within the state. La Crosse draws many of its workers from across the Mississippi River in Minnesota. Minneapolis–St. Paul and Duluth-Superior also extend their metroplexes into the Badger State.

Braving the Storm

You've never seen a storm until you've seen one on Lake Superior. Remember the **SS Edmund Fitzgerald,** the super-freighter that sank and took all hands with it in 1975? It's that kind of weather that curls the toes and runs the surf so high around the Apostle Islands that you'd think even Noah would have had a hard time surviving. Elder Hintz was caught far out on Michigan Island in such a storm, stranded for 4 days after a hiking excursion. Luckily I was able to stay with two National Park Service volunteers who were manning the lighthouse and visitor services there for the summer. We hunkered low, with no electricity (using gas lanterns/candles) and almost no water (no wells on the island). The waves crashed high up the island cliffs, rain lashed the pines, and wind—what a wind—seemed powerful enough to flatten the 100-foot lighthouse that was built in 1886. There are 143 steps leading up from the lighthouse keeper's dock to the cliff top. The waves made it up those steps faster than I could run.

When a Park Service boat finally showed up with extra supplies, I had to be ferried out aboard a rubber raft because the surf was still lashing over the pier. The runabout couldn't dock because of the high water, so the operation was a rescue mission worthy of Demi Moore in the movie *GI Jane.* Worth it? You bet.

bicycling during nonsnow months and for snowmobiling when it chills. Contact the Loomises at W394 US 10, Mondovi 54755 (800-926-5309; www.lazyl.com).

The *Crex Meadows Wildlife Area* is 0.5 mile north of the village of Grantsburg in west-central Burnett County. While off the beaten path, the "paths" into the wildlife area are actually all-weather, hard-surface roads. The site is only 90 minutes east of the Twin Cities via I-35. County Trunk F marks the western and northern borders, with County Trunk D making up the south portion. Grantsburg itself is easy to find—just take Highways 70 and 18. You'll find a wildlife area project headquarters at the southwest corner of the property, east of the junctions of Trunks D and F.

The marshes here were formed when glacial Lake Grantsburg retreated. The place was well utilized by the Fox, Dakota, and Ojibwe nations for cranberry and wild-rice gathering, as well as for hunting.

Today this is birders' paradise. Swing out your scopes for glimpses of all types of ducks: mallards, ring-necks, green-winged teal, and other species. On the grass prairie you can find grouse and some prairie chickens. Sandhill cranes and Canada geese abound. If you wonder about the 300 acres of plantings in the center of the wildlife area, don't worry. There's a reason. The corn is left standing for the migratory birds.

Clark County

One of the most poignant retreats in Wisconsin is the *HighGround Veterans Memorial Park,* about 4 miles west of Neillsville on Highway 10 (715-743-4224; www.thehighground.org). Overlooking a deep valley, HighGround was dedicated in 1988 as the state's official memorial to its Vietnam vets. It's a powerful place, where emotional reunions constantly occur among men and women who survived that ugly conflict.

A statue there features several wounded soldiers and a nurse. Under the nurse's cape hang 1,215 dog tags, each with the name of a Wisconsinite who died during the war. The wind causes the tags to tinkle gently, a sound that no one forgets. Memorials to World War II and Korean veterans also are on the site.

Douglas County

The city of *Superior* is the largest community in northern Wisconsin. Founded as a mining center, it is now a commercial hub for the North Woods counties. Hugging the south rim of Lake Superior, it is linked to Duluth, Minnesota, by the Richard I. Bong Memorial Bridge. The gracefully curving structure is named

Hit the Books

Wisconsin has nearly 400 public libraries, which are great resources for travelers seeking local history and information on what to see and do. The libraries are grouped into 17 regional districts. If you are looking for anything particular about the state, try the various university libraries, as well. Wisconsin authorized free public libraries in 1872. For more info, check out http://dpi.wi.gov/pld/wis_lib.html. Not helpful? You can narrow search results when you're signed in to search http://dpi.wi.gov.

after the World War II flying ace born in nearby Poplar, a 15-minute drive east of town. In the late 1980s Superior was used as a setting for a film starring Jessica Lange. The location scouts came to town several times seeking picturesque sites draped with birch trees. The advance crews fell in love with the entire community and convinced the director to expand his shooting operation around the vicinity.

The **SS Meteor,** the world's last remaining whaleback freighter, is anchored at the Superior docks off Barker's Island. You can climb its decks and investigate the pilothouse and galley. The old ore vessel gets its name from the odd-appearing whale shape that provided extra stability in rolling waters. The ship was launched in 1896.

The museum (715-394-5712 during the season; www.superiorpublicmuseums .org/ssmeteor/NewMETEORMAIN.htm) is open from 9 a.m. to 5 p.m. Mon through Sat and 11 a.m. to 5 p.m. Sun from mid-May through Labor Day. From September through mid-October, hours and days vary, so it is best to call to confirm. Free parking is available. Tickets for the SS *Meteor* are $6 for adults and $5 for seniors and students.

For a peek into Superior's Victorian-era past, the **Fairlawn Mansion and Museum** provides a wonderful look at the city's history. The 42-room house was constructed in 1890 and was also used as a children's home for four decades. The mansion, with its assortment of period furniture and accessories, is open from 9 a.m. to 5 p.m. Mon through Sat and from 11 a.m. to 5 p.m. Sun for much of the year. Tours are held on the hour; the last tour is at 4 p.m. Admission to Fairlawn is $8 for adults, $6 for seniors and students up to age 18. Kids under 6 are free.

There's always a hot time in Superior, at least during the summer, when the **Old Firehouse and Police Museum** is open from mid-May through Aug from 10 a.m. to 5 p.m. Mon through Sat and from 11 a.m. to 5 p.m. Sun; from Sept through mid-October 10 a.m. to 5 p.m. Sat and noon to 5 p.m. Sun. The old brick building, restored to its original yellow paint job, can't be missed at the junction of 23rd Avenue East and 4th Street (Highways 2 and 53). Admission is free. Among the artifacts on display is a 1906 steam pumper.

For the latest details on any hour, day, or price changes for these facilities, contact Superior Public Museums (715-394-5712; www.superiorpublic museums.org).

Douglas County's **Amnicon Falls State Park** is one of the state's most photogenic waterfalls, crying for a calendar cover shot. The 800-acre park is located on Highway 2, about 15 miles east of Superior (715-398-3000; www .dnr.wi.gov/org/land/parks/specific/amnicon). The Amnicon River divides around an island in the center of the park, with a covered bridge linking the banks. There are good photo vantage points from the bridge or from either shore.

One of the best trout flowages in the county is the **Brule River,** which passes through Douglas County from Solon Springs into Lake Superior. Presidents Grant and Cleveland enjoyed fly casting on the river, and Silent Cal Coolidge had his summer White House at a resort there for several years. Cal never talked much about his secret fishing holes, but local bait-shop owners will tell you everything you need to know about the entire stretch of river. Part of the waterway meanders through the rugged Brule River Forest.

Forest County

Larry the Logroller is Wabeno's famous attraction. The statue of a timber cutter stands 21 feet 9 inches tall, symbolizing the area's main industry as well as providing a mascot for the town's high school sports teams. The statue is next to the Wabeno High School band shell in town. Straight-backed Larry looks a little stiff, as if he has been chopping wood too long, but he's a good backdrop for a family portrait.

Laona is in the heart of the **Nicolet National Forest,** where many local loggers still work—cutting out about 200,000 cords of hardwood per year. The wood is sent to mills in the Fox River Valley to the south. The Nicolet Forest encompasses about 651,000 acres, within which are the headwaters for the Wolf, Pine, Popple, Oconto, and Peshtigo Rivers. The Nicolet was named after Jean Nicolet, the French explorer who "discovered" Wisconsin in 1634.

While in the Nicolet Forest, look for the MacArthur Pine, named for the famed general. The tree is one of the oldest in the nation, standing 148 feet high and with a circumference of 17 feet. The tree was old when Nicolet and his *voyageurs* were first finding their way to the southlands some 300 years ago. To find the tree, turn north onto Highway 139 just as you leave the village of Cavour to the west. (Cavour is 8 miles north of Laona on Highway 8.) Continue to Forest Road 2166 near Newald and turn west to FR 2167. Make a sharp turn north, and you'll spot the pine towering above its neighbors.

Laona has been putting on a *Community Soup* (www.laonahistory.com/ LaonaCommunitySoupPage.html) annually for the 70-plus years, the first Sunday of every August. Townsfolk donate the ingredients for the homemade vegetable soup, made in large cast-iron pots over an open fire. The only requirement for eating is that you bring your own bowl and spoon. Some of the fun is coming to the city park to watch the preparations, which begin about 6 a.m. The soup is simmered until noon, when serving starts. The recipe includes some secret ingredients, but generally it contains fresh onions, carrots, celery, potatoes, beans, and whatever else might be in the garden. The Soup is open from 9 a.m. to 5 p.m.

The soup-serving tradition started years ago when neighbors got together for a friendly outing. The attendance grew so large that the Laona Lions Club took over operations a few years ago to help coordinate the event.

Laona is also home to the *Camp Five Lumberjack Train*, a steam train that operates Mon through Sat from June to late August. Camp Five is a typical turn-of-the-20th-century lumber camp, with an environmental hike nearby and a country store on the grounds at the junction of Highways 8 and 32 (715-674-3414 in summer or 800-774-3414; www.camp5museum.org). The train ride through the woods is fun, giving kids the chance to see a working locomotive up close. Tickets are $19 for adults, $8 for children 4 to 12, and free for tykes 3 and younger. A family package costs $56.

Forest County has another interesting Rustic Road that extends through the woodlands for 7.4 miles off Highway 70. It meanders across Brule Creek along Fishel Road to Cary Dam Road to Lake View Drive, concluding in the hamlet of Alvin on Highway 55. The village is about 2 miles south of the Michigan border.

Iron County

The *Frontier Bar* on Highway 2 near Saxon is a loud, happy place. It's the jumping-off point on the Iron Horse Snowmobile Trail for a 20-mile run northward through the Bad River Indian Reservation in next-door Ashland County. Tucked off the highway, about 7 miles south of Lake Superior, the Frontier is the place to hang out, tell a few lies, and eat chili—not necessarily in that order. The Frontier outdoes fast-food joints with its hefty burgers. If you are the last of the big spenders, add some cheese for only a dime. In the wintertime the bar serves up a "snowshoe," schnapps with brandy. For details call (715) 893-2461 or visit www.frontierbarandcampground.com.

Travel Games

Roger Jasinski, former manager of the state's Department of Natural Resources (DNR) for the **Turtle-Flambeau Flowage** in Iron County, and Melanie Eklof put together a fun "young person's vacation guidebook" that is packed with trivia and games for kids. One of the best is unscrambling the names of northern Wisconsin wildlife. Jasinski retired in 2009, after 32 years of service to the DNR.

Try these on the tykes: 1) obbatc, 2) skatrmu, 3) esoum, 4) reshw, 5) tiewhaltide eerd, 6) punkihcm, 7) oxedrf, 8) wuckchodo, 9) love, and 10) raveeb. Okay, so you want answers? It's not going to be that easy. You figure 'em out, too! But okay, here's a sample to get you started: 5) white-tailed deer. That's enough for now. Get busy.

The flowage, by the way, once consisted of the Flambeau and Turtle Rivers, Beaver Creek, and 16 lakes. A dam was built in 1926 where the rivers met, flooding the lakes and the surrounding land. This formed one large lake called the Turtle-Flambeau Flowage. The dam was built to save water that could be used to generate electricity at other dams farther downstream. The flowage has subsequently become one of the state's major aquatic waterfowl breeding and migratory grounds. Bring a canoe, waders, camera, and binoculars.

Mercer is proud of its title, "the Loon Capital." The large birds have a distinctive, haunting call that echoes over the lakes and forests of Wisconsin. They are such a part of the North Woods world that Mercer dedicated a large statue to the fowl on Highway 51 at the southern outskirts of town. The 16-foot-high bird is in a little park adjacent to the town's information center. The big bird weighs 2,000 pounds and contains a speaker with a tape recording explaining all the loon calls and facts about the bird's habitat. There is a serious reason for the Mercer display as well. It is a reminder that the lakes in Iron County provide one of the few prime breeding grounds for the large waterbird.

Langlade County

The roar of white water is music to the ears of outdoors fans in Langlade, Marinette, Menominee, and Oconto Counties, where canoeing, kayaking, or rafting are more than just Huck Finn adventures. Using rubber rafts, the rides can be slow, easy drifting or furious careening along the Wolf, Peshtigo, or Menominee Rivers. The routes twist and turn through the pine woods, with action paced by the height of the water during each season. Commercial raft operators usually hit the water from Memorial Day through Labor Day on the Menominee and from mid-April to late October on the Peshtigo and Wolf.

The Menominee is dam controlled, which determines the amount of high water, so it's always good to call an outfitter before arrival to check on water levels.

Gear is simple. Wear tennis shoes or rubber-soled shoes because rafts have soft bottoms that can get slippery when racing the rapids. Regular riders often wear wet suits when the weather turns chilly. Windbreakers are important in early spring. There's no sense in being uncomfortable. Rafts hold from two to four persons, with trips ranging from 1 to 5 hours.

fun**facts**

Wisconsin has 64 state parks, state forests, and state recreation areas and 39 state trails. For information on the park system, contact the Bureau of Parks and Recreation, Department of Natural Resources, Box 7921, Madison 53707 (888-936-7463; www.dnr .wi.gov).

Newcomers to the rafting scene will enjoy a mild ride on Langlade County's Wolf River, which alternates between rugged boulders with gentle waves to bedrock that churns the water into a hearty froth. There are plenty of fast chutes for stomach-tingling action.

The higher stretch of the river between Hollister and Langlade offers long stretches of smooth water. In the lower section of the Wolf, the water picks up speed through Boy Scout Rapids. This is not a place for beginners, edging as it does into a rocky funnel that is strewn with boulders. A narrow channel follows, where rocks are close enough to shave a preteen. The run then slides back onto smooth water.

Quality outfitters include the **Wolf River Lodge** at W2119 Taylor Rd., north of Langlade (715-882-2182; www.wolfriverlodge.com) and **Shotgun Eddy's Rafting** on Highway 55 just south of Langlade in Menominee County

Wisconsin's Rustic Roads

For a really "back roads" look at Wisconsin, sample the state's **Rustic Roads.** These designated stretches of getaway lanes and byways retain the charm of a less-complicated era. There are 56 such designated roadways in the state, ranging from 2.5 miles to 10 miles in length. Most are paved, but some are gravel. These roads aren't built for the heavy-metals set, and the speed limit hovers around 45 mph. Consequently, be aware of slow-moving vehicles. For comprehensive info about the roads, check www.dot.wisconsin.gov/travel/scenic/rusticroads.htm or, contact the Wisconsin Department of Transportation, Box 7913, Madison 53707 (608-266-0649; www.dot.wisconsin.gov/travel/scenic/contact.htm).

(715-882-4461; www.shotguneddy.com). The rafting season open on May 1 and closes in September.

Lincoln County

For good reason, **Merrill** is called the "City of Parks." The town has nine major parks within its boundaries, making it the picnic capital of the north country. Green grass, brilliant flowers, huge shade trees, playgrounds, and shelters seem to pop up around every corner. For an excursion outside of town, **Council Grounds State Park** is located on Highway 107 only a few miles northwest of Merrill. Traditionally a gathering spot for Chippewa Indians, the area became the hub of the North Woods logging industry. Between the 1870s and early 1900s, hundreds of lumberjacks chopped and sawed the towering pines that once ruled the forestlands. Some 600 million board-feet of timber were eventually floated downstream on the Wisconsin River from Merrill's immediate vicinity during the boom days. Council Grounds park now is much quieter and trees have been replanted, so you barely can tell that this landscape once had the appearance of a crew cut. The park has some excellent swimming areas (keep an eye on the kids because there are no lifeguards), plus boating and cross-country skiing in season. There is also a breathtaking (literally) exercise trail that weaves in and out of the trees, so get in shape.

Marinette County

Few people outside Wisconsin know much about **Peshtigo.** In 1871, a raging forest fire destroyed much of Marinette County's drought-stricken timber, taking the town with it on October 8. The fire swept through the community on the same day as the Great Chicago Fire, which pushed the incident onto the back pages of the nation's newspapers. Yet the Wisconsin incident was more horrifying. Between 600 and 800 people died in the Wisconsin fire, more than five times the number who perished in Chicago.

The Peshtigo River meanders past the Badger Paper Mill, one of the mainstays of the town's economy. The river itself saved hundreds of people, who survived the 19th-century fire by leaping into the steaming water. The inferno is remembered in the **Peshtigo Fire Museum** (715-582-3244; www.peshtigofire .info), which is highlighted by a huge painting depicting that fateful day and the role of the river as a lifesaver. The museum is in an old church that replaced one burned in the forest fire. Its display cases are carefully filled with melted coins, broken dishes, and other artifacts donated by area residents. A mound near the museum is a common grave for 350 unidentified victims of the fire.

The museum is 1 block north of Highway 41 on Oconto Avenue. Turn at Ellis Street, and you'll see the building.

The town is laid out much as it was before the fire: along the east and west sides of the river. Streets are wide and lined with maples and oaks. Gone are the huge pines that ranged all the way from Green Bay toward the Michigan border.

Things are generally quiet now on the Peshtigo, but there's a 5-mile stretch of water called Roaring Rapids that puts a rafter's heart in his or her mouth. The river rolls through the thick forest, cutting like a hot knife through butter into Five-Foot Falls, which has a vertical drop of bedrock and only one way to go—straight ahead with a yell and all the pumping adrenaline you can muster.

The chute whops rafts into a sheet of smooth water near the left bank, but rowers have to watch out for upcoming boulders. Horse Race Rapids, where the narrow chute cuts through steep cliffs, is the longest ride on the river. High waves are kicked up over the rocks, and it takes lots of extra muscle and steering expertise to battle through without being swamped. That 30 or so yards of heart-murmur slides into several tight corners and drops over submerged rocks

Read All About It!

For the latest in what to see and do in any of the state's communities, turn to the local newspapers. Their entertainment sections, usually published by dailies on Wednesday and/or Friday, are excellent resources. If you are in a college town, pick up one of the school newspapers. The **Marquette University Tribune,** the **University of Wisconsin–Milwaukee Post,** the **Wisconsin Badger,** and others contain a wealth of information on concerts, sports events, gallery openings, lectures, films, and other activities.

The state also has several ethnic newspapers, most of which are published in the Milwaukee area. Each offers news and calendar information pertaining to its heritage, whether African-American, Hispanic, Jewish, Italian, or Irish.

Wisconsin Trails, a monthly four-color publication highlighting the state's scenery and attractions, has been a swell resource for the state's visitors for more than 35 years. Copies are available in most libraries. For more details or subscription information, contact the publication at 333 W. State St., Milwaukee (800-877-5280).

Key Magazine, a free publication distributed in Milwaukee area hotels, provides more valuable details on the entertainment scene. If you don't find a copy in your room, ask at the front desk or contact Beth Ewing or Roger Stafford at the publication's offices at (262) 242-2077.

So, as you can see, there are no excuses for sitting in your hotel room because you have no idea of what is going on. Get out there and do something!

into a quiet pool where you can get your head back on straight again, according to experienced rafters.

The Menominee River, which forms the border between the state of Michigan and Marinette County, is a good rafting locale, according to friends who take the whitewater route quite often. They suggest putting in at **Little Quinness Falls Dam** for a 2-mile run through heavy woods and into a short stretch of rapids. The first drop, according to ace rafter John Shepard, is about 7 feet on a "pour-over" called Mishicot Falls. There's a tricky backwash at the base of the waterfall, he warns.

The county is noted for its waterfalls, the bane of the lumberjacks but a boon to photographers. The loggers hated coming to the narrow rapids that could often cause jams, lost time, and deaths. Nobody enjoyed ramming the timber over the waterfalls. Today's visitor doesn't have to be concerned about those problems. Finding the best picture angle is enough.

The county's most picturesque falls are just off the meandering Parkway Road in the western stretch of the county. Some of the roughest falls in this area have been channeled or partially tamed over the past generations by artificial dams. To get to **High Falls Dam,** take High Falls Road off Parkway Road. The dam creates the 1,700-acre High Falls Flowage. Just to the north of the dam about a mile or so is **Twin Bridge Park,** which provides another good spot to see the High Falls Flowage. The park is also off Parkway Road. You need to be careful at Veteran's Falls (just off Parkway Road in Veterans' Memorial Park on the Thunder River) because of the steep slopes dropping down to the falls themselves. Be sure to wear hiking boots or other strong shoes. A picturesque little wooden bridge angling high over the rapids is a perfect setting for autumn camping and picnicking.

Hungry Hiking

Hungry after a day of hiking in the woods? Try these healthy snacks for late nights around the campfire: Brush halved pears with melted butter and place the pieces on a square of heavy-duty foil. Fill the center of the pears with chopped nuts and raisins. Dot the centers with some more butter. Seal the package and place on medium coals for about 10 minutes. Then dig in.

Now try this one: Core several apples and fill each cavity with a teaspoon of raisins. Top them off with sugar and cinnamon and dot with butter. Seal each apple in a square of foil and place on medium coals for about 45 minutes or until the apples are tender. You also can substitute marshmallows, cloves, or other goodies for the raisins. Be creative.

To see the Caldron Falls Dam, take Boat Landing 8 Road off Parkway. The dam creates the 1,200-acre ***Caldron Falls Flowage,*** where a boat launch is available. McClintock Falls is located in ***McClintock Park*** off Parkway Road. The falls is actually a series of rapids and white water with several bridges leapfrogging from bank to bank. This is one of the nicest picnic areas in Marinette County. Strong Falls is in ***Goodman Park,*** on the Peshtigo River off Parkway Road. Many hiking trails wander through the dense forest and brushland in the park itself. The park planners provided log shelters in the area, handy refuges in case of rain.

Other waterfalls in the county also are easily reached off the beaten path. To see ***Twelve Foot Falls,*** scene of several television commercials, take Lily Lake Road south off Highway 8 to Twelve Foot Falls Road. Several magnificent drops make up the waterway. Each has its own name: Horseshoe Falls, Eighteen Foot Falls, Eight Foot Falls, and Bull Falls. We like Horseshoe best because of the surrounding framework of trees.

The list continues, a fact making waterfall lovers gleeful. For Long Slide Falls, drive along Morgan Park Road to the east off Highway 141. A small sign marks the direction, so be alert or you might miss the turnoff. Park your car and take the short walking trail to the falls themselves. A county park with camping, swimming, and picnicking is up the road to the east. Piers Gorge is a whitewater rapids area along the Menominee River in the far northern section of the county. To get to the viewing area, take Highway 8 when it branches to the east off Highway 141, just before the Michigan-Wisconsin border. On the northeast side of the county's border with Michigan is Pemenee Falls, which is a really wild stretch of the Menominee. You'll find the spot just to the left as you enter Michigan on County Highway Z.

Dave's Falls is my personal favorite, located south of Amberg on the Pike River. There's a county park there with a neat wooden bridge arching high over the water. A 19th-century folk song tells the sad lament of how a logger named Dave died while breaking up a jam on the river in that location. Ever since that accident, the falls has carried his name.

If you're looking to spend a little time in the ***Crivitz*** area, be sure to check out ***Twin Bridge Resort and Supper Club.*** The vacation cottages are carpeted and have fully equipped kitchens, automatic gas heat, and bathrooms with showers. Public dining and cocktails are available, and breakfast is served on the weekend. Aluminum boats are accessible for lake fishing, sandy beaches await the swimmers and sunbathers, a golf course is nearby, and there are miles of leafy forest trails for hikers. Twin Bridge can also be enjoyed in the winter months. It is a winter playland for cross-country and downhill skiers, and there is easy access to more than 100 miles of well-marked groomed snowmobile trails. Anglers can ice fish for musky, northern, walleye, bass, or trout.

For information on Twin Bridge, call (715) 757-3651, visit www.twinbridge resort.com, or write Twin Bridge Resort, N9661 Parkway Rd., Crivitz 54114.

With all this water in Marinette County, remember that one-third of all the best trout streams in the state are located here.

Menominee County

One of the country's largest and most complete logging museums, the *Menominee Camp Logging Museum,* is located on Highway 47 and County VV, on the Wolf River at Grignon Rapids in *Keshena.* Unless you knew it was there, however, you might miss the facility. The camp (715-799-3757) is on the 230,000 acres of the *Menominee Indian Reservation* about 168 miles north of Milwaukee. Native American guides take visitors through the 7 log buildings that have been rebuilt in the heavy forest. A cook shack is complete with table settings and a well-stocked kitchen. The blacksmith shop, woodworkers' building, and bunkhouse are outfitted as well with the appropriate 19th-century details. The camp is open 9 a.m. to 3 p.m. daily Tues through Sat, May 15 to October 15. Admission is charged.

The museum is one of several economic-development packages in Menominee County aimed at making the tribe more self-sufficient. Other industries include a sawmill, bingo parlor, and a rafting outfitter to guide travelers on the 59-mile stretch of the Wolf River that meanders through tribal lands.

Oconto County

Southwest from Peshtigo is *Oconto,* on the sun-dappled shore of Green Bay. Camping for recreational vehicles is available at the *North Shore Recreation Area* on the edge of the bay, just a few minutes' walk to the banks. You can fish from land or use waders to get a few steps closer to the chinook and trout that swim in the murky waters offshore.

As with Peshtigo, Oconto's neighbor just to the north, a forest fire almost destroyed the town in 1871. A rain came just at the right time, as the flames were creeping to within a few blocks of some of the stately mansions that still can be seen along Park Avenue and its side streets. Edward Scofield, Wisconsin's governor from 1897 to 1901, lived in Oconto for a time. His home at 610 Main St. was built in 1868, next door to the Bond house, whose occupants ran a pickle factory. These magnificent old houses were among the dozens saved by that lucky downpour.

About 2 miles west of Oconto is *Copper Culture State Park* (715-757-3979; www.dnr.wi.gov/org/land/parks/specific/copperculture), where artifacts have been found from a clan of prehistoric people. Apparently these ancient craftworkers mined the copper from nearby deposits, made tools and other items from the precious metal, and traded with groups as far away as the Gulf of Mexico.

Oneida County

The hungry *hodag* lurks in the woods around *Rhinelander,* a town where tall tales could be true. At least the only place in the world where you'll see a hodag is in the logging museum in the city's Pioneer Park. The mythical monster was dreamed up in 1896 by some of the loggers who worked in the forests. They supposedly captured a 7-foot-long hairy beast with huge horns and teeth, keeping it "alive" in a pit behind the house of one of the practical jokers. Nobody was too upset to discover that the men had assembled the beast with ox hides and claws made from bent steel rods. The hodag had captured the town's interest and became a local legend.

The *Rhinelander Logging Museum* is at the junction of Highways 8 and 47 (715-369-5004; www.rhinelanderchamber.com/logmuseum). In addition to the hodag, the museum shows off equipment used by frontier woodcutters. The museum is open daily 10 a.m. to 5 p.m. from Memorial Day through Labor Day, and admission is free, but donations are gratefully accepted.

Adjacent to the logging facility is the *Civilian Conservation Corps Museum,* which should bring back memories to any now-elder who served in the CCC during the Depression of the 1930s. The replica of a typical camp located in a one-room schoolhouse was opened in 1983 for the 50th anniversary of the government-sponsored conservation work brigade. More than three million persons worked in the corps between 1933 and 1942, preserving and maintaining forests and waterways. Former CCC volunteers staff the museum from Memorial Day through Labor Day, telling about their work in the woods. Photos, uniforms, and tools from the era are displayed in the barracks and other buildings. Donations are accepted.

maps&more
maps

The Northwood Map Company has an Internet site that has a good breakdown of Wisconsin. Log on to the site at www.north woodmap.com. To order a copy of their publication, call (800) 236-MAPS. Price is $1 plus 75 cents for shipping.

On the last Saturday in September, the folks in Minocqua celebrate *Beef-O-Rama,* where anyone who wants to fix a giant pot roast (provided by the local chamber of commerce) can compete for prizes. Celebrity judges get to sample upward of 60 roasts before choosing a winner. Prior to announcing the victors, the chefs parade down the main street to a local park where the meat is made into sandwiches.

I took daughter Kate and one of her friends plus son Steve there for a party. We couldn't look at another roast beef for months.

Minocqua and Milwaukee, incidentally, have launched into a Sister City tourism promotion to encourage a rural-urban getaway experience.

Polk County

On the outskirts of St. Croix Falls along Highway 8 is the *Ice Age Interpretive Center* at Interstate Park. Some splendid geological formations in the park's canyonlands are sure to get camera shutters clicking. A highly instructive film on the impact of the glaciers throughout the region should capture the attention of even the most wiggly tyke. The center is open year-round from 8:30 a.m. to 4:30 p.m. during the summer, otherwise hours vary. You'll need a state park sticker for admission, which can be secured at the center (715-483-3747; www .dnr.wi.gov/org/land/parks/specific/chipmoraine).

But if the film still doesn't keep the kids' attention, drive 3 miles west on Highway 8 to *Fawn Doe Rosa Park,* where they can feed and pet deer and other animals. The park is open 9:30 a.m. to 8 p.m. mid-May through Sept. Call (715) 483-3772 if you need more information (or log on to www.fawndoerosa .com).

Price County

Timm's Hill, the highest point in Wisconsin, is 6 miles east of Omega, just before you get to the crossroads village of Spirit. Timm's Hill is 1,951 feet above sea level. An observation tower rears over the treetops for an even more expansive view of the countryside. On a blustery autumn day, middle son Steve and I climbed up there as the wind tugged our coattails. A hint: Don't look down. But once on the top, the sight was spectacular . . . even if it was a white-knuckler.

Wisconsin Concrete Park on Highway 13 South in *Phillips* is definitely a difficult—or should I say hard—place to miss. Some 200 statues made from concrete portray cowboys on horseback, deer, bears, Native Americans, and a plethora of other items from the imagination of the late Fred Smith. When Smith retired from logging, he took up sculpture and today is considered one of America's foremost folk artists. For a special effect Smith put bits of broken glass into his dozens of whimsical forms, all of which seem to smile back at the observer. The park is open year-round; admission is free. For information call (715) 339-6371 or (800) 269-4505 (www.friendsoffredsmith.org).

St. Croix County

Hudson looks much like the Hudson River Valley of New York State. At least that's what the original settlers in the area thought, so they figured the name would fit their community as well. The **Octagon House** is the local history center, at 1004 3rd St. (715-386-2654; www.pressenter.com/~octagon), on the north end of the town's business district off Highway 35. There's a magnificent old grand piano in the old home's living room. Looking at it, one would never guess that it was twice dumped into the Mississippi River on its delivery run here in the mid-1800s. The Octagon House is open May 1 to October 31, and then open for 3 weeks after Thanksgiving for a holiday display. The house is closed for the remainder of the year. The hours are Tues through Fri from noon to 4:30 p.m., and Sun from 2 to 4:30 p.m. Admission is $7 for adults, $3 for ages 13 to 19, $2 for children 6 to 12, and free for younger kids.

Near the city, a puffing, rumbling, rocking, and rolling engine swings quickly around the track. A full head of steam greets the passengers waiting for a ride on the **St. Croix Railroad.** Everyone piles on, a bit cramped maybe, but ready to roll. It's not a hard run, with only a 4-foot-high engine and several 6-foot-long passenger cars traveling more than 7,000 feet of track. But that's the

Lutfisk Lunching

Norwegian, Danish, and Swedish influences are still strong throughout Wisconsin's Northland, with more guys in hunting jackets nicknamed "Swede" than probably anywhere else in Wisconsin. And many of the churches in the North, especially around Burnett County's Grantsburg, still stage *lutfisk* suppers as fund-raisers. Vacationers will find these fjord feasts loads of fun.

Kokt lutfisk is dried cod that has been preserved in lye and soda and softened into a glutinous mass by letting it sit in saltwater for about a week. It is then boiled and served with a white sauce (*mjolksds*) along with boiled potatoes. Everything is liberally dosed with salt and white and black pepper. *Lefsa,* a rolled and sugared pancake, is the typical side dish.

For the times and dates of these suppers, check the local newspapers. Among them are the *Inter-County Leader,* which is published in Frederick in Polk County, and the *Burnett County Sentinel,* published in Grantsburg. The weeklies can be purchased at grocery stores, gas stations, bait shops, and similar retail outlets.

fun of it. The "toy line" railroad is Bob Ahrens's plaything, a train set to end all train sets, with an engine that burns crushed charcoal. In fact, the entrance to this place has a sign that reads CAUTION—MAN AT PLAY. He laid the aluminum rails himself, spacing them through his 8 acres of valleyland. The train runs the last Sun of each month from noon to 4 p.m. Call (715) 386-1871 for more information (www.stcroixrr.org).

The *Apple River* in Somerset is the best place in the state to try your hand, or bottom, at tubing. Numerous outfitters throughout the area rent inner tubes for swift rides along the flowage. The water isn't usually deep, but be sure to wear tennis shoes because of the rocky river bottom. Even kids can enjoy the ride, swirling as they do through the eddies and across quiet pools. The rental companies will pick you up at the end of the hour or half-day run. Watch out for sunburn, however. The glare from the stream can bake fair skin quicker than a microwave.

One good outfitter in the area, a member of the Hudson Area Chamber of Commerce (715-386-8411; www.hudsonwi.org), is the *Apple River Hideaway* near Somerset (715-247-3230 or 888-274-4045; www.tubetheriver.com). Rates for tubing are $15. Runs are offered during daylight hours Thurs through Sat.

Sawyer County

There was a time when the North Woods attracted another tourist element, one that was not really welcomed. Chicago mobsters often came to the quiet lakes and woods to escape the literal and figurative heat of the Windy City. They brought their nervousness with them, however. *The Hideout* was one of the most extensive retreats used by mobster Al Capone, who favored fishing almost as much as rum-running. Fieldstone pillars guard the entrances to a 400-acre estate near Couderay where he used to rest and recuperate. The architecture inside the grounds includes a gun tower, bunkhouse, cell, and other buildings utilized by gang members when they vacationed in Sawyer County. For a time, it was a restaurant, but unfortunately, the site is now closed to the public.

The world's largest muskie rears over the trees in *Hayward,* marking the site of the *National Fresh Water Fishing Hall of Fame.* The 5-story glass-fiber structure houses a large portion of the museum, with its dated outboard engines, lures, and stuffed fish. The lower jaw of the giant muskie is a platform on which several weddings have been held. Even if you aren't die-hard fish-erfolks, wandering among the exhibits makes a good layover for anyone on a rainy weekday afternoon when vacation time is running short. Admission is charged. The museum is open daily in June, July, and Aug from 9:30 a.m. to 4:30 p.m. In Apr, May, Sept, and Oct, the hours are 9:30 a.m. to 4 p.m. Only the offices are open in winter. The museum is located at 10360 Hall of Fame Dr., on the south side of Hayward at the corner of County Trunk B and Highway 27 (715-634-4440).

Hayward is also site of the **Lumberjack World Championships** held each July, with contestants from Australia, New Zealand, and the United States. They compete in axe chopping, tree climbing, bucksawing, and other robust events. This is a chance for you to wear red flannel shirts, overalls, and wide suspenders. Everyone else in town does. For information contact the Hayward Area Association of Commerce, Highway 63, Box 726, Hayward 54843-0726 (715-634-2484).

Trempealeau County

Trempealeau County's western boundary is the turgid, mud-black Mississippi River. Catfish roll to the surface, and muskrats splash in the backwater sloughs. The waterway, fed by the fast-flowing Black River, anchors the bottom of the county and gives life to its surroundings.

We love watching fat barges swinging downstream, loaded with grain, lumber, or petroleum products from the Twin Cities, heading to the far Southland and the Gulf of Mexico. The barges, shepherded by a rumbling tugboat, are aimed carefully for the entrance to **Lock and Dam No. 6** at Trempealeau, one of the major links on the upper river's navigational channels.

An overlook near a parking lot alongside the dam provides a great vantage point for watching the river traffic during the spring to autumn shipping season. You almost can stand on top of the barges as they are pushed through the locks. Then, all of a sudden, the barges drop down to the lower level and continue on their journey to New Orleans. In addition to the bigger vessels, more than 6,000 pleasure craft use the locks each year. Lines of little fishing boats, sleek canoes, and jaunty cabin cruisers hug the lock walls like a convoy of ducklings before they also are dropped or raised to the next level. The complex consists of a main lock and an auxiliary structure completed by the Army Corps of Engineers, plus a concrete dam and an earthen dike extending across the wet bottomlands. The foot of the spillway near the Minnesota side provides good fishing.

While in town, stay at the comfortably funky old **Trempealeau Hotel** (608-534-6898; www.trempealeauhotel.com). Owner Bill King takes very good care of his guests. Eight rooms are available above the restaurant for $40 to $49 a night. A shared bathroom is down the hall. Or you can opt for a suite with a whirlpool and bathroom in either the Doc West House or the Pines Cottage for $110 during the week and $130 on the weekend and holidays. Kingfisher rooms, 4 riverside motel rooms, are also an option. They go for $60 to $70.

OTHER ATTRACTIONS WORTH SEEING

Amsterdam Sloughs Wildlife Area, northwest of Siren

Crystal Cave, west of Spring Valley

Fire House & Police Museum, Superior

Fruit of the Woods Wine Cellar, Three Lakes

Gaslight Square, Minocqua

Irvine Park, Chippewa Falls

Lac du Flambeau Chippewa Museum & Cultural Center

Lac Du Flambeau Tribal Bingo

Scott Worldwide, Marinette

In the hotel's restaurant, try the signature walnut burgers, made from English walnuts. The Trempealeau also hosts a regular lineup of music.

North of Trempealeau is Galesville, at the junction of Highways 35/54 and 53. Folks around Galesville believe in the adage that an apple a day keeps the doctor away. Consequently, they celebrate their locally grown fruit with a 1-day event called an **Apple Affair.** The festival is held the first Saturday each October, luring visitors with the aroma emanating from a 10-foot apple pie served in the downtown square. The event is sponsored by the Galesville Area Chamber of Commerce with a bike tour, displays by area craftworkers, a country market with bushels of apple-based products, a popular omelet breakfast, and a bratwurst lunch. There is also plenty of live music.

Exhibits on the apple industry and the town can be seen at the **Historic Arnold House,** built in 1874, and **Galesville Public Library.** While in town, hike along McGilvray Road to see a century-plus-old bowstring bridge, listed in the National Register of Historic Places. For more information call (608) 582-2868 (www.galesvillewi.com).

Trempealeau National Wildlife Refuge (608-539-2311; www.fws.gov/midwest/Trempealeau/), near Trempealeau, is managed by the US Fish and Wildlife Service. There is no way that anyone could see the entire 6,000 acres of the refuge in a weekend or even a week, but take the kids along the 5-mile self-guided auto tour around the park that skirts the edge of the Mississippi River. There is also a well-marked 0.5-mile nature trail and a marsh to explore. White-tailed deer, bald eagles, ducks, geese, and other creatures can readily be seen.

Perrot State Park is another marvelous outdoor preserve to explore along the Mississippi River, located between the town of Trempealeau and the national refuge. Most of the trails here take hikers to the bluffs overlooking the river. Be aware that they have steep, challenging climbs up steps or stairways, so be sure to bring appropriate hiking boots or shoes. For a closer look at the river, we've always enjoyed the Riverview Trail, a 2.5-mile trek that is accessed from the campgrounds. If you are into cross-country skiing or mountain biking, the most challenging route is the 3.1-mile Prairie Trail. The park has 9 miles of cross-country possibilities and 7 miles open for bikers. Skate skiing, however, is only allowed on a marked 2-mile section in the campground area. Canoeing opportunities take guests deep into the watery preserve for the chance to spot all sorts of wildlife. Bring sunscreen and a hat because the day's rays can scorch tender skin. Perrot, dedicated in 1928, is one of the state's oldest parks and is named after French fur trader Nicholas Perrot, who traversed this area in the 1600s.

Vilas County

Life in the North Woods isn't just about bears and camping out. It can be civilized, too. After all, Jason Meinholz operates **Soda Pops** in Eagle River, serving dozens of different varieties of refreshing beverage (715-479-9424; www .soda-pops.com).

The town of **Eagle River** has long been one of the state's premier tourist attractions, playing up the "get away from it all" image that downstaters really appreciate. The highly touted Eagle River chain of 28 lakes is considered one of the world's largest such systems. It's all part of Vilas County's watery spread of 1,300 large, countable bodies of water, plus 73 rivers and smaller flowages.

Of course, the locals claim that the fish always bite up here and that the living is constantly easy. Yet drawing in that record muskie can still take a bit of work, to say nothing of the walleye, perch, and bass. Many fisherfolk these days advocate the catch-and-release form of outdoor entertainment, whereby finny critters attracted to the hook are freed to come back another day. That ensures fun for the next generation. Plenty of guides are available for showing vacationers the best locales for tossing in a line. Contact the **Eagle River Guides Association** for details on reeling in the big ones (715-479-8804; www.eagleriverfishing guides.com).

Winter in the Eagle River area is also loaded with plenty of outdoor

putonice

From Christmas through New Year's Day, the Eagle River Area Fire Department and volunteers construct an Ice Palace with more than 2,500 10-inch blocks of ice cut from Silver Lake. There is a new design each year. At night the palace is illuminated with colored lights. Call (800) 359-6315 (www .eagleriver.org/icecastle.asp).

opportunities, including ice fishing, of course. The county is called the Snow-mobile Capital of the World because of its extensive trail system, which reaches more than 500 miles. Nearby St. Germaine is a natural for the home of the *International Snowmobile Hall of Fame.* The facility is open 10 a.m. to 5 p.m. Mon through Fri and 10 a.m. to 3 p.m. most Saturdays. Check ahead, however, just to be sure—especially for winter hours (715-542-4463; www.snowmobilehalloffame .com).

If you take County M north out of Boulder Junction to County B West, you'll find yourself in Presque Isle. *Presque Isle Heritage Society Museum* (715-686-2481; www.thebradleyhouse.org), with a fine collection of artifacts and clothing from the area's logging days, is located in downtown Presque Isle. Continue your drive up Main Street and you'll discover the old Presque grade school, and down a grassy path is the historic "Shanty Boy Hill" cemetery. It is named so because of the ramshackle shanties and houses the loggers lived in while working in the forests. The largest walleye-rearing ponds, where more than 10 million walleye fingerlings have been produced for transplanting, can be visited daily. For more information about any of these attractions, call the Presque Isle Chamber of Commerce at (715) 686-2910, (888) 835-6508 or visit www.presqueisle.com.

Loon Business

The eerie cry of the *loon* is one of the most thought-provoking sounds in the North Woods. These powerful waterbirds have red eyes, a green-black head, a long beak, and black and white plumage. The common loon is the only one of the four types of loons found in Wisconsin. The others are denizens of Canada and Alaska. Trivia lovers want to know why the bird has red eyes. The color is caused by a pigment in the bird's retina that filters light when loons dive beneath the water's surface and allows for sight. And it is impossible to tell the sex of a loon without looking at its internal organs.

At the risk of driving you loony, here are some more loon facts:

- They weigh between 7 and 10 pounds.

- They require 0.25 mile of smooth lake surface in order to become airborne.

- A loon can fly upward of 80 mph.

- Loons are believed to mate for life. It is believed that loons return to the same lakes every year. First the male arrives and waits for the female. She usually lays two eggs.

- There are four types of loon calls (wail, tremolo, yodel, and hoot).

Don't get the wrong idea if I mention ***Hintz's North Star Lodge*** (715-542-3600; www.hintznorthstar.com) in Star Lake. We are not related to Bill Hintz, the young guy who purchased the old resort in 1984, but we've spent some pleasant vacation hours there. Daughter Kate and middle son Steve still talk about the frog-jumping contest they organized on the patio to the rear of the main building. Son Dan reeled in enough fish to keep us in brain food for the entire week. I read, loafed, swam, and sunburned for 7 glorious days.

The place was built in 1894 as a retreat for railroad and lumber magnates and their guests. Bill does his own cooking, which includes fresh walleye and regular weekday specials. While we usually ate in our own cabin, we tried his Sunday brunch, a table-groaner that included homemade sweet rolls, eggs, sausage, bacon, pancakes, chicken, fried potatoes, dessert, and a ton of salads and other fixings. The cabins at North Star Lodge range sleep from four to eight persons. Villas and apartments are also available.

Not far from Star Lake is ***Sayner,*** home of the ***Vilas County Historical Museum*** (715-542-3388; www.northern-wisconsin.com/museum), open daily from 10 a.m. to 4 p.m. The museum has an extensive collection of old and contemporary snowmobiles, seen in the winter through picture windows in the rear of the facility. The lighted display opens up to a snowmobile track that runs behind the building, so visitors can have a look even during a nighttime jaunt. A donation of $2 is suggested.

The world's first commercial snowmobile was built by the late Carl Eliason of Sayner, whose family now runs the hardware store and lumberyard across the street from the museum. In 1924 he used a small gasoline motor—attached to a long toboggan mounted on front and rear tracks—to help him get through the drifts. The idea caught on so well that now the snowmobile is the Northland's main form of winter recreational transportation. The prototypes of Eliason's vehicles are in the exhibit.

The annual ***World Championship Snowmobile Derby*** is always a big affair in Eagle River and celebrated its 40th anniversary in 2003. On the third weekend each January, pro racers flock to the track that has been coated with 16 inches of solid ice. Speeds of more than 100 mph have been clocked on the 0.5-mile banked oval. For information about upcoming derbies and ticket prices, call (715) 479-4424 or log on to www.derbytrack.com.

The complex was established by Audrey and Dick Decker, a lively couple who also run Deckers' Sno-Venture Tours. They have taken snowmobile riders to Finland, Iceland, Canada, Yosemite, and other exotic locales, as well as on lengthy trips around northern Wisconsin and into the Upper Peninsula of Michigan. A Decker tour is something special, bonding a disparate group of folks of all riding skills who come from around the country. The Deckers also put together special packages for corporate groups, providing long, challenging rides for CEOs and their staffs who want a different sort of getaway from the office. For tour information, check www.sno-venture.com. Some of the best memories I had on a 5-day Decker trip from Eagle River to Bayfield and back again were the roasted hot dogs in a warming cabin in Chequamegon Forest, grouse exploding out of the thickets near Iron River, and the sight of the vast frozen waters of Lake Superior just before the sun came up.

Gangsters led by bank robber John Dillinger once paused at the *Little Bohemia Resort,* near *Manitowish Waters* and 20 miles north of Minocqua on Highway 51. In 1934 the thugs were escaping from a holdup in Racine and made it to Little Bohemia for a rest stop. Apparently it was the only place open between Mercer and Minocqua, so the gang stayed for a long weekend.

Acting on a tip, the police arrived to smoke out the notorious crew. By the time the gunfire was over, three locals who had been sitting at the bar were shot dead, and several sobbing girlfriends had been left behind by the gang. The thugs had hightailed it into the woods and escaped. The current owner, Emil Wanatka Jr., is the son of the man who operated Little Bohemia when Dillinger checked in—and out.

It's much quieter these days, but you can still see a small building on the restaurant grounds that contains items abandoned by the criminals, including underwear, some tins of laxatives, and other odds and ends.

The building itself is peppered with about 100 bullet holes. For more history on Little Bohemia, call (715) 543-8800 or visit www.littlebohemia lodge.com.

Part of *Woodruff* lies in Oneida County, but the bulk of the community and its neighbor, Arbor Vitae, are on the southern edge of Vilas County. The

Snow Schlepping

Snowshoeing is a great way to see Wisconsin in the winter, whether in a local park or in the North Woods. Among the best places to see winter up close and real is along the shore of Lake Superior, especially with the sea caves of the Apostle Islands National Lakeshore. High Cliff State Park offers 1,147 acres to crisscross. The Peninsula State Park in Door County gets an average of 50 to 60 inches of snow each year, making it magnificent for snowshoeing. For snowshoe rentals nearby, contact *Nor Door Sport and Cyclery* in Fish Creek (920-868-2275, www.nordoorsports .com). There are 60 miles of snowshoe trails through upland and lowland forests, sedge marshes, bogs, and flowages in the Navarino Wildlife Area, and trails in the Kettle Moraine State Forest–Southern Unit are also winter perfect. For other suggestions, check www.travelwisconsin.com/Snowshoeing.aspx.

Wisconsin Curiosities

If you think Wisconsin is nothing but cows and cheese wheels, guess again. The state is replete with oddities and weird goings-on. To find the how, the what's, and the where's, read *Wisconsin Curiosities: Quirky Characters, Roadside Oddities & Other Offbeat Stuff* by Michael Feldman and Diana Cook (Globe Pequot, 2004). They'll tell about a talented worm that played basketball and the best place to find locally made limburger. The website www.weird-wi.com will connect the curious to other sites that describe the ongoing exploration for pyramids under Rock Lake or mysterious cobwebs that fell from the sky over Milwaukee, Green Bay, and several other eastern Wisconsin cities in 1881. Another site, www.associatedcontent.com, tells where to find Wisconsin's largest talking cow, as if there were a smaller talking bovine somewhere in the state. It also describes other peculiarities in the Cheese State. Mary Bergin of Madison is a member of the Society of American Travel Writers and knows Wisconsin like the, well, back of her hand. She offers a fun and fact-filled weekly travel column on her website, www.roadstraveled.com, plus lively stories in various state newspapers. Well, you get the picture.

crossroads towns share a common school district, with the main grade school in Woodruff. On the playground a block west of Highway 51 is a *giant concrete penny.* The town claims it is the world's largest coin, weighing in at 17,452 pounds and standing 10 feet tall. The statue was erected in 1957, recalling a fund-raiser for the local hospital that brought in a million-plus pennies. In 1952, kids in Otto Burich's geometry class wanted to see a million of something. So he suggested they count a million pennies and contribute the money as a kick-off donation for a clinic.

The medical facility was long sought by Dr. Kate Newcomb, the "Angel on Snowshoes," who delivered babies by the bushel-basket throughout the county regardless of the weather. Newcomb appeared on the old *This Is Your Life* television program and told about the fund-raising efforts. Naturally that led to more donations and the eventual construction of a clinic. Several years later, an uncle of actress Elizabeth Taylor gave the community more funds with which to build a larger medical unit. He had vacationed in the Woodruff–Arbor Vitae area for years and wanted to help the towns.

Woodruff celebrated its centennial in 1988, with a re-creation of the first *Penny Parade,* the one launching the children's efforts three decades earlier. Dr. Newcomb's refurbished home on 2nd Street, just around the corner from the school and the giant penny, also was opened as a museum.

Log rolling, wood chopping, and tree climbing are a few of the events presented on the grounds of *Scheer's Lumberjack Show* (715-634-6923; www .scheerslumberjackshow.com) in downtown Woodruff on Highway 97 East.

The program of logger skills is open mid-June through late August. Tickets are $9.95 for adults, and $7.95 for seniors and youngsters 4 to 7. Fred Scheer, a world-champion log roller; his brother Bob, a record holder in pole climbing; and their sister Judy, the seven-time world's record holder in women's log rolling, form the core of the entertainers' troupe. There are two different sites to view the timber talents. Days and times of the shows vary, so be sure to call for verification.

Washburn County

The ***World's Largest Warm-Water Fish Hatchery,*** according to the Wisconsin Department of Natural Resources, which runs the place, is located in Spooner. The sprawling facility is south of downtown on Highway 63, across two bridges.

The DNR has a nice picnic area on the grounds, where you can put up your feet and watch the fingerlings splish and splash. Several varieties of game fish are raised here for stocking North Woods lakes. It's enough to make you want to bring a fishing pole.

Places to Stay in Northern Wisconsin

MINOCQUA

Comfort Inn
8729 US 51 North
(715) 358-2588
www.comfortinn.com
Inexpensive to moderate
Pet friendly hotel with pool, meeting space, and morning grub.

New Concord Inn of Minocqua
320 Front St.
(715) 356-1800
(800) 356-8888
http://concordinnof
minocqua.com
Inexpensive to moderate
Comp breakfast with specialty baked items and bread; free high-speed and wireless Internet; business center includes printers, fax/photocopy machines; hot tub and indoor pool.

Pine Hill Resort
8544 Hower Rd.
(715) 356-3418
www.pinehillminocqua.com
Moderate
Tucked along the shores of Lake Kawaguesaga

and the Minoqua Chain of Lakes for some of the best muskie, walleye, and bass fishing up North, plus panfish for the kids; swimming beach, water trampoline.

Pointe Resort & Club
8257 US 51 South
(715) 356-7799
www.thepointeresort.com
Moderate to expensive
780 feet of shoreline on Lake Mionocqua, where the motto is "wake up to water and unwind to sunsets"; great summer as well as winter getaway with snowmobile trail access.

NEILLSVILLE AND ENVIRONS

The Heartland Motel
7 S. Hewett
(715) 743-4004
Inexpensive
Low rates, with access to nearby snowmobile and ATV trials; close to restaurants and gas stations for convenience and ease.

Bruce Mound Ski Hill Resort
N791 Bruce Mound Ave.
Merrillan
(715) 743-2296
Moderate
Near Neillsville in fun winter sports area offering chair lifts and snow tubing.

RHINELANDER

Holiday Acres
S. Shore Drive on Lake Thompson, 4 miles east of Rhinelander (take Highway 8 and follow signs)
(715) 369-1500
www.holidayacres.com
Moderate
Lakeside cottage rentals, guest rooms, and executive homes make this a top locale for conferences and reunion or family outings; highly reviewed by happy guests.

Brekke's Fireside Resort
4268 County Road P
(715) 369-3112
www.brekkesresort.com
Moderate
On Lake George, which offers fishing, boating, sand castles, and kickback feel; participates in Wisconsin's Travel Green program for environmental awareness.

Forsyth Sunlite Resort
2963 Nostalgia Ln.
(715) 362-2195
www.wisvacations.com
Cottages make for family fun, with fishing almost out the front door on Lake George; caters to ice-fishing fans and snowmobilers in the winter.

Three G's Resort
2823 Three Gs Dr.
(715) 362-3737
www.3gsresort.com
Moderate
Located in Oneida County along the 435-acre Lake George, which means plenty of room for walleye fishing; waterskiing only allowed from 10 a.m. to 7 p.m., making it perfect for a quiet getaway.

SHELL LAKE

Bashaw Lake Resort
3215 Lakeview Church Rd.
(715) 466-2310
(877) 306-3501
Moderate
Family owned resort with 4 cottages with kitchenettes, plus campground/RV park with hookups and sanitary dump station; on-site watercraft, including pontoon boats.

SPOONER

Best Western–American Heritage Inn
101 Maple St.
(715) 635-9770
(800) 780-7234
www.bestwestern.com/prop_50120
Inexpensive to moderate
Only commercial lodging in the Spooner area; indoor heated pool, spa, on-site game room; free breakfast; each room has free high-speed Internet access.

Country House Motel & RV Park
717 S. River St., US 63
(715) 635-8721
www.countryhousemotel.com
Inexpensive
Open for independent units but no tent camping permitted; 21 sites with water and electric hookups.

Inn Town Motel
801 River St.
(715) 635-3529
www.inntownmotel.com
Inexpensive
Offers hockey team discounts; discounts at area attractions if you take brochure from motel lobby to the site; reserve early for July Spooner Rodeo weekend (www.spoonerrodeo.com) because facility fills fast.

SELECTED CHAMBERS OF COMMERCE

**Chequamegon National Forest
Headquarters, US Department of
Agriculture**
500 Hanson Lake Rd.
Rhinelander 54501
(715) 362-1300
www.fs.usda.gov/cnn

**Eagle River Chamber of Commerce
Information Center**
201 N. Railroad St.
Eagle River 54521-1917
(800) 359-6315
www.eagleriver.org

Hayward Area Chamber of Commerce
101 W. 1st St.
PO Box 726
Hayward 54843-0726
(715) 634-8662
www.haywardareachamber.com

**Minocqua–Arbor Vitae–Woodruff
Chamber of Commerce**
8216 US 15
Minocqua 54548
(715) 356-5266
(800) 446-6784
www.minocqua.org

Mississippi Valley Partners
PO Box 1
Wabasha, MN 55981
(888) 999-2619
www.mississippi-river.org

Rusk County Information Center
205 W. 9th St. South
Ladysmith 54848
(715) 532-2642
(800) 535-7875
www.ruskcountywi.com/visitor-center
.php

**Shawano Area Chamber of
Commerce**
1263 S. Main St.
Shawano 54166
(715) 524-2139
www.shawanocountry.com

**Waupaca Area Chamber of
Commerce**
c/o Parks and Recreation
221 S. Main St.
Waupaca 54981
(715) 258-7343
www.waupacaareachamber.com

**Persen's Dunn Lake
Resort**
7815 Dunn Lake Rd.
(715) 635-9557
Moderate
Family-oriented, clean, and
quiet; kitchen; radio alarm
clock in the rooms.

Tall Timbers Resort
1324 W. Point Rd.
(715) 635-3326
www.washburncounty
.com/talltimbersresort/index
.htm
Inexpensive

Big McKenzie Lake; with
Weber grill and 14-foot
canoe with each cabin; pet
friendly with prior approval
and small deposit.

WOODRUFF

Hiawatha Trailer Resort
1077 Old 51 South
(715) 356-6111
www.hiawathatrailerresort
.com
Near shopping centers,
water ski shows, go-karts,
water slides, minigolf,

antique shops, summer
playhouse; or merely sit
under a tree and read.

**Indian Shores / Shoreline
Inn**
7750 Strongheart Rd.
(715) 356-5552
www.indian-shores.com
Moderate
Easy place to "unplug and
unwind," as they say in
these parts; on north shore
of 3,600-acre Tomahawk
Lake, the largest lake in
Minocqua Chain; rent a

cottage, pop-up trailer, or RV site.

Madeline Lake Resort
8902 Madeline Lake Rd.
(715) 356-7610
www.madeline-lake-resort
.com
Moderate
Cabins, seasonal RV site; American Legion State Forest surrounds 22-acre resort with woods, grassy areas on Madeline and Carroll Lakes with more than 1,200 feet of lake frontage for swimming and loafing.

Places to Eat in Northern Wisconsin

AMERY

A&W Restaurant
326 S. Keller Ave.
(715) 268-2117
Inexpensive
www.awrestaurants.com
Nothing beats a frosty mug of root beer in summer; plus chili dogs, and cheeseburgers.

Village Pizzeria of Amery
210 Keller Ave. North
(715) 268-7010
www.thevillagepizzeria.net
Inexpensive
Eyeing cheese, sausage, mushroom, green pepper, and black olives? Yummy— and open daily.

Wollers Shoreview Supper Club
796 100th St.
(715) 268-8774
www.shoreviewsupperclub
.com
Moderate
Overlooks Pike Lake for Sunday brunch, happy hour; USDA choice steaks and Canadian walleye.

BAYFIELD

Greunke's Restaurant
17 Rittenhouse Ave.
(715) 779-5480
www.greunkesinn.com
Inexpensive to moderate
Downtown Bayfield for blueberry pancakes, burgers, salads, and soups for lunch; trout and pizzas add pizzazz for dinner; lots of Coca-Cola memorabilia, a working Wurlitzer organ, and an antique soda fountain.

Maggie's Restaurant
257 Manypenney Ave.
(715) 779-5641
www.maggies-bayfield.com
Inexpensive to moderate
Try the avocado and blue-fin crab salad; varieties of pizza; Mexican-style shredded pork sandwiches; crème brûlée and ice cream made on the premises; and, oh, those Wisconsin cheeses, too.

Wild Rice Restaurant
84860 Old San Rd.
(715) 779-9881
www.wildricerestaurant
.com
Award-winning, top-flight chefs; on rim of Lake Superior; impressive floor-to-ceiling "wine cube" with hundreds of bottles.

CHIPPEWA FALLS

Golden Eagle Restaurant
16760 County Highway X
(715) 723-2948
Inexpensive
Hearty portions, strong coffee, and homemade desserts; cheerful, longtime servers.

James Sheeley House Restaurant
236 W. River St.
(715) 726-0561
www.jamessheeleyhouse
.com
Moderate
House chef-made sides and sauces; building listed on the National Register of Historic Places; salted-in-the-shell peanuts in the saloon.

EAGLE RIVER

Aerio Club
1530 Highway 45 North
(715) 479-4695
Dates from the 1930s; Friday- and Wednesday-night fish fry; Saturday-night prime rib.

Chanticleer Inn
1458 E. Dollar Lake Rd.
(800) 752-9193
www.chanticleerinn.com
Moderate
See deer carefully treading across the ice in winter; menu includes a noted burger, plus lobster and Friday fish and salad. The inn is also a regular snowmobilers' stop.

Riverstone Restaurant
9 N. Railroad St.
(715) 479-8467
www.riverstonerestaurant
.com
Artisan breads; small plate;
catering; lots of awards for
cooking; bistro lunch.

HAYWARD

Angler's Bar & Grill
10547 Main St.
(715) 634-4700
Inexpensive
www.anglershavenresort
.com
Popular spot on Main
Street for more than 65
years; outdoor patio dining
and a beer garden; kitchen
closes at 10 p.m. nightly.

Karibalis Restaurant
10563 N. Main St.
(715) 634-2462
Inexpensive
Building dates from
1922; Hayward's largest
salad bar and delectable
walleye sandwich; lounge
and outdoor deck for
comfortable seasonal
dining.

Norske Nook
10436 SR 27
(715) 634-4928
www.norskenook.com
Inexpensive to moderate
Since 1973, pies here
have been plus-good;
Norwegian foods with
Yankee flair such as lefsa
wraps; this one of several
Nooks, with others in
Osseo, Rice Lake, and Eau
Claire.

MANITOWISH WATERS

**Pea Patch Motel &
Saloon**
305 W. Park Ave.
(715) 543-2455
www.thepeapatch.com
Inexpensive
"Best damn burgers";
snowmobilers, the saloon
is next to Wisconsin
Snowmobile Trail #8.
Usually crowded, open
daily.

Smokeys
10004 County Rd. West
(corner of Highways K
and W)
(715) 543-2220
Moderate
Rack of lamb, sirloins,
cold-water lobster tails,
plus fudge brownie a la
mode to satisfy the wildest
sweet tooth.

Swanberg's Bavarian Inn
County Trunk West
(downtown)
(715) 543-2122
Moderate
Wine and beer lists,
extremely powerful martinis;
chicken, pork, seafood,
steaks and pastas; cozy
fireside setting; accessible
by snowmobile (Trail #6) or
boat through Koller Park in
the summer; reservations
appreciated.

MINOCQUA

**Albee's Yacht Club Bar
& Grill**
8290 Highway 51 South
(715) 356-1366
www.twitter.com/Albees
YachtClub
Moderate

Excellent view of Lake
Minocqua; best with drinks
and dinner; carryout; gas
for autos.

**The Belle Isle Sports Bar
& Grille**
301 Front St.
(715) 356-7444
www.thebelleisle.com
Inexpensive to moderate
Live music makes the place
rock; go for the steaks;
loads of specials, so be
sure to ask.

Bosacki's Boat House
305 Park St. (at the Bridge)
(715) 356-5292
Moderate
Breakfast, lunch, and
dinner; original building was
built by the Jossart family
in 1896; one of one of the
longest bars in town, which
makes for elbow room to
look at the lake.

Mama's Supper Club
10486 Highway 70 West
(715) 356-5070
www.mamassupperclub
.com
When mama says, "eat!"
you better—and it's always
delicious; open daily, with
a well-stocked Sunday
brunch.

**Paul Bunyan's
Northwoods Cook Shanty**
8653 Highway 51 North
(715) 356-6270
www.paulbunyans.com
Inexpensive to moderate
Lumberjack-size meals
in a backwoods setting
with hamburgers, grilled
chicken, and fried walleye
sandwiches; this Bunyan's
is a relative of that one in

the Wisconsin Dells, with a similar feel.

PHILLIPS

Club 13 Restaurant & Lounge
784 N. Lake Ave.
(715) 339-3456
www.club13online.com
Moderate
Popular hideaway for anglers and snowmobilers, depending on the season; wide range of entrees, soups, salads, and sandwiches; business and social groups meet here for parties, so be prepared to find some evening crowds; sponsors summer air show among other events.

Harbor View Restaurant
Highway 13 North
(715) 339-2626
www.harborviewonline.com
Casual pub and eatery, with sand volleyball outside; lots of music; polar bear plunge.

RHINELANDER

The Al-Gen Dinner Club
3428 Faust Lake Rd.
(715) 362-4223
Moderate
Woodsy feel, with a rustic ambience, offering steaks, roasted chicken, fish, homemade soup, Friday-night fish fry, and comprehensive wine list; cocktail lounge and the dining room are closed Mon.

Rhinelander Cafe & Pub
33 N. Brown St.
(715) 362-2918
www.barandrestaurant
central.com/rhinelander-cafe-pub
Inexpensive
Always sandwich time here with burgers, dogs, turkey, and chicken; fishing in the summer and snowmobiling in the winter.

Wolff's Log Cabin
721 W. Kemp St.
(715) 362-2686
Inexpensive
Just like home, according to travelers who know hash and eggs; Friday night buffet.

RICE LAKE

Dana's Beer Cheese Bar & Grill
2 N. Main St.
(715) 234-2527
Inexpensive
Known for burgers; good place to stop while fishing in the area.

Lehman's Supper Club
2911 S. Main St.
(715) 234-2428
www.lehmanssupperclub
.net
Moderate
Located across from the Cedar Mall; when hungry, ask for a full rack of barbecued ribs or try the walleye; closed Mon.

ST. CROIX FALLS

Dalles Restaurant & Lounge
720 S. Highway 35
(715) 483-3246
Moderate to expensive
Excellent prime rib for relaxing meal after canoeing in the area or visiting Interstate Park; 45 minutes east of the Twin Cities.

Grecco's
115 Washington Ave.
(715) 483-5003
www.greccos.com
Moderate
Presents "eclectic infusion of global cuisine and wine," presenting a chef's tastings menu weekly; "chef in a box" meals can be shipped; seared duck breast or pepper-crusted New York strip make the visit a plus.

Logger's Bar & Grill
2071 Glacier Dr.
(715) 483-2504
www.loggersgrill.com
Inexpensive
Friday fish fry, homemade pizza and soup, sandwiches, and lunch and dinner specials; drink deals in the spacious bar, which is decorated with logging tools, mounted deer heads, and photos of the old days in the lumber camp; pool tables and a game area.

SUPERIOR

Barker's Island Inn
300 Marina Dr.
(715) 392-7152
www.barkers-island-inn
.com
Moderate
Steak and seafood
specialties; good view
of Lake Superior; open
daily for lunch and
dinner; conference center
attached.

Golden Inn
24 East St.
(715) 395-2565
www.goldeninnrestaurant
.com
Inexpensive to moderate
Chinese and American fare;
numerous combo specials,
with Szechuan delicacies
among the most popular;
also Hong Kong–style lo
mein and related dishes for
different flair.

Fullers Family Restaurant
5817 Tower Ave.
(715) 392-7510
Inexpensive to moderate
Burgers, chicken, seafood,
soups, tasty salads, and
mouthwatering cakes and
pies; breakfast begins at
6:45 a.m.

The Shack Smokehouse & Grill
3301 Belknap St.
(715) 392-9836
www.shackonline.com/
restaurants
Moderate
Hickory pit barbecue
plus salads, sandwiches,
seafood, and choice
steaks, plus French onion
soup; huge wine cellar;
watch out for the "mega-
tini" drink special.

Thirsty Pagan Brewing Company
1623 Broadway
(715) 394-2500
www.thirstypaganbrewing
.com
Inexpensive to moderate
Brews 9 varieties of beer,
plus seasonal batches;
extra-delicious pizza and
a hearty menu for kids;
regularly scheduled music.

EASTERN WISCONSIN

The eastern portion of Wisconsin near Lake Michigan has the greatest concentration of population in the state, but there are still secret treasures of travel waiting there for you. For an extensive overview of what the nation's inland coast has to offer, take the Lake Michigan Circle Tour. For 1,000 miles the route carries tourists through Wisconsin, Michigan, Indiana, and Illinois. Wisconsin's 300-mile connection begins at Highway 32 south of Kenosha and concludes at Highway 41 in Marinette. Many lakeshore towns have designated "spur" routes off the main Circle drive, to show off their home neighborhoods.

The route is marked by 3-by-3-foot green and white signs set about every 5 miles. In most areas the route meanders close to city beaches, harbors, and marinas, so be sure to bring a fishing pole and sunscreen. Angling licenses can be secured at most bait and tackle shops, so don't let the initial lack of the right paperwork be an impediment.

For your reference, here's the Wisconsin leg of the Circle route: Highway 32 through Kenosha, Racine, Milwaukee, and Port Washington to its interchange with I-43 north of Port Washington; I-43 to the interchange with Highway 42 south-west of Sheboygan; Highway 42 through Sheboygan to the

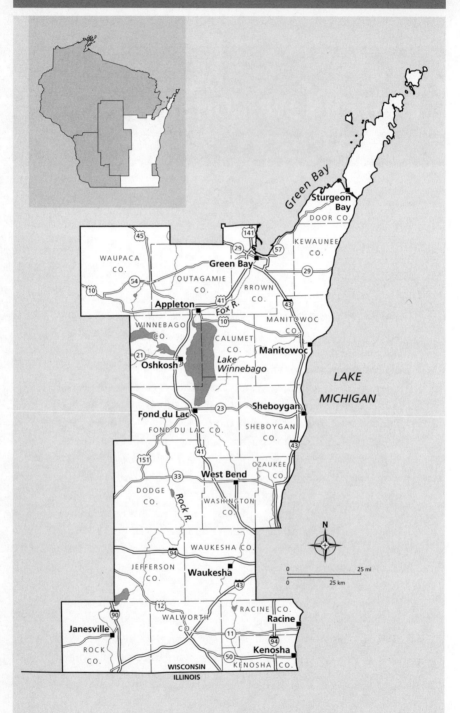

EASTERN WISCONSIN'S TOP HITS

American Club	Old World Wisconsin
Aztalan State Park	Outagamie Museum and Houdini Historical Center
Bristol Renaissance Faire	
Chain O'Lakes	Peterson's Hamburgers
Emma Carlin Hiking Trail	Pioneer Village
Experimental Aircraft Association Air Venture	Point Beach State Forest
	Rock Aqua Jays
Green Bay Packers Hall of Fame	Seven Mile Fair & Market Square
Hoard Historical Museum and Dairy Exhibit	Southern Kettle Moraine Forest
	Walleye Weekend
Hobo's Korner Kitchen	Washington Island
Houdini Plaza	Wisconsin Maritime Museum

junction with I-43 northwest of Sheboygan; I-43 to its interchange with Highway 151 southwest of Manitowoc.

Take Highway 151 to downtown Manitowoc, then to Highway 10 and its junction with Highway 42 north of the downtown. Drive Highway 42 through Two Rivers, Kewaunee, and Algoma to Sturgeon Bay; Highway 57 up the east side of Door County to Sister Bay; Highway 42 down the east shore of Green Bay back to Sturgeon Bay.

Then move on Highway 57 to its junction with Highway 29 in Green Bay; Highway 29 through downtown Green Bay to its interchange with Highway 41 in Howard; Highway 41 west along the shore of Green Bay to Marinette and the Michigan border.

You'll go through communities in Kenosha, Racine, Milwaukee, Ozaukee, Sheboygan, Manitowoc, Kewanee, Door, Brown, Oconto, and Marinette Counties on your Circle adventure. En route you'll hit restaurants, museums, lodgings, and other attractions that blend in perfectly with the lakefront milieu.

Brown County

The *Oneida Nation Museum* in *De Pere* (www.oneidanation.org/museum), a Green Bay suburb, offers keen insights into the lives of this Native American tribe, which came to Wisconsin in the 1820s. There's a hands-on room in which kids can play a drum and try on an eagle-feather headdress. The museum is located at the intersection of Highways E and EE. It's open June through Aug from 9 a.m. to 5 p.m. Tues through Sat, closed Sun and Mon. The museum is closed every Sat from Sept to May. Call (920) 869-2768 for more details. The tribe also operates a giant bingo parlor and casino adjacent to its Radisson Hotel across from the airport in Green Bay.

The De Pere Historical Society maintains **White Pillars,** the state's first bank building (www.deperehistoricalsociety.org). The structure, located at 403 N. Broadway, was built in 1836 to house the currency and records of the De Pere Hydraulic Company. The firm was then building a dam across the Fox River in De Pere. Over the generations the old bank building was alternately a barbershop, an Episcopalian meetinghouse, and a newspaper office before becoming a home. It was returned to its original look in 1973. The bank is open Mon through Thurs from 2 to 6 p.m. and Fri 11 a.m. to 3 p.m., or by appointment. Admission is free. For more information call (920) 336-3877.

While in Green Bay, don't miss the remodeled **Green Bay Packers Hall of Fame** (www.packers.com/lambeau-field/index.html), located in Lambeau Field, 1665 Lombardi Ave. The museum hours on nongame days are 9 a.m. to 6 p.m. Mon through Sat, Sun from 10 a.m. to 5 p.m. The site is almost a shrine, honoring all the players who have worn the gold and green of the city's pro football team over the years. You can even try kicking your own field goal there. In July and August the team has practice sessions open to the public in the nearby stadium. (A giant statue of a ball-grabbing Packer atop a football that used to stand on the lawn in front of the old museum building is now in front of the Neville Public Museum, 210 Museum Place.) Call (920) 499-4281. Admission is $10 for adults, $8 for seniors 62 and older, and $5 for kids 6 to 11.

The **National Railroad Museum,** just off Highway 41, is a nationally known train museum. While train buffs may already be aware of the history of its rolling stock, the rest of us might not be as knowledgeable. One locomotive on display, called "Big Boy," weighs in at 600 tons and is 133 feet long. Another engine pulled Gen. Dwight Eisenhower's command train in World War II.

For details on the railroad museum, call (920) 437-7623 or look over www .nationalrrmuseum.org. The facility is open year-round from 9 a.m. to 5 p.m. Mon through Sat and from 11 a.m. to 5 p.m. Sun. Jan through Apr the museum is closed on Mon. From May 1 through September 30 and weekends in Oct, train rides, an additional $2, are offered at 10 and 11:30 a.m. and at 2:30 and 4 p.m. Summer admission is $9 for adults, $8 for seniors (62 and older), $6.50 for youngsters 4 through 12, and free for kids 3 and younger. During the winter season, October 1 through April 30, admission is generally half price because the train ride is not available.

For flower and plant lovers, the **Green Bay Botanical Garden** is a definite must-see. The garden is located on a 60-acre site adjacent to the Northeast Wisconsin Technical College campus on the west side of Green Bay. The rolling hills, spring-fed pond, and excellent soil make it an ideal dwelling for a wide spectrum of plants, from formal rose gardens to the fairytale-like atmosphere of the children's garden. Impressive architecture includes graceful bridges, domed gazebos, and even an English cottage. Workshops, programs, and special events are offered throughout the year. The garden is open daily May through Sept, 9 a.m. to 5 p.m. Apr through early June, and from 9 a.m. to 8 p.m. mid-June through the end of Aug. For more information on autumn, winter, and spring hours, call (920) 490-9457 or log on to www.gbbg.org.

For eating, **Chili John's** (920-494-4624; www.chilijohns.com) is famous for its namesake food, ranging from spicy enough to curl hair to milder versions for daisy-weights. The place has been in the same family for three generations. It's located at 519 S. Military Ave. in the Beacon Shopping Center, at the intersection of Highway 54. Takeout is available. Some wags claim you can use the hottest version for fueling a motorboat, but don't believe 'em. Just eat and be satisfied.

Dodge County

Dodge County is rich in farmland, layered with rolling hills, and spotted with lakes. Westford, Mud Lake, Shaw Marsh, Theresa Marsh, and Horicon Marsh wildlife areas and the **Horicon National Wildlife Refuge,** as well as Fox, Emily, Beaver Dam, and Sinissippi Lakes, are the county's pride and joy. Outdoors fans flock here regardless of the season for bird watching, hunting, fishing, or just plain loafing.

Our favorite canoeing jaunt is deep into the Horicon Refuge, angling for bullheads and watching for blue herons and sandhill cranes. The wildlife refuge has several large rookeries of each, accessible only by water. The **Blue Heron Landing,** near the Highway 33 bridge over the Rock River, has canoe rentals April through September and pontoon boat tours from May through the end of September.

Call (920) 485-4663 or visit www.blueheronlanding.com or www.horicon marsh.com for details. Public boat-launching sites are located at River Bend Park below the Horicon Dam in town, Ice House Slough off Chestnut Street, Arndt Ditch Landing off Highway E northwest of Horicon, and Burnett Ditch Landing on the west side of the marsh.

AUTHORS' FAVORITES

Aztalan State Park, Lake Mills

Experimental Aircraft Center Museum, Oshkosh

Golden Rondelle (Johnson's Wax), Racine

Great Lakes Dragaway, Union Grove

Green Bay Packers Hall of Fame, Green Bay

Hoard Historical Museum and Dairy Exhibit, Fort Atkinson

Lake Michigan shoreline

Lambeau Field/Stadium tour, Green Bay

National Railroad Museum, Green Bay

Old World Wisconsin, Eagle

Oneida Nation Museum, DePere

Orchards in Door County

If you have kids too little to take into the marsh, let them fish for bullheads from the grassy west-side riverbank across from the John Deere plant, near the Highway 33 bridge west of downtown. Pubs in the neighborhood offer pickled eggs and pig's feet, two gourmet treats for the macho set.

Canada geese use the county's cornfields and swamps for a regular autumn pit stop on their way south. They fly from the Hudson Bay in Canada to their winter layover where the Ohio River joins the Mississippi. Up to 100,000— sometimes more—birds are counted in the marsh each year. Consequently, on some weekends, traffic is bumper-to-bumper along the county roads ringing the marshes as rubberneckers strain to see the giant fowl. Some of the feathered fliers weigh in at an impressive 18 pounds or more, with a wingspan of 6 feet. If you can, take a middle-of-the-week jaunt around the Horicon instead of a Saturday or Sunday run. You'll be able to stop and stare to your heart's content at the sky-blackening flocks without worrying about backed-up traffic.

The town celebrates its link with the environment during ***Horicon Marsh Days*** in July, with activities ranging from street sales to a drum-and-bugle-corps competition that attracts groups from around southeastern Wisconsin. In September the Autumn Art on the Marsh show is held in Discher Park, on Cedar Street. The show provides an opportunity to stock up on Christmas presents.

Founded in 1907, the ***J. W. Jung Seed Company*** in Randolph is another Dodge County attraction, located 40 miles northeast of Madison. Each winter, while planning for planting, gardeners eagerly look forward to the company's nationally distributed mail-order vegetable and flower catalogs. The firm prints its own catalogs, up to 2.5 million copies a year, with 5,000 orders for seeds and plantings per day during the peak spring season. Few people realize that tours of Jung are available if you reserve ahead (800-247-5864; www.savor wisconsin). There's also the opportunity for green thumbs to stop in at the company's garden store, open 8 a.m. to 5 p.m. Mon through Sat. It's a marvelous place to purchase shrubs, evergreens, seeds, fruit trees, and plants.

Specialists are on hand to answer questions about plantings, soil conditions, and all those similar tough details that are necessary to help create the perfect vegetable or flower garden. To ensure the continuation of its fine stock, the company has test plots for many varieties of plants, from gladioluses to seed corn.

The firm's founder, J. W. Jung, died in 1988 at age 100. Even after he had hit the century mark, however, Jung was often out speaking to his customers, spending a full day at work. The company currently is run by grandson Richard Zondag and other members of the family.

The *Dodge County Fairgrounds* (920-885-3586; www.dodgecountyfair grounds.com) in *Beaver Dam* has racing and demolition derbies at various times in the summer. The track is 3 miles east of Beaver Dam on Highway 33.

For a quieter but a buzzing good time, there's the *Honey of a Museum,* N1557 Highway 67, 2 miles north of *Ashippun.* More than 2 million pounds

TOP ANNUAL EVENTS

JUNE

Walleye Weekend
Fond du Lac
(920) 923-6555

JULY

Big Fish Bash
Racine
(262) 634-1931

Experimental Aircraft Association Air Venture
Oshkosh
(920) 230-7800

Laura Ingalls Wilder Children's Day
Old World Wisconsin, Eagle
(262) 594-6300

Sawdust Days
Oshkosh
(920) 235-5584

Shopko Americafest (Fourth of July)
Green Bay
(920) 437-5972

NOVEMBER

Festival of the Trees
Racine
(262) 634-6002

DECEMBER

Snowshoe Workshop at Retzer Nature Center
Waukesha
(262) 896-8007

of honey are produced each year at the apiary located there. Spigots in the museum allow you to taste the different flavors of honey, from tart wildflower to bitter brown buckwheat and smooth golden clover. Honey is sold in a shop on the grounds, with numerous varieties from plain to that spiced with apricot bits. The museum (800-558-7745; www.honeyacres.com) is open year-round from 9 a.m. to 3:30 p.m. Mon to Fri. From mid-May through October 30, it is also open from noon to 4 p.m. Sat and Sun.

If all that noise isn't one's cuppa tea, then it's time to delve back into history where it is really quiet. The **Rock River Archaeological Society** was established in 1998 to study the ancient Native American heritage of Dodge County and nearby areas. The group holds meetings, leads tours, and hosts events that help participants better understand the land and waterways of the region. Especially interesting are visits to the numerous effigy mounds that can be found throughout the county.

The group meets at 7 p.m. on the third Wed of each month between Sept and May at the Department of Natural Resources service center on Highway 28 between Mayville and Horicon. Contact them through their website at www.dnr.state.wi.us/org/land/wildlife/reclands/horicon/edcntr/rrarchsoc/.

Door County

Door County (920-743-4456; http://doorcounty.com) has often been called the Cape Cod of Wisconsin. The rocky coast juts like a thumb into the frosty waters of Lake Michigan, separating the lake from Green Bay. It's a harsh landscape, but one that artists love. Scandinavian farmers and fishers settled the vicinity, appreciating its environmental kinship to their homeland. We like the county no matter the season. Spring has the fragrance of cherry and apple blossoms. Summer's hard heat is beaten only in the cool woods or by swimming.

We just wish that some of the small towns were not becoming so commercialized, with what appears to us an overabundance of mini-malls featuring crafts, candles, ribbons, and trendy hiking wear. All these shops have become too much of a good thing. So we prefer to hit the back roads, where it's more relaxing.

Autumn's colorama in Door County is considered among the best in the state. A drive around the peninsula in October provides the last opportunity to scour the county's antiques shops before they close for the snowbound winter. Winter? Well, there's cross-country skiing, followed by a huddle in front of the fireplace with a hot toddy.

The city of **Sturgeon Bay** (920-743-6246 or 800-301-6695; www.sturgeon bay.net) is the entry point for the county, where Highways 42 and 57 link to

At Death's Door

The stretch of water between the tip of the Door Peninsula and Washington Island, 7 miles offshore, is called the ***Porte des Morts Passage.*** This literally means "Passage of Death" or "Door of Death," from which Door County gets its name. The rockbound coast, the shoals, and the reefs have chewed up dozens of ships over the generations. While the name is appropriate, it originally had nothing to do with shipwrecks. Early French traders called the treacherous passage by that handle in honor of a group of Native American friends who died there during a storm.

cross the ship channel. To get there any other way, you'll have to swim, sail, or fly; all of which are excellent options, of course, if you have your own fins, yacht, or plane. Regardless of the transport mode, the county has facilities to accommodate anyone's arrival.

Door County is noted for its many excellent inns and guesthouses. Among the best in Sturgeon Bay are the ***White Lace Inn,*** 16 N. 5th Ave. (920-743-1105 or 877-948-5223; www.whitelaceinn.com), the ***Bay Shore Inn,*** 4205 Bay Shore Dr. (800-556-4551; www.bayshorein.net), the ***Inn at Cedar Crossing,*** 336 Louisiana (920-743-4200; www.innatcedarcrossing.com), and the ***Scofield House,*** 908 Michigan (920-743-7727; www.scofieldhouse.com). In Ephraim, try the ***French Country Inn,*** 3052 Spruce Ln. (920-854-4001; www.frenchcountry-inn.com/accommod.html). ***Inn on Maple,*** 414 Maple Dr., Sister Bay (920-854-5107; www.innonmaple.com) is an excellent lodging on the peninsula. One of the most popular in Door County is Jan and Andy Coulson's ***White Gull Inn,*** 4225 Main St., Fish Creek (888-364-9542; www.whitegullinn.com). Hospitality and moderate pricing are the name of the game for all these accommodations.

Of all the Door County traditions, the ***fish boil*** is the most famous, harkening back to the area's Scandinavian heritage. Almost every roadside restaurant and inn offers some version of this popular summer "event." The chef boils a huge pot of salted water over an outside blaze. Depending on his or her inclinations as to what ingredients go in when, next usually comes seasoning, potatoes, and onions that cook for about 15 to 20 minutes. Bunyan-size chunks of whitefish are then boiled in the mix for another 7 to 10 minutes or so. No eyes of newt or wing of bat are needed—this is your basic stick-to-the-ribs food. The water bubbles over from the pot, causing a dramatic explosion of steam and great photo opportunities. The boil carries off all the fats with the scalding foam.

You can then sit down for a breeze-touched picnic. Add homemade bread and jam, coleslaw, corn on the cob, and a slab of freshly baked Door

Backpacking Only

Newport State Park is a semiwilderness on the far tip of Door County. A century ago the logging village of Newport stood where the park is now. The village eventually died and reverted to fields and forests. While hiking there we've found the ruins of several cabins and foundations of houses far back among the pines. The park has 11 miles of shoreline along Lake Michigan, including a 3,000-foot-long beach.

The best part about the park is that it allows only backpacking at its campsites, which range along the lakeside for quiet, if not five-star-resort, comfort. But we never went for that, preferring to rough it. The dawn up from the side was worth the strain of humping in all our gear. The wildflowers in spring and the explosion of leaf color in autumn mean repeat trips. The park is located 5 miles northeast of Ellison Bay on Highway 42. Then turn east on County Highway NP. The park is open daily from dawn to dusk year-round. For further information contact the Park Superintendent, Newport State Park, 475 S. County Highway NP, Ellison Bay 54210; (920) 854-2500; www.dcty.com/newport.

County cherry or apple pie. A la mode helps make this concluding part of the meal truly decadent. But what the hey? Mmmm, grand! For a listing of several regional restaurants offering this combo of showmanship and good eats, check out www.doorcountyvacations.com/html/generalInfo/fishBoils.htm.

Washington Island is reached by ferry only from Gills Rock on the Door County mainland. The island has been discovered by tourists, which has led to an overabundance of gift shops near the harbor mouth. But once you get away from the ferry landing, the island is delightfully pretty. Spend a day driving around the island's back roads or rent a bike at the dockside. I was running late during one exploration and had to catch the night's last ferryboat. With about a minute to spare, I got from the north end of the island to the south end. I don't recommend a careening drive like that on a regular basis because the roads are too twisting and narrow. But at least I made the boat landing in time.

Rock Island is the next island out from Washington, also reached by ferryboat only. No cars are allowed in this state park, so be prepared to hike. Without the noise of autos to compete with the surf and the wind rustling the beech leaves, you can spot the deer and other wildlife that live on the craggy spit of rock and sand. Pack a lunch and sit on the north beach looking out over the lake. The view is tremendous. Archaeologists have been poking around the island for several years, discovering ancient Native American villages and burial places, as well as checking out abandoned pioneer settlements. The sites are well marked, but don't go around digging on your own. They're all legally protected.

Fond du Lac County

Ripon (www.ripon-wi.com) proudly struts the fact that the Republican Party was formed here when a group of disgruntled politicians met on March 20, 1854. The building in which they got together is now called the *Little White Schoolhouse.* The building on Blackburn Street is open daily throughout the summer and early autumn.

The city of *Fond du Lac* is on the southern rim of Lake Winnebago, with a large white lighthouse at the Lakeside Park to act as a focal point for outdoor events. The city's *Walleye Weekend* each June attracts anglers from all over the Midwest to compete for cash prizes and the adulation of fellow fishing fanatics. For details call the Fond du Lac Convention and Visitors Bureau, (920) 923-3010 or (800) 937-9123 (www.fdl.com), or the Fond du Lac Festival at (920) 923-6555.

Jefferson County

The *Emma Carlin Hiking Trail* (www.dnr.wi.gov/org/land/parks/specific/kms/trails.html) is one of the state's best for hiking and biking, beginning in a parking lot on County Trunk Z, south of Highway 59 and only 2 miles east of Palmyra. The trail offers 3 loops of varying distances, with a pond, meadows, and plenty of wildlife. Eagles are often spotted high in the air over the aspen and basswood groves that are scattered between the oak stands. Sometimes turkey vultures can be seen swooping and soaring overhead as well.

After a brisk hike on the trail, indulge in all the creature comforts at the *Fargo Mansion Inn* (920-648-3654) in *Lake Mills.* Enoch Fargo, a descendant of the stagecoach family, built the home at the turn of the 19th century. It became the town's social center, complete with towers, woodwork, a lavish foyer, and a huge kitchen with a walk-in freezer. The neighbors were amazed when Fargo put in a cement sidewalk out front, supposedly the first in Wisconsin.

After a succession of owners, including one family that hosted 80 foster children (over the years, not all at once), the building was listed on the National Register of Historic Places in 1982 and made into a guesthouse in 1986. Five bedrooms are on the second floor, reached by a staircase worthy of

findthebadger

In case your geography is a bit askew and you need to locate the Badger State on a map, Wisconsin is bounded on the north by Michigan's Upper Peninsula and Lake Superior, on the west by Iowa and Minnesota, on the south by Illinois, and on the east by Lake Michigan.

Cinderella. The rooms are named for former occupants of the mansion. Several suites have been added to the building's third floor by owner Barry Luce and his partner, Tom Boycks. The inn has tandem bikes for use in the summer, for pedaling along the nearby Glacial Drumlin Trail. Prices at the inn are moderate and include a continental breakfast.

Near Lake Mills is **Aztalan State Park** (920-648-8774; www.stateparks .com/aztalan.html) and the southern unit of Kettle Moraine Forest. On summer weekends dirt-bike racers zoom near the park on a twisted, turning motocross track that can be seen from I-94. Their roaring engines, however, can't be heard at the site of a prehistoric village to the south. The tribe that settled here is thought to be an outpost of ancient mound builders who lived in southern Illinois.

Artifacts found throughout the region show that the inhabitants were great traders. Shells, precious metals, and implements not indigenous to this part of Wisconsin have been found in farm fields and along riverbanks. The artifacts and pioneer tools are displayed at the **Lake Mills–Aztalan Histori-cal Society Museum** (920-648-4632; www.orgsites.com/wi/aztalan), 3 miles east of Lake Mills on County Trunk B. Two pioneer churches and other 19th-century pioneer buildings are on the museum site, which is open noon to 4 p.m. Thurs through Sun from mid-May through late September. There is a modest charge.

The state has erected a palisade where the village once stood, similar to one that archaeologists say protected the tribe from marauding enemy bands. Excellent markers and signage around the grounds tell the story of the Aztalan tribe. A picnic site is nearby at the foot of a hill leading down to a creek. On one of our excursions there, the kids spent half a day fishing after reading how the Native Americans used the same waterway for their fish traps and netting. It is possible that this community was somehow related to the Cahokia Mounds people of southwestern Illinois. Archaeologists have discovered many similar artifacts and building styles at both sites.

Fort Atkinson is home of the **Hoard Historical Museum and Dairy Exhibit,** 401 Whitewater Ave. (920-563-7769; www.hoardmuseum.org). The museum is open Memorial Day through Labor Day, Tues through Sat from 9:30 a.m. to 4:30 p.m. The museum is closed Sun and Mon year-round. The exhibits trace the development of the American dairy industry, with plaques honoring famous scientists and dairy operators. Fort Atkinson has long been famous as a dairy and agricultural publishing center, where such important magazines as *Hoard's Dairyman* are produced.

The Hoard Museum also traces the action of the US Army and militia in the Black Hawk War of 1832. Several skirmishes took place in Jefferson County between pursuing troops and their quarry, the Fox and allies who were led by the famed warrior Black Hawk.

Young Abraham Lincoln was one of the militiamen who chased the Native Americans to the Mississippi River, where they were massacred while trying to escape by swimming across. A large map in the museum shows where soldiers and Native Americans camped as they jockeyed back and forth.

The town also has a replica of Fort Koshkonong, originally built to protect settlers during the Black Hawk War.

Nearby are several prehistoric Native American markers, one of which resembles a huge panther. That intaglio (a design cut into the surface of the earth) was probably constructed around AD 1000. The Fort Atkinson form is believed to be one of only two such earthworks remaining in the world (another intaglio in the shape of a panther is in Ontario). The design is rare, because most of the patterns made by the Native Americans were in mounds, rather than in depressions in the ground. The intaglio is located on the west bank of the Rock River, on Highway 106 at the west edge of town. Actually, you will have to use your imagination in "seeing" the beast, because at least 25 feet of the tail was destroyed by construction of a driveway in 1941. The depression is grass covered, near some hedges and sidewalks at 1236 Riverside Dr.

On Highway 26 on the south side of town is the ***Fireside Dinner Theatre*** and restaurant (800-477-9505; www.firesidetheatre.com), which stages live theater-in-the-round productions, many of which are well-known musicals. The theater is popular with tour groups. The country's top folk and acoustic musicians perform regularly at the ***Cafe Carpe,*** a club operated by well-known singer Bill Camplin and co-owner Kitty Welch at 18 S. Water St. West (920-563-9391; www.cafecarpe.com). It's not quite a throwback to the coffeehouse days of the 1960s, but it's close enough. The Cafe Carpe has a soothing ambience, good vibes, and hearty, reasonably priced food. A place to call a musical home.

In Watertown, on the county's north side, is the restored building that was the nation's first kindergarten, celebrating its 150th anniversary in 2006. A German teacher, Margarethe Meyer Schurz, brought this form of teaching youngsters to the United States in 1856. The structure was originally in downtown Watertown but was moved to the site of the ***Octagon House Museum*** in 1956. Both museums are open daily. Summer hours are 11 a.m. to 4 p.m.; winter hours are 11 a.m. to 3 p.m. (919 Charles St.; 920-261-2796; www.water townhistory.org/octagon.htm). Admission is $7 for adults, $4 for students 6 to 17, and $6 for seniors and AAA members. Kids 5 and younger get in free.

Also while in Watertown, stop for ice cream at ***Mullen's Dairy Bar and Eatery*** on W. Main Street (920-261-4278; www.mullensdairy.com/

Mullens_Dairy/handmade.html). The dairy still produces its own creamery products. Scattered around the room are old advertising materials, glass milk bottles, and similar items from the company's past. It's open Mon to Fri from 9 a.m. to 9 p.m. and weekends until 10 p.m.

Wedl's Hamburger and Ice Cream Parlor, 200 E. Racine St. (920-674-3637), on the corner with US 18, 1 block east of downtown in Jefferson, is burger nirvana. Wedl's is open from 10:30 a.m. to 9:30 p.m., from mid-March until mid-October. This tiny shack (and its predecessors) has been a staple for Jefferson burger fans since the 1920s. A couple of hot, steamy kids flip burgers on a small grill in the cramped shack. But they do a great job. Fast, as well. I always ask for fried onions. The mix can't be beat, even though you don't want to talk closely with anyone for a while. Wooweee! Be prepared to wait, especially on summer evenings, because the place is so popular. There's no indoor seating, so perch outside on a long bench stretching alongside an adjacent building, which houses an ice-cream parlor. On the way home to Milwaukee, I once drove 6 hours from Minneapolis to Jefferson, just for a couple of Wedl's cheeseburgers.

Kenosha County

Kenosha County is tucked into the far southeastern corner of the state, where Lake Michigan laps along its miles of beach frontage. The rolling waters provided opportunities for trade and fishing, so pioneer settlers plunked down their log cabins along the shoreline. Eventually, a string of mansions grew up along the lakeside, especially in **Kenosha,** the county seat. They include the **Kemper Center,** once a girls' school, renovated as a conference center and banquet hall, at 6501 3rd Ave. (262-657-6005; www.kempercenter.com), home of an annual Oktoberfest in October, usually featuring the Dorf Kapelle Village Band; and the **Kenosha County History Center** and its famous lighthouse, 220 51st Place (262-654-5770; www.kenoshahistorycenter.org).

If gazing at older buildings isn't your forte, perhaps fishing is. The county boasts the largest catch rate of coho salmon and lake trout along the Wisconsin side of Lake Michigan. **Cohorama,** a celebration of that fabled fighting fish, is usually held in mid-June and features a fishing contest. What else?

The primo hamburger joint in town is **Ron's Place,** 3301 52nd St. (262-657-5907; www.ronsplacekenosha.com). It's inexpensive, with a delicious half-pound burger called the "5x5" that is guaranteed to show up any national fast-food chain's poor excuse for a sandwich. The burger is worth every penny. Ron's has other eats as well, of course, but when it comes to burgers, I won't eat anywhere else in Kenosha.

The **Bristol Renaissance Faire** in Bristol Township is a fun step way, way back into history. Jugglers, whipcrackers, troubadours, poets, and minstrels put on shows on weekends from mid-July through Labor Day. The 80-acre site is near the Illinois-Wisconsin border just off I-94. From Chicago take I-94 west to Highway 41 north and exit at Russell Road.

From Milwaukee take I-94 east, exit at County Road V, and follow the Frontage Road. There's usually a College of Wizards, bawdy comedy, games of skill (get the kids to slay a dragon), and a sword fight or two. For tickets call the Faire at (847) 395-7773 or log on to www.recfair.com/bristol.

Kenoshans appreciate their well-maintained beaches, although they are not staffed by lifeguards. Folks of all ages love swimming, tanning, and loafing at **Alford Park,** 2901 Alford Dr. (Highway 32); **Eichelman Beach,** 6125 3rd Ave.; **Pennoyer Park,** 3601 75th Ave.; **Simmons Island Park,** 5001 Simmons Island; and **Southport Park**, 7825 1st Ave.. You'll also have to bob about on your own; no flotation devices can be used in swimming areas.

Locals also love their parks and nature areas. **Anderson Park,** 8730 22nd Ave., has a playground, as well as baseball and soccer fields. In the summer, the public swimming pool here is busy with 2 water slides. In the winter, an ice-skating rink is set up. A 95-acre fishing pond also attracts young anglers, helped by grandparents. **Charles Nash Park,** 5909 56th St., is geared toward the active Kenoshan, with its 52 acres hosting 4 baseball diamonds, a soccer

Great to Hike

Bong Recreation Area is named after Wisconsin native Richard I. Bong, the number-one fighter pilot for the United States during World War II. In the mid-1950s the government purchased 5,540 acres in Racine and Kenosha Counties for an air force base. The project was abandoned at the end of that decade. In the 1960s, 1,000 acres of the vacant land were purchased to convert to forestland and a county park. In 1974, 4,515 additional acres were set aside as the state's first recreational area that included nontraditional uses of parkland. For instance, sky gliding, dog training, hot-air ballooning, and model-rocket launching are allowed. But we go for the hiking opportunities around the park's small lake.

The Blue Trail (South Loop) is one of the most interesting treks, taking us along a nature trail with excellent signage. The marshy areas in the middle of the recreation site are excellent for bird watching, so bring some binoculars. This is an easy trek for little kids. From I-94 get off at the Highway 142 exit and drive west about 8 miles. The park is 1 mile west of Highway 75. Kenosha is the largest nearby city, 17 miles to the east on Lake Michigan. For more information contact the site manager, Bong State Recreation Area, 26313 Burlington Rd., Kansasville 53139, (262) 878-5600; www.dnr.state.wi.us/org/land/parks/specific/bong/.

field, horseshoe pits, playground, and skateboard park. Yet it does have a spacious picnic area for after-game gatherings. The 24-acre *Kennedy Park,* 4051 5th Ave., also has a picnic area, with a hiking/biking trail to use for working off the brats and burgers. *Lincoln Park,* 7010 22nd Ave., features the lovely *Warren J. Taylor Sunken Garden,* with its 50-plus varieties of annual plantings in 31 formal beds. During nice weather, you can almost stumble over the wedding parties using the grounds as photo backdrops.

For more details call the parks department (262-663-4080) or log on to www.kenosha.org/departments/parks.

The community has 2 marinas, each with beautiful nearby beaches for swimming. The *Simmons Island Marina* (262-657-5565) and the *Southport Marina* (262-653-9089) host boaters from around Lake Michigan, who appreciate the accommodations there for their vessels. On balmy summer Saturdays, the lakefront is home to *Harbor Marketplace,* an extended farmers' market that offers fresh produce and entertainment (262-605-1004).

Speaking of food, don't miss dropping by *Tenuta's Delicatessen and Liquors,* a real down-home Italian grocery store on the west side of town at 3203 53rd St. (262-657-9001; www.tenutasdeli.com). Go for the two-for-one wine buys found at the rear of the store, augmented by homemade meatballs, pasta, and other wonders from the vast coolers. Mmmmm, great.

Kewaunee County

Algoma (www.algoma.com) is a photographer's dream on early summer mornings, especially as the state's largest charter fishing fleet sets out from the harbor. The city claims record lake-salmon catches every year just offshore. Who's to argue when boat after boat returns with hefty catches after a full day on the choppy Lake Michigan waters? It's not uncommon to haul in 20-pound chinooks off Algoma Shores.

Von Stiehl Winery, at 115 Navarino St. in Algoma (920-487-5208 or 800-955-5208; www.vonstiehl.com), is open for tours daily from 9 a.m. to 5 p.m. May through Oct. The winery store is open throughout the year, with complimentary tastings. Tours run every half hour May through Oct, from 9 a.m. to 5 p.m. Tickets are $3.50 for adults and $3 for seniors; kids under 16 are free. Perusing the collection of toy trolls on display is almost as much fun as visiting the sampling room. The winery specializes in sweet and semisweet wines and has won several national and international awards.

Kewaunee County (www.kewaunee.org) can promise dolls, wine, and huge fish. It also can show off the *World's Largest Grandfather Clock,* located on Kewaunee's north side. The old timepiece, which stands 35 feet tall,

is the trademark of **Svoboda Industries** (920-388-2691 or 800-678-9996; www
.mastersofwood.com), a 100-year-old firm that specializes in all sorts of wood
products. The clock is on the facade of the factory, chiming every 15 minutes.
The Svoboda plant is located on Highway 42 North and makes smaller versions
of the grandfather clock in addition to furniture, carvings, and other wooden
household accessories.

Manitowoc County

The county fronts the rolling waters of Lake Michigan, with a string of towns
along the shore that look like diamonds, with lights sparkling at night. The
coastline, although lost in darkness, glimmers when you're putt-putting along
in a powerboat. The best view is from 0.5 mile or so offshore on a lazy summer evening.

The city of **Manitowoc** (www.co.mainitowoc.wi.us) must be one of the
few towns that has its own submarine. The USS *Cobia,* acquired by the **Wisconsin Maritime Museum** from the US Navy in 1970, has been outfitted just
as it was during combat in World War II. Recorded battle sounds, accurate to
the shouts of "dive, dive, dive," lend reality to the tight quarters. The 311-foot-
long vessel had a distinguished career, sinking 13 Japanese vessels in 1944 and
1945. After being decommissioned, the sub was assigned as a training ship
for Milwaukee's submarine reserves unit. Manitowoc secured the *Cobia* as a
memorial to the factory workers who built 28 subs in city plants during the war.

The museum itself celebrates life on Lake Michigan, with exhibits of shipwrecks, model vessels, diving gear, photographs, and artifacts. It opened in
1969 but moved to new quarters in 1986, a building complete with a "street"
that includes a ship chandlery, post office, and other storefronts.

One of the most interesting displays is a full-scale section of a sailing ship
as it would have appeared during construction in 1854. The beams, spikes, and
caulking are all in their proper places, detailing the intricate work that went
into the rugged lake vessels.

The museum (920-684-0218 or 866-724-2356; www.wisconsinmaritime.org)
is located at 75 Maritime Dr. in downtown Manitowoc. The museum is open 7
days a week year-round: 9 a.m. to 6 p.m. in the summer and 9 a.m. to 5 p.m.
in Sept and Oct; winter (November through mid-March) hours are 10 a.m. to 4
p.m. Mon to Fri, and 9 a.m. to 4 p.m. Sat and Sun. The museum is closed on
major holidays. Tickets for both the museum and the USS *Cobia* submarine tour
are $12 for adults, $10 for children, and free for youngsters under 6.

The **Best Western Lakefront Hotel** (920-682-7000 or 800-654-5353; www
.bestwesternwisconsin.com/manitowoc-hotels) is the place to eat in Manitowoc,

Landho!

The first sailing vessel to reach the upper Great Lakes was the *Griffon,* a galleon captained originally by famed explorer René-Robert Cavelier, Sieur de La Salle. In 1679, he visited several of the Door County islands and collected furs. However, the ship went down in a raging storm on its return trip to Niagara. Subsequently, the *Griffon* also was the first of many recorded vessels to be sunk on Lake Michigan.

In 1779, the British warship *Felicity* sailed into Milwaukee's harbor after stopping to show the Union Jack flag at several Native American encampments along the western rim of Lake Michigan. The ship, loaded with weaponry, was manned by Gaelic-speaking Scottish and Irish soldiers from the 84th Regiment of Foot, Royal Highland Emigrants based at Fort Michlimackinac. In Milwaukee, they warned the few itinerant French traders there not to ally themselves with the rebellious "Bostons" who were stirring up trouble farther east during the Revolutionary War.

"Roaring Dan" Seavey was the only person arrested for piracy on the Great Lakes, being brought to justice in 1907 after hijacking a schooner on the Michigan side of the lake, dumping its crew overboard and then reselling its valuable cargo of cedar in Chicago. A revenue cutter was sent out from Milwaukee to hunt down the miscreant, noted for other nefarious activities on Lake Michigan, including smuggling poached venison and transporting ladies of the evening from port to port. After a spirited chase back and forth across the lake, Seavey was captured. However, he was acquitted on the piracy charge, testifying that he won the ship in a poker game and the fact that the vessel's owner did not show up for the trial. He died "a lonely man" in a Peshtigo nursing home on Valentine's Day, 1949, at age 84, according a newspaper of the day. The almost-pirate is remembered now with Roaring Dan's Rum, produced by Milwaukee's Great Lakes Distillery, the city's first distillery since Prohibition ended.

featuring fish and steak. General menu prices are moderate. The inn is on the shore in downtown Manitowoc and offers short "getaways" such as the Waterfront Retreat and Castaway Package. The latter includes a box lunch for fishing or sailing, two of the most popular sports in town.

Speaking of eating, it's obvious that no one need ever go hungry in Manitowoc, especially when strolling into ***Beerntsen's Confectionary*** at 108 N. 8th St. (920-684-9616; www.beerntsens.com). This quaint candy shop with its ice-cream parlor has been a tradition in the city since, well, let's say since when chocolate was invented. In 1932, Joseph Beerntsen founded the company, which is now in its third generation of the family. The Beerntsens opened a second outlet in Cedarburg in 1984. Homemade temptations line the shelves in all their caloric splendor. Beerntsen's hot fudge is so lusciously thick and rich, it makes a lava flow look like skim milk. Hours are 10 a.m. to 10 p.m. daily year-round.

Mishicot is a Native American word for "place of shelter." The city is tucked into farmland at the junction of Highways 147 and 163. Lake Michigan is about 10 miles to the east. ***River Edge Galleries*** (920-755-4777; www.river edgegalleries.com) has one of the most extensive collections of the work of Wisconsin fine artists of any state showplace, regularly displaying Karen Gunderman, Patrick Farrell, and other state personalities. The 2-story gallery on the East Twin River is located at 432 E. Main St.

A great state-owned property along Lake Michigan in Manitowoc County is perfect for anyone who enjoys rambling outside and communing with the birds and bees. Although maintained by the county, the 123-acre ***Fischer Creek State Recreation Area,*** 4319 Expo Dr. (www.dnr.state.wi.us/org/land/ parks/specific/fischercreek), offers wooded bluffs, expansive grasslands, and creature-filled wetlands, along with almost a mile of Lake Michigan shoreline on which to tramp. No camping is allowed, but for other details on what to see and do, call the Manitowoc parks folks at (920) 683-4530.

Point Beach State Forest (920-794-7480; www.dnr.state.wi.us/org/land/ parks/specific/pointbeach) is just south of the power plant. It covers more than 2,800 acres of prime timber bordered by 6 miles of sand dunes along Lake Michigan. The woods contain beech, hemlock, maple, yellow birch, and numerous other varieties of trees. There are 127 wooded campsites, 70 with electricity, and all are a short walk to the beach. For campsite reservations call (888) 947-2757. They are open year-round.

Wildlife is abundant, ranging from deer and fox to mink and muskrat. Naturalist programs are held regularly there throughout the summer. The lighthouse is a major attraction at Rowley Point, in operation since 1953.

The ice-cream sundae was supposedly invented in Two Rivers (www.ci .two-rivers.com), about 6 miles north of Manitowoc on Highway 42. On a steamy Sunday in 1881, Ed Berner, owner of a local soda fountain, was asked to top off a dish of ice cream with chocolate sauce. The sauce was usually used only for sodas, but the new concoction took off in popularity once the town's youngsters tried it. A glass vendor saw potential in the product and ordered special sets of canoe-shaped dishes for Berner, calling them sundae dishes. A plaque marking the event stands downtown. Berner's fountain at 1404 15th St. is gone now, replaced by a parking lot for Kurtz's Vintage Wine Cellar.

Outagamie County

The fate and future of Outagamie County, linked to Calumet and Winnebago Counties to the south, are closely tied to Lake Winnebago and the Fox River. Since pioneer times the county has been a commercial center. The waterways brought explorers, settlers, and traders into the heart of Wisconsin from Green Bay and Lake Michigan.

The **Outagamie Museum and Houdini Historical Center,** run by the county historical society, is different from many of its sister museums around the state. This facility concentrates on the industrial and corporate heritage of the Fox River Valley. The displays cover electricity, papermaking, financial services, agriculture, and communication, as well as local history. *Tools of Change,* depicting technology's impact on culture between 1840 and 1950, is fascinating. The standing exhibit is a must-see for kids, who can tour a machine shop, a doctor's office, and other "rooms" to see how various tools are used. First edition books written by Pulitzer Prize–winning author Edna Ferber are also on display. The museum is located at 330 E. College Ave. in Appleton (920-733-8445; www.myhistorymuseum.org). Admission is $7.50 for adults, $5.50 for seniors and students, $3.50 for children 5 to 17, and $20 for a family. A ticket includes admission to the Houdini Historical Center. Hours are 10 a.m. to 4 p.m. Tues through Sat and noon to 4 p.m. Sun. The museum is closed Mon between Labor Day and Memorial Day and on holidays.

A few years ago, the state's tourism motto was "Escape to Wisconsin." That led to all sorts of bad jokes, of course. But the **Houdini Historical Center**

Wildlife at the Edge

If nature is your game, then the **Riveredge Nature Center** is the place to stroll. It's one of our most popular near-to-home getaways for bird watching, deer sighting, and woodchuck counting. The center is a 350-acre stretch of woodland and prairie along the Milwaukee River. The property offers 12 miles of hiking and cross-country ski trails. In addition, naturalist programs, photo shows, and environmental classes keep outdoors lovers occupied. We trekked the property, with a special kinship for the trails along the river because of the scenery and wildlife-viewing opportunities. Bring bug goop for muggy summer hikes; swarms of pesky skeeters can be an irritant.

The main property behind the old barn that serves as center headquarters is ablaze with prairie flowers in spring and summer and is lacking the mosquito problem that you might encounter along the riverbank trails. I've never seen so many daisies as are on display at the center. The yellow carpet seems to spread from horizon to horizon. The center is only 1 mile east of Newburg on County Highway Y. Trail fees are $4 for adults and $2 for kids ages 4 to 13, with a family rate of $12. Guests are asked to register at the visitor center. The center is open 8 a.m. to 5 p.m., Mon through Fri, and noon to 4 p.m. on Sat.; closed Sun. Contact Riveredge Nature Center, 4458 County Highway Y, Saukeville (262-375-2715; www.riveredge.us). Send mail to Box 26, Newburg 53060-0026.

is no laughing matter. The museum wing, dedicated to Appleton's favorite son, has a wide selection of his memorabilia and artifacts. Demonstrations and hands-on exhibits let you test your own agility and ability. Let me tell you that "escapism" isn't as easy as it looks.

To tour *Appleton* (www.appleton.wisconsin.com), exit Highway 41 on College Avenue and park at the city ramp at the Paper Valley Hotel. Walk down the steps at Jones Park for a look at the locks and dam on the Fox River and cross the river on the Oneida Skyline Bridge. Return to the Appleton Center office building and walk through it to *Houdini Plaza,* which commemorates Appleton's famous native son, magician Harry Houdini. There is a sculpture in the plaza of the noted performer, who was born in the city in 1874 as Erich Weiss. The young man took the name of the famous French magician Houdin when he launched his career as an escape artist.

Appleton is also home to Lawrence University and the Fox City Performing Arts Center, a 2,100-seat proscenium-style theater. The center has an extensive schedule of local and national performers. For a lineup call (920) 730-3760 or check www.foxcitiespac.com.

Ozaukee County

Take a step back 100 years, whizzing over the crest of County Road I. The Wisconsin frontier of the 1840s pops out of the farmland at the Ozaukee County *Pioneer Village* (www.co.ozaukee.wi.us/OCHS/PioneerVillage.htm), on the north edge of Hawthorne Hills Park in Saukville.

Twenty settlers' buildings from around the county, including houses, barns, the Cedarburg railroad station, a chapel, and trading post, were moved to the site and reassembled into a village, bordered by an 1860s split-rail fence from the Alvin Wiskerchen farm. The rails are mostly cedar, but there are some oak and ash as well. The village is open from noon to 5 p.m. Sat and Sun from Memorial Day through mid-October. The last tour is 4 p.m. Curators demonstrate pioneer skills such as log trimming, weaving, bread baking, and iron working. All the buildings are furnished in styles from the 1840s to the early 1900s, depending on the structure.

There's nothing fishy about *Port Washington* (www.visitportwashington .com), 25 miles north of Milwaukee on the shores of Lake Michigan, except that it offers excellent angling for coho and lake trout. The city has a relatively new marina, built in 1982, that has a fish-cleaning station at the waterfront, plus boat-launching facilities. You also can fish from the breakwater and along the piers. Keep an eye on the kids, however, because the chill lake water runs deep and fast even close to shore. Fourth of July fireworks are popped off at the marina, making a blazing spectacle over the harbor entrance.

Port Washington celebrates what it claims is the ***World's Largest One-Day Outdoor Fish Fry*** on the third Saturday of each July. Having attended several of these events, I'm not one to offer a challenge. You want fish, you get fish. Seemingly tons of it. Plus the usual french-fried potatoes as a side delight. Fish-fry aficionados love the smoked fish eating contest, an activity we prefer to pass up.

The local firefighters usually have a hose war, trying with their streams of water to push a beer barrel across a wire strung between two poles. The opposing side attempts to push it back, making for a wet time for all participants. A hint: Don't stand close. The teams sometimes will playfully squirt the crowd, especially if it's a hot day.

Port Washington has several excellent restaurants. Among the best for casual, down-home cooking is ***Harry's Restaurant,*** 128 N. Franklin St. (262-284-2861; http://portwashington-wi.patch.com/listings/harrys-restaurant-2). A discerning diner can get by with a hearty meal for under $10. It's located on the community's main street, and it's an easy stroll to the marina to watch the early-morning fishing fans returning with their catches. This place is especially popular with cyclists, who often line up outside and wait for a high-energy taste treat.

Another destination for cyclists is ***"the Port,"*** where they come with food in mind after a long trek. Dockside Deli, 222 E. Main St. (262-284-9440; www.docksidedeli.com) serves breakfast and lunch, with cookies to die for, including a delight known as the Snickerdoodle.

The city's downtown chamber of commerce building on Grand Avenue is called the ***Pebble House.*** On the National Register of Historic Places, the old home was built in Greek Revival style with rubble stone walls 20 inches thick. The foundation of the building was constructed of pebbles and rocks collected along the shoreline by original owners Elizabeth and Henry Dodge in 1848. The house was moved to its current location in 1985, pebbles and all. To reach the chamber of commerce, call (262) 284-0900 (www.ci.port-washington.wi.us).

The last remaining authentic covered bridge of what had been 40 in the state is in Ozaukee County's ***Covered Bridge County Park*** (www.co.ozaukee.wi.us/history/bridge.html). The bridge over Cedar Creek was built in 1876 and "retired" from service in 1962. You'll find the structure by going west of downtown Grafton on Highway 60 to the junction with Highway 143. Turn north there on Covered Bridge Road.

In 1999 Donald Tendick Sr. donated 142 wooded acres interspersed with rolling farmland to Ozaukee County, with the idea that a park be developed.

Although the philanthropist died in 2000, his memory lives on with Tendick Nature Park (www.co.ozaukee.wi.us), located on County Highway O, approximately 2 miles north of Saukville. Its amenities include an archery range, disc golf course, access to the Milwaukee River for canoeing, nature trails, hiking/ski trails, and a winter sledding hill.

HoBo's Korner Kitchen, 100 E. Main St. in Belgium (262-285-3417; www .howdea.net/hobos-home.htm), is one of those truck stops where the food is plentiful, the conversation boisterous, and the music preference is country-western. There is plenty of room to park, move, stretch, and grin. The stop is directly to the west of Highway 43, the main four-lane road to Sheboygan, at exit 107. On Friday there is an all-you-can-eat codfish fry, including fries, two slabs of bread, coleslaw, a cup of soup, and enough tartar sauce to fill a 10-gallon pail. If you want to go fancy, try the Poor Man's Lobster with vegetables and potatoes.

Curley's Restaurant, at 745 Main St. in Belgium (262-285-3100), is located in a building built in 1887 by J. B. Krier, the son of a Luxembourg immigrant. At that time, it was the Belgium House. Today, Curley's Restaurant now carries the name of Curley Peiffer, who operated Curley's Tavern in this building in the early 1940s until he retired in 1968. The renovated casual-dining space is now owned by Afla Irani, who was born in Mumbai (formerly Bombay), India. Emphasizing cross-culturalization, Irani put up photos of the Luxembourg royal family near the restaurant's bar area. Steaks are popular, along with house specialties such as chicken Wellington and citrus-crusted swordfish. As with Hobo's, there's a marvelous Friday fish fry.

Racine County

Racine (www.racine.org) has long been host to one of the county's largest colonies of Danish immigrants. And someday a poet will compose an ode honoring the delightful, delicious Danish kringle, the most delectable pastry of them all. Racine is the Kringle Capital of the Universe, with at least 11 bakeries where even a quick stop adds pounds to thighs and hips. The Racine Chamber of Commerce estimates that the bakeries, most of which are run by families of Danish descent, produce upward of a million kringles annually. Many are shipped around the world for Christmas giving.

Kringles are oval-shaped layers of buttered dough, weighing about 1.5 pounds. They feature a variety of fillings, such as pecan, walnut, raspberry, chocolate, rhubarb, cheese, cherry, apple, custard, and even peanut butter.

Today's kringles are smaller than the 3-by-8-foot pastries made in 19th-century Denmark. Austrians taught Danish bakers the technique of layering thin

Green between the Toes

Milaeger's Inc.'s greenhouses in southeastern Wisconsin are among the largest in the state, located at 4838 Douglas Ave. in Racine or at 8717 Hwy. 11, Sturtevant. Both properties are open from 9 a.m. to 8 p.m. Mon through Fri, 8:30 a.m. to 5 p.m. Sat, and 9:30 a.m. to 5 p.m. Sun. Guests are free to browse amid the potted this-'n'-thats that are growing everywhere. Perennials are the big things here, with a total of 71 greenhouses to check out. We've always dreamed that our plants would be this lush. Call (262) 639-2040 (www.milaegers.com).

sheets of butter and dough, letting the concoction sit for a day or so before flattening it with large rolling pins. Most of the initial work is still done by hand, but better rolling machines and high-tech ovens ensure easier production and consistency. Some large plants can make 1,500 kringles an hour, a boon during holiday time.

Stop in for a take-home munch at *Bendsten's Bakery,* 3200 Washington Ave. (262-633-0365; www.bendstensbakery.com); *Larsen Bakery,* 3311 Washington Ave. (262-633-4298; www.larsenbakery.com); *Lehmann's Bakery,* 9117 Duirand Ave. (262-632-4636; www.lehmanns.com); or *O&H Danish Bakery,* 1841 Douglas Ave. (866-637-8895 or 800-227-6665; www.ohdanishbakery.com) or 4006 Durand Ave. (866-554-1311).

When in Racine (www.racinedowntown.com) ride through the city's historic downtown and business district aboard one of the lakefront trolleys. They operate daily from Memorial Day through Labor Day, Tues to Thurs 10 a.m. to 4 p.m.; Fri and Sat 10 a.m. to midnight; and Sun 10 to 4 p.m., There are also special pub-and-grub tours of local restaurants and bars on Friday and Saturday nights during the summer. Call (262) 637-9000 or (800) 317-4333. Speaking of the lakefront, we always enjoy taking Lighthouse Drive between Three Mile and Four Mile Roads in Racine. The Wind Point Lighthouse there is a familiar sight for Racine residents and has been painted and photographed so often it probably has its own museum wing somewhere. Built in 1880 for a cost of $100,000, the 112-foot tower helped guide ships into the Racine harbor during its merchant fleet heyday. Before the lighthouse was built, a solitary tree on the point served as sentinel. The building now serves as the municipal offices for the village of Wind Point, surrounded as it is by the larger city of Racine. Note that the interior is not open to the public, but the grounds are available for strolling. Stunning views of Lake Michigan seen from the area are worth at least one Kodak Moment. I suggest you go for more.

The *Golden Rondelle* at the S. C. Johnson & Son Inc. plant in Racine offers tours on Friday by reservation. Contact the Guest Relations Center at the company, 1525 Howe St., Racine 53403 (262-260-2154; www.racinecounty .com/golden). The Golden Rondelle Theater was initially used by Johnson Wax at the 1964 World's Fair in New York as part of its display building.

Tours of the firm's main administration building, designed by Frank Lloyd Wright, also start at the Golden Rondelle Theater.

The Johnson company, better known as Johnson Wax, was started in 1886 as a manufacturer of parquet floors and moved into the wax business when customers asked for ways to protect their under-foot investment. Currently, the firm markets more than 200 products and carries out continuous research. A display of these items fills an exhibit room.

Racine's theater scene is known throughout the region for its wide selection of drama and music. Among the community's creative venues are the *Prairie Performing Arts Center,* 4050 Lighthouse Dr. (262-260-3845), and the *Racine Theater Guild,* 2519 Northwestern Ave. (262-633-4218). The *Over Our Head Players* operates the *Sixth Street Theater,* emphasizing contemporary comedy. The latter's playhouse is located at 318 6th St. (262-632-6802).

The *Racine Art Museum,* affectionately known as "RAM," is the repository of a significant collection of contemporary craft works, showcased in major exhibitions of new work, as well as with a permanent collection. RAM emphasizes ceramics, fibers, glass, metals, and wood. Such artists as ceramic sculptor Toshiko Takaezu are highlighted, showcasing 14 human-size sculptures in his Star Series. Wisconsin artists Dona Look, Alex Mandli, Michael Pugh, and Tom Rauschke are also featured. For details and schedules of exhibits, lectures, and workshops, contact RAM, 441 Main St., (262) 638-8300, or check its website at www.ramart.org.

The *Seven Mile Fair & Market Square in Caledonia* is a bizarre bazaar. As in the old Arlo Guthrie song "Alice's Restaurant," you "can get anything you want" (at Seven Mile Square). Antique hammers, old postcards, collector buttons, car parts, discounted beauty products, tools by the ton, and the occasional fresh vegetables in season fill the booths. I remember the good old days when the entire 10 acres was outdoors and bargain hunters flocked there rain or shine. Today a large metal building houses several hundred exhibitors, with an overflow outside. The new place doesn't quite have the feel that the old locale did, when it was a cross between the Arab Quarter in Jerusalem and Coventry Gardens. Now there is more of a Shopping Network atmosphere to the place. But don't let that turn you off, because Seven Mile Fair is still wonderful for meandering. You can get lost for hours wandering up and down the aisles.

Wright Way Wingspread

Frank Lloyd Wright considered **Wingspread,** 33 E. Four Mile Rd., the last of his "prairie houses." The building, on Racine's north side, is now a major international conference center and think tank sponsored by the Johnson Foundation, where scholars, politicians, and others gather to debate great topics and to freshen their minds. I've taken in several programs over the years at the facility, with discussions covering the Arab-Israeli conflict to the state of higher education. Wingspread was once the private residence of H. F. Johnson, of Johnson Wax fame, and is the largest house of this design that famed architect Wright ever assembled. Tours are free, offered 9:30 a.m. to 3:30 p.m. Tues through Thurs. No tours are held if a conference is in progress. Call (262) 639-3211.

I once purchased a complete set of handmade antique iron fireplace utensils (tongs, shovel, brush, wood carrier) for some outrageously low price.

Start in the 60,000-square-foot Market Square, which offers antiques and collectibles (one person's junk is another's treasure).

Specialty vendors lay out a menu of Mexican and Chinese foods, plus cheesecakes, ribs, and (on Fri) a magnificent fish fry. In the old days, you were lucky to get a hot dog. So I guess progress has made a difference.

The sprawling facility is open outdoors on Sat and Sun from 7 a.m. to 5 p.m. Apr through Oct and from 9 a.m. to 5 p.m. Nov through Mar. Admission is $1.50 for adults and $1 for seniors; youngsters 11 and under are free. Free admission to Market Square on Fri. The fair is located at 2730 W. Seven Mile Rd., just off I-94. Look for the marked exits if you are on the freeway. The place is always an "almost-home" landmark whenever we drive back north from Chicago to Milwaukee. The expanse of parking lots and the signage always signal that home and hearth are getting close. Call (262) 835-217 (www.7milefair .com).

Burlington is proud of its reputation as home of the world-famous **Burlington Liars Club** (262-763-4640; www.burlingtonliarsclub.com), which annually hosts a competition to see who can tell the tallest tales and the biggest lies. The awards are usually given out in a local restaurant, after judges cull through thousands of submissions. Submit your best "lie" with a $1 entry fee to the Burlington Liars Club, PO Box 156, Burlington 53105.

The community also calls itself "the Chocolate City" because of its chocolate plant. Annually in mid-May, the locals host **Chocolate Fest** to celebrate the city's history of chocolate manufacturing. The Nestlé Corporation has a plant in town and is a large supporter of the event. Everywhere you turn is chocolate to eat or buy: dark, light, white, flavored—everything to satisfy the most discerning sweet tooth. Festgoers love watching a carver produce intricate designs from large hunks of the luscious stuff. A lucky raffle winner can even be awarded his or her weight in chocolate. Each night, bands on several stages ensure that everyone is up and moving. Hypnotists, comics, and magicians also hold forth. Be sure to watch the chainsaw artist produce whimsical bears and other critters from large logs. A carnival, bike ride, run/walk, and fireworks round out the fun. For details log on to www.chocolatefest.com.

I always stock up on chocolate whenever taking a drive along any one of the seven official Rustic Roads that grace the county. You never know when you might need a snack. Among the best tours in the state is the drive north from Burlington along Honey Lake Road, Maple Lane, and Pleasant View Road. This route eventually takes you to County Highway D and on to Highway 83. The **Wehmhoff Woodland Preserve** on the route is a great place for muskrat watching. Another scenic backcountry expedition is along Oak Knoll Road from County Highway DD to County Highway D, adjacent to the Honey Creek Wildlife District. Wheatland Road from Highway 142 south to Hoosier Creek Road and on to County Highway JB is also pleasant on a warm summer afternoon. Stop for fishing along the Fox River.

Nitro-powered dragsters, with plenty of accompanying fire and smoke, screech down the track at the **Great Lakes Dragaway** in Union Grove (262-878-3783). Broadway Bob Metzler (yep, that's his name) held sway as owner-manager-fan-magnifico from his timing tower overlooking the rubber-scarred pavement where jet cars rock and roar. He's now retired, but the facility is still going strong. The track is in the eastern outskirts of the city, easy to find with all the signage or simply by following your ears. Parachutes often have to be used to slow down the vehicles at the end of their 0.25-mile runs.

Whenever we need a motor fix (not tune-up, folks), the Great Lakes Dragaway is the place to go. The Hintz clan has regularly made it to the track—one of the best in the Midwest—for a day of watching the action. One time, Steve (middle son) and elder Hintz were allowed access to the timing tower. The whole thing rocks when the race cars framing it on the track below rev their engines. Flames shoot skyward, smoke is everywhere—and then they're off! Our eardrums still reverberate at the memory.

Several years ago, daughter Kate and elder Hintz collaborated on writing a series of drag-racing books for a children's publisher. Naturally, Great Lakes was on the list of must-see places to revisit. We actually tooled down the track (not at 200 mph, however), talked with drivers and pit crews, chatted with management, and generally had a grand time amid the turbo-jet vehicles and funny cars. Kate, being a modern young woman, naturally knew the difference between a piston head and camshaft. So she carried on a great conversation. But I admit, I was lost by the time we got to the intricacies of pressure gauges.

You can even rent the track's "Back 40," a long open field, for weddings, family reunions, and other shindigs. Call (847) 436-0333 or (262) 878-3783 (www.greatlakesdragaway.com).

Rock County

Rock County is the sixth largest county in Wisconsin, located along the Illinois border. Enter the state on I-90 from the Lincoln State, where there is a Wisconsin Tourist Information Center at Rest Area 22. You'll get loads of details on activities and attractions in the county and elsewhere in Wisconsin. The information building is open 8 a.m. to 4 p.m. Sat through Thurs and until 6 p.m. on Fri from mid-May through Oct. From Nov to mid-May, the facility is open only from 8 a.m. to 4 p.m. Tues through Sat.

The county has more than 1,500 sites listed on the National Register of Historic Places. Two towns in the northwestern part of the county are considered historic districts. The entire community of **Cooksville** (at the junction of Highways 138 and 59), with its splendid redbrick buildings, is on the list. Most of nearby **Evansville** (intersection of Highways 213 and 14) is also a historical site. Ask at the tourist information center for locations and details on similarly designated sites in the vicinity.

Beloit is the first major town you'll encounter, home of the **Hanchett-Bartlett Homestead.** The museum, at 2149 St. Lawrence, is on the city's west side. It's an old Victorian-era farmhouse built in the 1850s, featuring period furniture. The grounds include an old one-room schoolhouse. The museum (608-365-7835; www.beloithistoricalsociety.com) is open Fri through Sun from 1 to 4 p.m., June through September.

At **Beloit College** the **Logan Museum of Anthropology** is packed with prehistoric tools, axes, and clubs; arrowheads; and other artifacts from early Native Americans. Beloit College, chartered in 1846, and its surrounding neighborhood are also listed on the National Register of Historic Places. The Logan Museum (608-363-2110; www.beloit.edu/logan) is open 11 a.m. to 4 p.m. daily, except Mon. Admission is free. Since the facility is on a college campus, it is closed on the usual school holidays. You can also take a self-guided tour of 23 effigy mounds built from AD 700 to AD 1200 by Native Americans.

The **Angel Museum,** 656 Pleasant St., houses what is considered the world's largest collection of angels, with more than 12,000 figures. Among them are 900 black angels donated by broadcast star Oprah Winfrey. The museum is open from 10 a.m. to 4 p.m. Tues through Sat, Feb through Dec. It is closed in Jan. Call (608) 362-9099 (or visit www.angelmuseum.org) for holiday hours.

For a quick picturesque drive from Beloit, drive northeast out of town on County Road X to the little crossroads communities of Shopiere and Tiffany in the Turtle Creek Valley. The latter town has a photogenic five-arch bridge over Turtle Creek. The "Tiffany Bridge" is the only such remaining five-arch railway bridge in the world. Then angle north to Janesville on either I-90 or Highway 51,

funfacts

Wisconsin has about 110,000 miles of highways and paved roads. In 1917 the state was the first to adopt the number system for highways, a practice soon followed elsewhere.

exiting on Highway 14 to the *Lincoln-Tallman House,* a villa built in 1857.

The old home includes many household conveniences that were the marvels of their day. For instance, running water was supplied by an attic storage tank rather than by the typical outside pump. The place even had its own working observatory. Abraham Lincoln slept here in 1859, long after his forays in the Jefferson County Indian wars.

The site (608-752-4519 or 608-756-4509; www.rchs.us/lincoln-tallman-house) is open daily from 9 a.m. to 3 p.m., June through Sept, and weekends from 9 a.m. to 4 p.m. in the summer. Holiday tours are held daily from November 20 through December 31, although they are closed on Christmas. Tours of the property are led hourly beginning at 10 a.m., with the last one at 3 p.m. Admission is $8 for adults, $7.50 for seniors, and $4 for children in kindergarten through high school.

North of downtown along Parker Drive is *Traxler Park,* where the *Rock Aqua Jays* national champion waterskiing team demonstrates its skills at 7 p.m. Sun and Wed nights in June and July, and 6:30 p.m. in August on the Rock River. For information contact Forward Janesville, (608) 757-3171 or (800) 48-PARKS. The website is www.rockaquajays.com.

Sheboygan County

The *Rolling Meadows Sorghum Mill* in Elkhart Lake is the largest working plant in the state. Tours of the facility are held during business hours from Memorial Day through October 31. Once inside, you'll see how the manufacture of sweet sorghum has evolved from the use of horse presses to modern equipment. A mill is adjacent to a broom factory that opened in the early 1990s, with an exhibit showing the manufacturing evolution of brooms. Talk with owners Richard and Cheryl Wittgreve for all the latest in the wonderfully sticky business of sorghum making. And they sweep up afterward, of course! The handicap-accessible mill is located at N9030 Little Elkhart Lake Rd. To get to the mill, drive north of Plymouth on Highway 57 to County Road MM, then west 2 miles to Little Elkhart Lake Road, go north 0.25 mile and find the facility on the west side.

The *Kettle Moraine State Forest—Northern Unit,* with forest headquarters in Campbellsport (262-626-2116; www.dnr.wi.gov/org/land/parks/specific/kmn), is a warren of hiking and biking trails through the rocky, rolling countryside formed by glaciers 10,000 years ago. Learn how the topography came together by visiting the *Henry S. Reuss Ice Age Visitor Center* (920-533-8322; www.dnr.wi.gov/org/land/parks/specific/kmn/iac.htm). The center is open weekdays from 8:30 a.m. to 4 p.m., and weekends and holidays from 9:30 a.m. to 5 p.m. The center, with its 20-minute film on the Ice Age, extensive exhibits, and great views, is closed Christmas Eve and Christmas Day. The Ice Age center is located 0.5 mile west of Dundee on Highway 67. The knowledgeable staff there provides information focusing on the forest, as well as naturalist tours.

The late and great actor/racer Paul Newman used to roam the pit area at the *Road America* track in Elkhart Lake, an hour's drive north of Milwaukee. He often stopped in to drive, sign autographs, and greet friends such as the Andrettis, Unsers, Sullivans, and other top drivers who turned out for the September running of the Road America race. Don't miss the lineup of other events held on the twisting course throughout the summer, such as the AMA Suzuki Superbike Double Header and the High Performance NASA Weekend (800-365-7223; www.roadamerica.com).

The track is one of the greatest locales for people watching in eastern Wisconsin, as well as for watching classic race vehicles. You get there from Milwaukee by taking I-43 north to Highway 23, and then going west to Highway 67. Take 67 north to County Trunk J. Road America gates are 2 miles up the road on the left side. Watch out for the Wisconsin Highway Patrol, which keeps a close watch out for motorists thinking they are on the speedway. The grandstand near gate 4 provides some of the best viewing, near the Corvette Corral.

A stroll along the *Rotary Riverview Boardwalk* on Sheboygan's Lake Michigan waterfront can be a relief from the roaring engines at Elkhart Lake. The jaunt, on S. Franklin Street, goes past a historic fishing village that was once a vibrant part of the city harbor. A pleasant time for such a walk is on Sheboygan Bratwurst Day, always the first Saturday in August. Enter the eating contest: Participants see how many double-brat sandwiches they can wolf down in 15 minutes.

The *Kohler Design Center* (800-4-KOHLER [456-4537]; www.us.kohler .com/designkb/designcenter/designcenter.jsp) in the village of Kohler, opened in 1985, showcases the innovative bathroom appliances built by the company that gave its name to the town. The firm is one of the world's leading manufacturers of plumbing accessories. One wall in the center is creatively stacked with red, white, black, and gray toilet bowls and bidets, framed by bathtubs, whirlpools, and similar appliances in a display called the Great Wall of China. The exhibit takes the mundane and transforms it into nifty art. Marine engines and other implements made by the company also are shown off. The center is open 8 a.m. to 5 p.m. Mon through Fri and 10 a.m. to 4 p.m. Sat, Sun, and holidays. Admission is free.

Kohler itself is a planned community just to the west of Sheboygan, built at the turn of the 20th century to house plant staff. Winding streets, ivy-covered walls, and streetlights provide a charming element. The old dorm where the workers lived has been converted into a posh resort called *The American Club.* Prices match the elegant ambience.

The annual pre-Thanksgiving chocolate festival, called "In Celebration of Chocolate," at the American Club is a study in delightful decadence. The secret to a successful foray at the groaning board is developing a slow, easy pace around the torte table, picking up speed at the chocolate-covered fruit, and then gaining momentum

funfacts

Wisconsin's shoreline extends 381 miles along Lake Michigan. For those wanting to learn the metric system, that translates to 613 kilometers. The shore along Lake Superior is 292 miles. The two vary greatly in appearance: There are high bluffs and sandy beaches along Lake Michigan, while Lake Superior offers more low-lying hills and pebbled beaches.

at the cakes. I've learned this through experience and training (building up stamina with chocolate-covered cherries over several months of a preseasonal holiday push). The chefs make their own chocolate, which is whipped, whirled, and swirled into everything imaginable when it comes to desserts.

One of the American Club ballrooms is set aside for the early-December festival. Ablaze with candles and dazzling with crystal, the site is transformed. I like to vary my chocolate selections with sherbet and fresh pears or apples. This freshens the mouth and prepares me for the next go-around. Be aware that this is more of a social, to-see-and-be-seen soiree rather than a stampede to the trough. It is inexcusable, although tempting, to fill one's pocket or purse with leftovers.

For resort packages that include the festival, call the American Club for all the details at (920) 457-8000 or (800) 344-2838, or log on to www.american clubresort.com/Hotels.

From culinary art to art-art, it is always relaxing to visit the *John Michael Kohler Arts Center,* 608 New York Ave., which was established in 1967 to encourage and support innovative explorations in the arts. The center is proud of being a lab for the creation of new works, an originator of exhibitions, and a performing-arts producer. It offers a wide range of art-related activities in a space that never seems to slow down. Check its offerings by calling (920) 458-6144 or peruse its website at www.jmkac.org.

For the sports-minded, the nearby *Whistling Straits* golf course north of Kohler (800-618-5535; www.destinationkohler.com/ws/ws.html) was host of the 2004 PGA Championship, the 2007 US Senior Open, and the 2010 PGA Championship; as of press time it will also be the site of the 2015 PGA Championship and 2020 Ryder Cup. Designed by Pete Dye, the facility opened in 1998, offering two rugged courses along the Lake Michigan shoreline. Duffers have to work hard here for that special hole-in-one.

Walworth County

Delavan is Circus City in a state that gave birth to more than 135 shows over the past 150 years. Between 1847 and 1894, the city was winter quarters for 28 of those circuses, including P. T. Barnum's first. You'll know the town's favorite image once you pull into downtown: A statue of a giant rearing elephant stands on the town square. To get all the skinny on the city, check out www.ci.delavan.wi.us.

Delavan's Spring Grove Cemetery and Old Settlers Cemetery has about 100 famous entertainers and less-well-known workers and administrative personnel buried there.

For a fine scenic overlook of the nearby Ice Age Trail, visit the *Whitewater Lake Recreation Area* ranger station, west of Walworth County Highway P on Kettle Moraine Drive. Walk up the moraine on a dirt road past the gravel pit, and take the roadway about 0.5 mile to the first open viewing area on the ridge's crest. One hundred feet below are Rice and Whitewater Lakes and rolling moraines that reach to the horizon. The view is magnificent.

An artesian well on Clover Valley Road, about 3 miles south of Whitewater, is popular with hikers and others who appreciate fresh, cold water. The place has been known for the past 80 or more years.

The lakes area of Walworth County, especially around Lake Geneva, is a popular resort area for Chicagoans and other Midwesterners. Fontana, Williams Bay, and *Lake Geneva* are small, touristy towns bordering the main lake. Larger facilities such as Lake Lawn Lodge (with several major Native American mounds on its property), Interlaken, the Abbey, and Americana Resort are well known for their spas, massages, tennis courts, horseback riding, restaurants, and meeting/convention rooms with rates to match. Try the more manageable, laid-back *Eleven Gables Inn* on Lake Geneva (493 Wrigley Dr.; 262-248-8393; www.lkgeneva.com). Only 2 blocks from downtown Lake Geneva, the bed-and-breakfast inn has an unobstructed view of the water and its own pier for swimming and fishing.

The *Geneva Inn,* 2009 S. Lake Shore Dr., on the eastern shore of Lake Geneva is another great layover for the road-weary. The property has 37 guest rooms, each snug and cozy, along with a marvelous restaurant with lakeside dining and lip-smacking meals. The Geneva Inn offers all sorts of packages throughout the year, making it easy for budgeting. Call (800) 441-5881 or check its website at www.genevainn.com.

For a different sort of stay, there's the *End of the Line Caboose.* I don't know if you would call the place a motel or hotel because accommodations are in real cabooses (caboosi?). Each railcar has its own bathroom, beds, and the usual guest amenities. The registration lobby is called the Roundhouse, and the Side Track gift shop has an assortment of railroad-themed gift items. The place is located at 301 E. Townline Rd. (262-248-7245; www.kiskijunction.com/RentaCaboose.htm).

For Scandinavian food there's *Scuttlebutts,* at 831 Wrigley Dr. (262-248-1111) on the lakefront. This family restaurant lays out the largest stacks of Swedish pancakes in town. *Popeye's Galley and Grog* and *Popeye's Restaurant* on Lake Geneva's waterfront opened in 1972. Call (262) 248-4381 or visit the website (www.popeyeslkg.com) to review its range of menu items. In the nearby quiet of tiny Williams Bay, *Chef's Corner Bistro* (262-245-6334; www.chefscornerbistro.com) on Geneva Street has excellent homemade soups and German cooking. Chef's Corner is open only for dinner. *Kirsch's* in the

OTHER ATTRACTIONS WORTH SEEING

Bear Den Zoo, Waterford

Bjorklunden Chapel, Baileys Harbor

Blackwolf Run Golf Course, Kohler

Door County Maritime Museum, Gills Rock

Door County Maritime Museum, Sturgeon Bay

Jackson Harbor Maritime Museum, Washington Island

Manitowoc Museum of Sculpture

Olde Stone Quarry County Park and Potawatomi State Park, Door County

Racine Zoological Gardens

River Bend Nature Center, Racine

French Country Inn, W4190 W. End Rd., has won *Wine Spectator's* Award of Excellence several times.Call (262) 245-5756 (www.kirschs.com).

For a different way to see Lake Geneva, the **Lake Geneva Cruise Line** (800-558-5911) has a hiking tour in conjunction with a spring and autumn luncheon cruise. A shoreline footpath extends all 23 miles around the lake, only 3 feet from the water.

For the full lake package, park at the Riviera Boat Docks in Lake Geneva. Numerous ticket options are available. You'll be cruising past the Victorian-era homes of the Wrigley chewing-gum heirs, the Swift meat-packing clan, and the Montgomery Ward Thorne family.

Even with all that walking, it's an easier job than the one held by the "mailgirls" on the *Walworth II*. Working as regular summertime postal carriers, the two women leap from moving boat to dock and back again while delivering mail to homes on the lake. They have to jump to shore, run the length of a pier, drop off the mail, and leap back on the moving vessel before it gets too far away. The delivery process is a tradition that has been going on for more than 75 years.

Nobody has fallen into the water in recent years, but all the eager tourists on the early-morning run take bets on the possibility of a damp plunge. Many different tours are available, starting at $22 for adults without a meal. A sunset dinner cruise is $53 for adults. When not jumping from boat to pier, the mailgirls act as guides, describing the mansions along the shore. The cruise line operates an impressive schedule during the season, departing from Lake Geneva Cruise Line docks. Call (262) 248-6206 for reservations and schedules, or check out www.cruiselakegeneva.com.

Washington County

Washington County is just north of Waukesha and Milwaukee Counties, taking in the northern unit of the Kettle Moraine Forest. Follow the Kettle Moraine Drive by car or bike over landscapes carved out by glaciers 15,000 years ago. **Holy Hill** is the most prominent physical attraction in the county, perched high overlooking the surrounding countryside. The church looks as if it slipped off a page from a Bavarian calendar. Carmelite priests maintain a retreat center there, where you can get a great view of the forestland.

The surrounding farms and villages were first populated by Irish immigrants, including my great-grandfather and his brothers. When they emigrated from Ireland around the time of the Civil War, English agents in Canada asked them to stay there when they paused to pick up supplies. "Not on your life," swore great-grandpops Russell. "I've lived under English rule long enough," he added as a parting shot and boarded a Lake Michigan steamer bound for Milwaukee.

From Beer City he hoofed it into the Holy Hill area, where other relatives from the Auld Sod had already settled. His experience is typical of that of many of the people still living there.

The town of Erin is a rural township with country roads named after Irish cities and provinces. Each year the old traditions are renewed with a hilarious **St. Patrick's Day Parade.** The floats, horses, and marchers travel about a 3.5-mile course through the countryside, beginning at the Town Hall (corner of Highways 167 and 83) and concluding at the corner of County Trunk K and Donegal Road. To give you an idea of the "seriousness" of the event, one recent parade featured My Wild Irish Nose, a float built like a giant green schnoz; a green llama; a hillbilly band made up of grandmothers; and similar silliness. The only orange you'll ever see on parade day is the color of Washington County trucks loaded with snow fences. For information call (262) 673-6226.

The Irish cemetery at K and Emerald Drive is crowded with Whelans, Fallons, Purtells, McGraths, O'Neills, Coffeys, Mahoneys, McConvilles, Sullivans, and Hagertys. The wind sighs off the hilltops as you drive from the unfenced graveyard along Emerald, another of the state's Rustic Roads.

Waukesha County

Old World Wisconsin, operated by the Historical Society of Wisconsin, is on the map when it comes to tourist attractions. Yet its ongoing displays, programs, and activities often are overlooked. That's a shame, because Old World is a great place to touch the living history of Wisconsin. More than 40 buildings from around the state, originally built by immigrant settlers, have been relocated to the rolling Kettle Moraine highlands. Old World calls itself "America's Largest Outdoor Museum of Rural Life."

A motorized tram takes visitors around the 576-acre site. You can get on or off at leisure to explore the farm sites and buildings dotting the landscape. I like the museum because each community is separated from the other, to preserve the national identity. Interpreters in the appropriate costumes demonstrate crafts and chores you'd find in a typical mid-19th-century household. There are plenty of cows, pigs, sheep, chickens, ducks, and other critters in the pastures and pens to keep up the interest of city kids.

Seasonal events help keep the Old World feeling on the appropriate track: spring plowing, summer planting, and autumn threshing with the era's appropriate horse-drawn equipment; Fourth of July oratory, parades, and band concerts. We've always found it fun in the winter to cross-country ski around the buildings and over the fields. Many of the structures are open for visiting, even when the snow is drifting around the doorway. Each offers homemade ethnic cookies or breads, plus hot cider or hot chocolate to ward off the cold.

The museum (262-594-6300; oldworldwisconsin.wisconsinhistory.org) is on Highway 67 outside the village of Eagle, about a half-hour drive south of I-94. It is open daily from May 1 to October 31 from 10 a.m. to 3 p.m. Admission for adults is $16, students/seniors are $14, children 5 to 17 are $9, and a family pass for $43 includes all-day tram transportation and an electronic tour guide.

The *Clausing Barn Restaurant* is an octagonal barn built in 1897. It is a cafeteria-style restaurant (262-594-6320; http://oldworldwisconsin.wisconsin history.org/Visit/Restaurant.aspx).

Adjacent to the museum are the 16,600 acres of the *Southern Kettle Moraine Forest,* with a drive that tests your skill as a motorist. The ridges and valleys throughout the region were created by Ice Age glaciers. Today's roads barely tame the landscape as they loop and swirl over the ridges.

Not far from the edge of the state forest is the Genesee Depot, home of famed theatrical couple Alfred Lunt and Lynn Fontanne. Driving into the main courtyard of the sprawling complex called *Ten Chimneys* brings alive their flamboyant stage era. Lunt, who died in 1977, and Fontanne, who died in 1983, furnished their house with antiques and interesting art objects.

Visitors can now either tour the 3-story main house, which consists of 18 rooms ($28), or explore the entire estate ($35). Hours are 10 a.m. to 4 p.m. Wed through Sun, May through mid-November (262-968-4110; www.tenchimneys .org).

Drive north from Eagle on Highway 67, cross I-94 on the overpass, and head into *Oconomowoc.* At the turn of the 20th century, the town was a popular resort for Chicago-area business tycoons and their families, who flocked to the numerous lakes dotting the vicinity. Their elegant mansions border Lac La Belle and line the streets leading away from the water. Contemporary Oconomowoc has outgrown its quaint stage and is now a bustling community surrounded by subdivisions. The main street, however, has several excellent galleries, antiques shops, and crafts stores that carry unusual items.

The *Fabric Gallery of Wisconsin,* 204 E. Summit Ave. (262-560-110; www.fabricgallerywi.com) has a creative team of experts who can help with custom furniture, window treatments, and interior accessories. The facility is closed Sun and Mon. The *Oconomowoc Gallery, Ltd.,* 157 E. Wisconsin Ave. (262-567-8123 or 800-494-2878), carries wildlife art, contemporary and traditional fine art, sculpture, vintage French posters, creative custom framing, and gifts. *A. C. Troyer Gallery,* 148 E. Wisconsin Ave., also has a wide variety of

Wisconsin on Ice

The **Kettle Moraine glacial areas** of southeastern Wisconsin are fabulous for the hiking and skiing opportunities. The state has some 46,000 acres of forestland with various forms of landscape created during the Ice Age. Wisconsin's ice sheets retreated only a mere 10,000 years ago. Among the most obvious landmarks are the **moraines.** These are hills or snakelike ridges marked by debris left when the glaciers retreated. In other words, they are a glacial garbage dump. One of the moraines in the region is 100 miles long and 300 feet high. The moraines that mark the most advanced position of the glaciers are called terminal moraines.

Drumlins are long ridges or oval-shaped hills formed by glacial drift.

Kames are steep, conical hills created when meltwater flowed into funnel-like holes in the ice. The water carried debris that piled up like sand in an hourglass. Some of Wisconsin's kames tower more than 100 feet above the surrounding flatlands.

Kettles are depressions in the ground, formed when blocks of ice that were buried by earth and rock eventually melted. The ground collapsed when the ice melted. Such hollows are now lakes, marshes, or small valleys.

Eskers are ridges of sand and gravel that were dumped by rivers flowing underneath a glacier.

fine art (262-354-0804). At 7:30 p.m. each Wed and Sat in June, July, and Aug at the City Beach Band Shell, the Oconomowoc American Legion Band a revs up a concert for the folks who come to the lake edge to listen. Bring your own lawn chair or blanket for a night outing. Sometimes bug spray is necessary, and dress accordingly for the weather.

We've always thought that the **Golden Mast Inn** (262-567-7047 or 800-232-8688; www.weissgerbers.com/goldenmast) has one of the best views in the state, having written about the place for *Wisconsin Trails* magazine. Owned by German restaurateurs Hans and Maria Weissgerber and sons Hans Jr. and Jack, the Golden Mast looks out over Okauchee Lake with its convoys of ducks and dozens of sailboats. The food matches the scenery, with loins and schnitzel as house specialties. The place is located on Lacy's Lane at Okauchee Lake, just off Highway 16 on Oconomowoc's east side. The restaurant is one of four the family owns in Waukesha County.

The **Olympia Resort & Conference Center** (800-558-9573 or 262-369-4999; http://olympiaresort.com) to the south of Oconomowoc is well known in southeastern Wisconsin as a great place for a comfortable rejuvenation. But the place is a secret to many outsiders. Massages, steam rooms, pools, facials, exercise classes, and meals help keep visitors trim and alert. We enjoy the eucalyptus room whenever we have a head cold; the pungent steam quickly clears our heads and soothes the lungs. Rates are reasonable.

The *Hawk's Inn,* 426 W. Wells St. (262-646-4794; www.hawksinn.org) in nearby Delafield was built in the 1840s as a stagecoach stop. It has been refurbished as a museum, open from May through Oct. Tours are from noon to 4 p.m. Sat.

County seat *Waukesha* has made strides to keep its downtown alive and interesting, not wanting to be caught in the all-too-often downward spiral of smaller towns. There are numerous interesting shops, including one with magician's supplies. A gazebo/bandstand, called the Silurian Springhouse, was built as a hub for the one-way streets, which zoom off in several directions. This makes it difficult for a downtown drive-through, especially if you are unfamiliar with the area. I'd suggest you park and walk.

Waukesha means "fox" in Potawatomi, the language of one of many tribes that lived here over the generations. There are several mounds, built by earlier Native Americans, on the front lawn of the refurbished Central Library. The mounds are the only remaining ones of dozens that had been around the county prior to settlement. Most of the others have been plowed up or built over in the years since whites came into the region.

The 50-plus mineral springs in and around Waukesha made it the center of the state's 19th-century spa trade. The regenerative effects of the water were supposedly discovered by Col. Richard Dunbar, a local landowner. The good gentleman was not feeling well while out for a stroll one afternoon and took several drinks from a spring he discovered on his jaunt. Dunbar then napped under a nearby tree and allegedly woke up cured of everything that ailed him. From then on, bathhouses and health facilities sprang up, touting the wonders of Waukesha's water.

Background on these old properties can be found at the *Waukesha County Historical Museum,* 101 W. Main St. (262-521-2859; www.waukesha countymuseum.org). The facility is open from 10 a.m. to 4:30 p.m. Tues through Sat. Admission is $6 for adults; $5 for seniors; students, $3; and free for kids 5 and under. The region's pioneer history is explored, along with the growth and development of Waukesha and its outlying areas. To see firsthand how the good old days really were, visit *Nashotah House,* 2777 Mission Rd. (414-646-6500; www.nashotah.edu), in nearby Nashotah. The complex is now an Episcopal seminary, but self-guided tours of its historic buildings are available when you make a reservation through the school's development office.

On the east side of town is the *Inn at Pine Terrace.* High on a hill overlooking Oconomowoc's lakes, the property is appropriately secluded and comfortable, with a great breakfast. The inn is located at 351 E. Lisbon Rd. (262-567-7463; www.innatpineterrace.com).

Waupaca County

Waupaca is a fantastic year-round getaway for anyone who loves the outdoors. The best-known attraction is the *Chain O'Lakes,* which consist of 22 interlocking, spring-fed lakes that range in size from 2.5 to 115 acres. The waterways—packed with fish, of course—are from 8 to 100 feet deep. The first settlers arrived in the area in 1849 to establish a flour mill to serve neighboring homesteaders. In honor of the earlier Native Americans who lived in the region, the new residents selected the name Waupaca, supposedly after a local tribal leader, Wa-Puka (meaning "watching"). Historians, however, claim the name was derived from *waubeck seba,* meaning "clear water."

Regardless of whence the name, the town of Waupaca knows how to have fun. In mid-June is the Strawberry Festival, followed on July 4 with Hometown Days. A Fall-O-Rama is held in mid-September. For details on events and activities, contact the Waupaca Area Chamber of Commerce, 221 S. Main St., Box 262, Waupaca 54981 (715-258-7343 or 888-417-4040; www.waupacaarea chamber.com).

Waupaca is home to *Hartman Creek State Park,* which includes the Whispering Pines picnic area. Located 5 miles west of town on Highway 54, the 1,320-acre park offers tent and RV camping (101 sites) and a group campground.

Glacial oak hills, lakes, and ponds offer a plethora of color-photo opportunities while you are hiking or biking. Contact the park offices (715-258-2372; www.dnr.wi.gov/org/land/parks/specific/hartman) for the latest information on wildlife discussions led by naturalists. Some 5 miles of the state's 1,000-mile Ice Age Trail system are also within the park boundaries. When cross-country skiing in the park, remember that the glaciers retreated from here a mere 10,000 years ago.

For a more "motorized" vacation stop in Waupaca County, *Iola* holds an annual *Old Car Show and Swap Meet* early each July. More than 2,500 show cars are displayed, with hundreds of pre-1983 vehicles up for sale. Call (715) 445-4000 (www.iolaoldcarshow.com). Admission is charged. Iola is located at the intersection of Highways 49 and 161. You can't miss the showgrounds—just follow the hundreds of bright posters and arrows leading to the site or pull the family sedan into a procession of flashy sporters that usually putt-putt around town during the show weekend. They'll get you to the right locale.

Winnebago County

The **Bergstrom-Mahler Museum** in **Neenah** has more than 1,500 glass paperweights on display as part of the Evangeline Bergstrom collection. The display features handmade weights from French, English, and American manufacturers dating back 100 years. The museum offers research facilities for other collectors by appointment. The library is filled with material, and there is a workroom in which to look over samples and talk with curators. The museum is located at 165 N. Park Ave. (920-751-4658; www.bergstrom-mahlermuseum .com). Admission is free.

The **Doty Cabin** on Webster and Lincoln in Neenah is a replica of the home of Wisconsin's second territorial governor, James Duane Doty. The building houses numerous pioneer artifacts, including many of the governor's own possessions. The cabin is open noon to 4 p.m. from mid-June to mid-August and Memorial Day and Labor Day weekends. Call the Neenah Parks and Recreation Department at (920) 751-4614 for more information. Admission is free.

Oshkosh, home of OshKosh B'Gosh, is also home of the world's largest event of its kind: the **Experimental Aircraft Association (EAA) AirVenture,** held at the end of July at Wittman Field. The event attracts upwards of 700,000 guests. Warbirds, mini-aircraft, gliders, and regular private planes jam the fields surrounding the airport. The EAA aviation center museum is located at 3000 Poberezny Dr. (920-426-4800; www.airventure.org), with hundreds of aircraft and accessories on display.

From Oshkosh drive northwest on Highway 110 to tiny Fremont, where some of the best cheese curds in Wisconsin can be found at the **Union Star Cheese Factory** (7742 County Rd. II; 920-836-2804; www.unionstarcheese .com). Non-Wisconsinites always wonder about the lumpy-looking curds, which make a delightfully squeaky sound when chewed. The curds are especially good with smoked catfish, crisp rye crackers, and freshly squeezed lemonade or a just-tapped beer. The factory is open Mon through Sat from 7 a.m. to 5 p.m., and Sun from 10:30 a.m. to 5 p.m.

Places to Stay in Eastern Wisconsin

APPLETON

Candlewood Inn
4525 W. College Ave.
(920) 739-8000
(866) 270-5110
www.candlewoodsuites
.com
Moderate
Has fully equipped kitchen,
television with DVD player,
and recliner for comfortable
reading ease.

Comfort Suites / Comfort Dome
3809 W. Wisconsin Ave.
(920) 730-3800
(800) 228-5150
fax (920) 730-9558
www.comfortsuites.com/
Wisconsin
Moderate
Book early and save;
located close to I-41 and
Highway 96 intersection for
easy on-off traveling.

Copperleaf Boutique Hotel
300 W. College Ave.
(920) 749-0303
www.copperleafhotel.com
Moderate
Perfect for romantic
getaways, especially in the
Copper King Room or the
Silver Whirlpool Suite.

Country Inn & Suites by Carlson
355 Fox River Dr.
(920) 830-9868
www.copperleafhotel.com

Moderate
Free Internet, airport
shuttle, and fitness center
to work off traveler fatigue.

Hampton Inn
350 Fox River Dr.
(920) 954-9211
(800) HAMPTON (426-
7866)
fax (920) 954-6514
http://hamptoninn.hilton
.com/Appleton
Moderate
Minutes from downtown
River Walk, with napping
follow-up on plush king-
size beds; free business
center, complimentary
breakfast, indoor pool for
afternoon splashing.

Residence Inn
310 Metro Dr.
(920) 954-0570
fax (920) 731-6343
www.marriott.com/hotels/
travel/atwri-residence-inn-
appleton
Moderate
Within walking distance
of Fox River Mall, with
complimentary *USA
Today* and *Appleton Post
Crescent* newspapers;
high-speed Internet service
for business and personal
use.

BAILEY'S HARBOR

Bailey's Harbor Yacht Club Resort
8151 Ridges Rd.
(920) 839-2336
(800) 927-2492
www.bhycr.com
Moderate to expensive
Located on 27 acres along
shore of Lake Michigan

with range of rooms,
including junior and 1- and
2-bedroom suites, plus
classic state room with
kitchenettes, sitting areas,
and patio.

Cedar Beach Inn
8006 State Highway 57
(920) 559-1877
Educates guests on
sustainability by purchasing
used bikes and lawn
chairs at garage sales
while recycling ones that
are no longer safe; 5 cozy
bedrooms; plus whirlpool.

CAMPBELLSPORT

Inn the Kettles
W977 Highway F
(920) 533-8602
www.bedbreakfasthome
.com/innthekettles
Moderate
Marvelous views of lake,
with nearby swimming,
hunting, fishing, boating,
downhill skiing, and
snowmobiling; or just stay
put and enjoy quiet time
away with significant other.

CLINTONVILLE

Clintonville Motel
297 S. Main St.
(715) 823-6565
www.travelwisconsin.com/
item_detail/Clintonville_
Motel.aspx
Moderate
Close to Bucholtz Park
on Highway 45 for quiet,
comfortable overnight.

Landmark Motel
5 N. Main St.
(715) 823-7899
(866) 830-6115 (toll free)
www.thelandmarkmotel
.com
Inexpensive
Continental breakfast
available for get-up-and-go;
refrigerators in all rooms,
free local calls, plus ironing
boards and irons; parking
for RVs and semis.

Kress Inn
300 Grant St.
(920) 403-5100
www.kressinn.com
Located on scenic St.
Norbert College campus,
free shuttle service to
Austin-Straubel Field
Airport; the Bemis
International Conference
Center is across the
street; next-door Abbey
Restaurant provides room
service; one dog allowed,
but let hotel know before
arrival.

DELAVAN

Allyn Mansion Inn
511 E. Walworth Ave.
(262) 728-9090
www.allynmansion.com
Moderate to expensive
A 3-room Queen
Anne/Eastlake mansion,
built by architect E.
Townsend Mix for the
Alexander Allyn family in
1885; 10 marble fireplaces,
gasoliers, and other original
features, plus loads of
Victorian-era antiques; wine
and cheese at 6 p.m. on
weekends.

EGG HARBOR

**The Alpine Inn &
Cottages**
7715 Alpine Rd.
(920) 868-3000
(888) 281-8128
www.alpineresort.com
Moderate to expensive
On shoreline of Egg
Harbor; 36-hole golf
course, basketball, pier;
daily, seasonal, and
weekly rates depending on
season.

EPHRAIM

Edgewater Resort
10040 Water St.
(920) 854-2734
www.edge-waterresort.com
Moderate
Private shoreline pier,
outdoor hot tub, and
pool; walking distance to
picturesque downtown;
famed for traditional fish
boil.

FISH CREEK

Parkwood Lodge
2775 Highway 42
(920) 868-2046
(800) 433-7592
www.parkwoodlodge.com
Moderate to expensive
Range of accommodations
from singles to family
suites; seasonal packages;
located near Peninsula
State Park and numerous
other Door County
attractions.

**Peninsula Park View
Resort**
3397 Highway 42
(920) 854-2633
(920) 363 4086
www.peninsulaparkview
.com
Moderate
Across the road from the
Highland Road entrance
into Peninsula State
Park; family-owned; cozy
and comfortable; Better
Business Bureau A+ rated
lodging.

GREEN BAY

AmericInn of Green Bay
2032 Velp Ave.
(920) 434-9790
www.americinn.com/hotels/
WI/GreenBayWest
Inexpensive to moderate
Fee Wi-Fi in all rooms
and common areas;
strategically located only 5
miles from Lambeau Field,
which makes this ideal for
Packers fans.

Bay Motel
1301 S. Military Ave.
(920) 494-3441
www.baymotelgreenbay
.com
Inexpensive to moderate
Pets welcome with a
deposit; 53 rooms just 1
mile from Lambeau Field,
so book this popular
caravansary early as
possible on Green Bay
Packers home dates;
home-style, comfort food in
the kitchen.

Quality Inn & Suites
321 S. Washington St.
(920) 437-8771
www.qualityinngreenbay
.com
Moderate
Located downtown; two dozen restaurants, pubs, and nightclubs within walking distance; in summer, strolling and bike along the Fox River Trail, reached across the street from the hotel; extended stay rates available if visiting the nearby Saint Vincent's Hospital, Bellin Hospital, Saint Mary's Hospital, or Aurora Bay Care Hospital.

St. Brendan's
234 S. Washington St.
(866) 604-7474
www.saintbrendansinn.com
Moderate to expensive
Inn's on-premise Irish pub has 15 imported beers on tap; outstanding Irish coffee; regular music; sister hotel to County Clare in Milwaukee; probably only hotel restaurant in the city offering shepherd's pie and "Grandma Flanigan's" Guinness pot roast.

Wingate Inn
2065 Airport Dr.
(920) 617-2000
www.wingatehotels.com/
GreenBay
Moderate
On the grounds of the Austin-Straubel International Airport, close to nearby offices and corporate parks; executive boardroom accommodates10 guests;

express check-in and check-out; in-room coffeemaker for early-rising convenience.

JANESVILLE

Best Western Janesville
Milton Avenue
(608) 756-4511
(800) 334-4271
www.bestwestern.com
Moderate
Large rooms and indoor pool under dome make it great for snowy wintertime; whirlpool, video game area.

Hampton Inn
2400 Fulton St.
(608) 754-4900
Moderate
www.hamptoninn.hilton
.com
Plush, king-size beds in some room make comfortable sleeping; special deals for AAA members.

KENOSHA

Harborside Inn & Kenosha Conference Center
5125 6th Ave.
(262) 658-3281
http://bestwestern
wisconsin.com
Moderate to expensive
On the shores of Lake Michigan, halfway between Milwaukee and Chicago; close to Kenosha attractions and businesses such as Jelly Belly® Center, Carthage College, University of Wisconsin–Parkside; free high-speed Internet.

Value Inn
7221 122nd Ave. (I-94, exit 344)
(262) 857-2622
www.valueinnmotel.com
Moderate
Easy access truck and bus parking; front desk is staffed 24 hours a day

MANITOWOC

Best Western Lakefront Hotel
101 Maritime Dr.
(Highway 42)
(920) 682-7000
(800) 654-5353
www.bestwestern.com
Moderate to expensive
Great base for fisherfolk, scuba divers, boaters, and hikers. Favorite Manitowoc attractions are not far away, including the Wisconsin Maritime Museum, Beernsten's Confectionary, the Capital Civic Center, and the Lincoln Zoo; business travelers are close to Busch Agricultural, Eck Industries, and the Manitowoc Company; pets welcome for small fee.

Birch Creek Inn
4626 Calumet Ave.
(920) 684-3374
(800) 424-6126
www.birchcreekinn.com
Moderate
Originally a 1940s motor inn, now totally redone with cozy and unique rooms; gay friendly.

SELECTED CHAMBERS OF COMMERCE

Algoma Chamber of Commerce
1226 Lake St.
Algoma 54201
(920) 487-2041
(800) 498-4888
www.algoma.org

Door County Chamber of Commerce
1015 Green Bay Rd.
Sturgeon Bay 54235
(920) 743-4456
(800) 52-RELAX (73529)
www.doorcounty.com

Fond du Lac Convention & Visitors Bureau
171 S. Pioneer Rd.
Fond du Lac 64935
(920) 923-3010
(800) 937-9123
www.fdl.com

Forward Janesville
51 S. Jackson
Janesville 53547-8008
(608) 757-3160
www.forwardjanesville.com

Fox Cities of Wisconsin Convention & Visitors Bureau
3433 W. College Ave.
Appleton 54914
(920) 734-3558
(800) 236-6673
www.foxcities.org

Green Bay Convention & Visitors Bureau
1901 S. Oneida St.
Green Bay 10596
(920) 494-9507
(888) 867-3342
www.greenbay.com

Kenosha Area Convention & Visitors Bureau
812 56th St.
Kenosha 53140-3735
(262) 654-7307
(800) 654-7309
www.kenoshacvb.com

Racine County Convention and Visitors Bureau
14015 Washington Ave.
Sturtevant 53177
(262) 884-6400
www.realracine.com

Sheboygan Area Convention and Visitors Bureau
621 S. 8th St.
Sheboygan 53081
(920) 457-9491
(800) 457-9497
www.sheboygan.org

RACINE

Racine Marriott
7111 Washington Ave.
(262) 886-6100
fax (414) 886-1048
www.marriott.com/Racine
Moderate

Five floors, 216 rooms, 6 suites; pets allowed; one concierge level; full-service business center; ask about the local restaurants that offer dinner delivery here.

SISTER BAY

County House Resort
715 N. Highland Rd.
(920) 854-4551
(800) 424-0041
fax (920) 854-9809
www.countryhouseresort
.com
Moderate

On 27 secluded, wooded acres on a rolling bluff with 1,100 feet of Green Bay shoreline, with rowboats, multispeed bikes, nature trail; comp coffee in lobby, free Wi-Fi.

STURGEON BAY

Bridgeport Resort
Business Highway 42/57
(920) 746-9919
(800) 671-9190
www.bridgeportresort.net
Moderate
Center of historic Sturgeon Bay; sauna, pool with waterfall; 2- and 3-bedroom suites, with each guest room featuring a whirlpool, a fireplace, and a complete kitchen.

WAUPACA

Green Fountain Inn
604 S. Main St.
(715) 258-5171
(800) 603-4600
www.greenfountaininn.com
Moderate
Bed-and-breakfast was private home dating from 1908 and renovated in 1994; plenty of beer and imported wines in Secret Garden Cafe.

Rustic Woods Campground
E2585 S. Wood Dr.
(715) 258-2442
www.rusticwoods
campground.com
Inexpensive
Grounds offers 150 seasonal campsites and 30 week/weekend sites, with bar and restaurant;

amenities include small lake for fishing, a game room, basketball court, volleyball court, and horseshoe pits.

Village Inn–Waupaca
1060 W. Fulton St.
(715) 258-8526
Moderate
www.reservation.magnuson
hotels.com
Convenience is primary here, with nearby Michaels Hospital, Riverside Hospital, Wisconsin Veterans Home, Expo Center, Thyssen Krup Foundry, and University of Wisconsin–Stevens Point.

Places to Eat in Eastern Wisconsin

ALGOMA

Breakwater
527 4th St.
(920) 487-3291
Inexpensive
Noted for family-style chicken dinner, and hamburgers also get raves; perfect stop before charter-boat fishing for salmon.

DE PERE

A's Restaurant & Music Cafe
112 N. Broadway
(920) 336-2277
www.asmusiccafe.com
Inexpensive to moderate
A's lives up to its name, with musical styles ranging from jazz and blues to

cabaret and rock on most Fridays and Saturdays; steaks very popular.

Pasquale's International Cafe
305 Main St.
(920) 336-3330
Inexpensive to moderate.
www.pasqualesintlcafe.net
Chicago-style Italian fare, including Italian beef, ravioli, pasta Alfredo, and ribs, plus mouthwatering corned beef; wall murals by local artist Cheryl Bowman, with scenes reminiscent of the World War II.

EGG HARBOR

Olde Stage Station Restaurant
7778 Egg Harbor Rd.
(Highway 42)
(920) 868-3247
Moderate
Said at one time to be an authentic, old-time stagecoach freight haulers' stop, now famous for pizzas; boasts having the largest selection of tap and bottled beers in Door County; late-night menu offered from 10 p.m. to midnight daily; be aware that Olde Stage is closed Tues and Wed during the winter.

Pelletier's Rest & Fish Boil, Fish Creek
4199 Main St.
(920) 868-3313
www.doorcountyfishboil
.com
Moderate
Get there early to watch the fish-boil process, fun

starts at 5 p.m. nightly during season; also has yummy homemade corned beef hash, eggs Benedict, and French crepes for breakfast.

ELKHART LAKE

Lola's on the Lake
The Osthoff Resort
Corner of Lake and East Streets
(920) 876-5840
Moderate to expensive
Panoramic views of Elkhart Lake, with an eclectic, award-winning menu and one of the area's most extensive wine lists; Lola's main entrance is located off of S. East Street in the resort complex.

Sal's Elkhart Inn
91 S. Lincoln St.
(920) 876-3133
www.elkhartlake.com
Moderate to expensive
Fine dining in an Old-World atmosphere, with building dating to 1886; known for its monster steaks; reservations suggested.

EPHRAIM

Old Post Office Restaurant
10040 Highway 42
(920) 854-4034
www.oldpostoffice-doorcounty.com/
Inexpensive to moderate
Yep, this was a post office in the old days when residents could only access the village via water; cupboard in the main room is stocked with homemade jellies, dish towels, and other gift items; reservations requested for the fish boils; freshly baked cherry pie worth walking on aqua to get to; these days; outdoor seating is available during good weather.

FISH CREEK

The Cookery
4135 Hwy. 42
(920) 868-3634
www.cookeryfishcreek.com
Moderate
Start with an artichoke tapenade, continue with whole wheat linguine with wild shrimp, and conclude with a fab dessert; wine bar happy hour 3 to 6 p.m. daily.

White Gull Inn
4225 Main St.
(920) 868-3517
(888) 364-9542
www.whitegullinn.com
Moderate
This historic inn and restaurant, established in 1896; eggs Benedict to die for, but also granola; traditional Door County fish boils Wednesday, Friday, Saturday, and Sunday evenings from May through October and on Friday evenings the rest of the year; some recipes handed down over the generations.

Wild Tomato Wood-fired Pizza and Grille
4023 WI 42
(920) 868-3095
www.wildtomatopizza.com
Inexpensive to moderate
Kid-rated five-star pizza place; gluten-free crusts available, just ask; excellent fresh produce; social mission emphasizes respect for all, so guests are in good hands; owner has degree in European pastries and chocolate.

GILLS ROCK

Shoreline Restaurant
12747 Highway 42
(920) 854-2950
Moderate to expensive
Home-style cooking with gourmet touch; open daily May through Oct and some days in late April and to mid-November, so call for hours.

GREEN BAY

Black & Tan Grille
130 E. Walnut St.
(920) 430-7700
www.blackandtangrille.com
Moderate
The Black & Tan, a heady mix of Guinness stout and beer, was the inspiration for the name; housed in the historic Bellin Building; specials include king salmon, yellowfin tuna, game and seafood dishes, and fresh seasonal vegetables.

Sideline Sports Bar & Grill
1049 Lombardi Access
(920) 496-5857
http://sidelinesportsbar greenbay.com
Inexpensive
Satisfy burger cravings and get sports here all the time,

on the road named after the Green Bay Packers' legendary coach, Vince Lombardi; 33 televisions tuned to games; dance club nightly offers music from '70s to '80s.

Titletown Brewery

200 Dousman St.
(920) 437-BEER (2337)
www.squareriggergalley
.com
Opened in 1996 in former offices of the Lake Shore Division of the Chicago & Northwestern Railway dating from 1893; good beer, too.

JACKSONPORT

Square Rigger Galley at Square Rigger Lodge

6332 Highway 57
(920) 823-2408
(866) 439-4578
www.squareriggergalley
.com
Moderate
Near Whitefish Dunes State Park; huge fish boils feature cherry pie a la mode, or substitute grilled chicken; kids' menu is also available.

JANESVILLE

Prime Quarter Steak House

1900 Humes Rd.
(East US 14)
(608) 752-1881
www.primequarter.com
Moderate to expensive
Management prizes USDA prime beef, husky baked potatoes, and salad bar presenting nearly two dozen items. For a

challenge, try finishing the 40-ounce steak in less than 1.25 hours; open daily.

Speakeasy Lounge and Restaurant

19 N. High St.
(608) 531-0012
www.gospeakeasylounge
.com
Moderate
Seasonal menus featuring best of Wisconsin's ag products; nightly specials but beware the colossal martini brownie sundae.

Wedges

2006 N. County Road East
(608) 757-1444
Moderate
Regular specials, including a Saturday-night prime rib dinner; karaoke nights and live music often scheduled.

KEWAUNEE

The Cork Restaurant & Pub

306 Ellis St.
(920) 388-2525
Inexpensive to moderate
Wide range of food and prices; a hopping place with occasional live music and always nightly specials; bread pudding with Irish whiskey sauce is always a safe bet; handicap accessible.

KOHLER

The American Club

Highland Drive
(920) 457-8000
(800) 344-2838
www.destinationkohler.com
Moderate to expensive

AAA Five Diamond resort with several award-winning restaurants on-site or on its nearby golf courses, including the showcase Immigrant Restaurant and more casual Horse and Plow; Craverie Chocolatier Cafe serves ice cream and sorbet in 14 flavors; numerous food and beverage festivals throughout the year, usually featuring major chefs.

MANITOWOC/TWO RIVERS

Courthouse Pub

1001 S. 8th St.
(920) 686-1166
www.courthousepub.com
Plays theme off the real courthouse across the street, with box lunches regularly sent over to presiding officials; seasonal menu; bar opens at 3:30 p.m., excellent microbrewery for finicky tasters.

Legend Larry's

921 S. 10th St.
(920) 458-WING (9464)
www.legendlarrys.com
Inexpensive
As they say here, "Eat chicken, dude" and try the wings; provides the office sauce for the US Chicken Wing Eating Championship; outlets also in Green Bay and Sheboygan.

Lighthouse Inn Hotel & Restaurant

1515 Memorial Dr.
(920) 793-4524
www.lhinn.com
Moderate to expensive

Deep-fried lake perch a house favorite; the Gull's Nest Lounge perfect while waiting for table or night on the town; open daily for breakfast, lunch, and dinner; look for the lighthouse.

Machut's Supper Club
3911 Lincoln Ave.
(920) 793-9432
www.machuts.com
Moderate
Opened in 1961, still a family place with monster kids' menu; dinner entrees and sandwich fare for range of offerings.

KENOSHA

Ashling on the Lough
125 56th St.
(262) 653-0500
http://ashlingonthelough
.com
Moderate
In heart of Kenosha's historic shopping district; pub trivia, live music, good pours of Guinness; sister pub to St. Brendan's Inn, Green Bay; County Clare in Milwaukee; and 52 Stafford, Plymouth.

Frank's Diner
508 58th St.
(262) 657-1017
www.franksdinerkenosha
.com
Inexpensive
Breakfast specials every weekend; place dates from 1926; always crowded but great fun, with plenty of personalities; good biker bar.

Mangia Restaurant
5717 Sheridan Rd.
(262) 652-4285
www.kenoshamangia.com
Moderate to expensive
Cozy, charming, and romantic; try the foccacia bread, the stracotta of veal; and the spaghettini del pescatore; four-star chef Tony Mantuano is James Beard winner.

The Wine Knot Bar & Bistro
5611 6th Ave.
(262) 653-9580
www.wine-knot.com
Moderate
Friendly neighborhood wine bar, plus lamb chops, filet mignon, seafood, and duck breast; live music, usually jazz, is a regular feature starting around 9:30 p.m.

OSHKOSH

The Granary Restaurant
50 W. 6th St.
(920) 233-3929
Moderate
Tucked into downtown Oshkosh, located in the historic old Schmidt building, within walking distance of Convention Center; ace steaks.

Robbins Restaurant
1810 Omro Rd.
(920) 235-2840
www.robbinsrestaurant
.com
Moderate
A taste of home cooking for seafood, chops, and steak; hosts local organizations' lunches and dinners—one of the main places in town to see and be seen.

PLEASANT PRAIRIE

Ray Radigan's
11712 Sheridan Rd.
(877) 606-9779
www.rayradigans.com
Moderate to expensive
Founded in 1933, still thinking and talking steak; closed Mon; takes reservations, which are highly recommended on weekends.

PLYMOUTH

Antoinette's
18 W. Mill St.
(920) 892-2161
www.antoinettesplymouth
.com
Inexpensive to moderate
Casual dining, fantastic chicken noodle soup, wraps and sandwiches, plus hearty pizza.

52 Stafford, An Irish Inn
52 Stafford St.
(920) 893-0552
www.52stafford.com
Moderate to expensive
The 1892 building listed on the National Register of Historic Places; true Irish feel; lots of live music, plus, Irish root soup, and Black Angus burgers; dinner and room packages are available; closed Sun.

RACINE

Chartroom Restaurant and Bar
209 Dodge St.
(262) 632-9901
www.thebigfork.com/
restaurants/chartroom-
racine-wi
Inexpensive to moderate
Live music; specializing
in fish; open daily, with
reservations recommended
for weekends.

DeRango's Pizza Palace
3840 Douglas Ave.
(262) 639-4112
www.derangos.com
Moderate
Hearty Italian foods such
as chicken parmigiana,
lasagna, manicotti (either
cheese or meat), rigatoni,
and other pasta.

Ivanhoe Pub & Eatery
231 Main St.
(262) 637-4730
www.theivanhoepub.com
Moderate
Historic pub building, now
renovated and upscale
yet still friendly and comfy;
helpful kilt-clad servers
always on hand.

Kewpee
520 Wisconsin Ave.
(262) 634-9601
www.kewpee.com
Inexpensive
Fast food with a smile,
dating back generations;
burgers, fries, and malts;
look at the doll exhibit
ranging around the room.

SHEBOYGAN

Brisco County Wood Grill
539 Riverfront Dr.
(920) 803-6915
http://briscocountywoodgrill
.com
Moderate
Black Angus beef slow
cooked over a charcoal
and applewood fire;
delicious margaritas and
mind-blowing mai tais,
well-stocked wine cellar of
imported, domestic, and
Wisconsin microbrews;
open daily.

City Streets Riverside Restaurant
712 Riverfront Dr.
(920) 457-9050
www.citystreetsriverside.net
Inexpensive to moderate
Short walk to the city's
dock and marina area;
features wonderfully piled-
high sandwiches, plus
refreshing soup and crisp
salads.

Field to Fork
511 S. 8th St.
(920) 694-0322
www.fieldtoforkcafe.com
Inexpensive Serves
breakfast and lunch with
ingredients from area
farmers; fair-traded coffee,
three soups made daily;
attached to Il Ritrovo
grocery store.

Trattoria Stefano
522 S. 8th St.
(920) 452-8455
www.trattoriastefano.com
Moderate
Founded in 1994; uses
local ingredients for
everything from appetizers
to desserts; all bread
baked in-house daily
for carb fix; extensive
collection of handpicked
Italian wine; closed Sun.

STURGEON BAY

Glas
67 E. Maple St.
(920) 743-5575
www.glascoffee.com
Inexpensive
Green roof filters rainwater
and creates a cooling effect
for the building (*glas* is
Gaelic word for "green");
also features organic
coffee, milk, tea, fruit and
vegetables.

Perry's Cherry Diner
230 Michigan St.
(920) 743-9910
http://cherrydiner
.homestead.com
Inexpensive to moderate
Re-created look and feel
of a traditional 1950s-style
casual eatery, but with
full contemporary menu
for breakfast, lunch, and
dinner; conclude a meal
with Perry's Cherry Pie;
groovy era music.

Scaturo's Baking Company & Cafe
19 Green Bay Rd.
(920) 746-8727
www.scaturos.com
Moderate
Door County icon, casual
eatery offering fresh-from-
the-oven pastries and
breads; open daily.

WATERTOWN

Mullen's Dairy Bar and Eatery
212 W. Main St.
(920) 261-4278
www.mullensdairy.com
Inexpensive
Family kickback place with wide tables and comfortable chairs, offering sandwiches and soups; hours vary during the seasons, so call ahead.

WAUPACA

Simpson's Restaurant
222 S. Main St.
(715) 258-8289
www.simpsonswaupaca.com
Moderate
Try the pickled mushrooms and remember to spread the grilled garlic on the warm, buttered bread; Friday fish among the best in the state.

Waupaca Woods Restaurant
815 Fulton St.
(715) 258-7400
http://waupacawoods restaurant.com
Inexpensive
Located behind the Waupaca Woods Mall; breakfasts geared to the working guy/gal who go for the grilled kielbasa sausage and two fresh eggs served with hash browns or American fries.

MILWAUKEE & ENVIRONS

The Potawatomi Indians called **Milwaukee** the "Gathering Place by the Waters," indicating a neutral ground. Tribes from around the Midwest could relax on the shaded banks of the Milwaukee and Menomonee Rivers and compare notes on buffalo hunting, just as today's conventioneers do about sales figures. Wild rice was thick in the swamps, and a large bluff separated the river valley from Lake Michigan. The hard, sandy beach was perfect for racing horses.

Of course, that was all before the first European settlers moved into the region. The explorer-priest Father Jacques Marquette pulled his canoe up on the riverbank in 1674 (a site now called Pere Marquette Park, located behind the Milwaukee County Historical Society, 910 N. Old World 3rd St.; 414-273-8288; www.milwaukeehistory.net). He was followed later by French trappers, who in turn were followed by Yankee land speculators. Next came the settlers. Soon the swamps were gone, the bluff was covered with houses, and the beach was a lakefront park.

Yet Milwaukee still retains that gathering-place image, proud of the potpourri of heritages that make up the roster of residents. Any visitor to the city finds that out immediately.

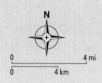

N

0   4 mi

0   4 km

Brown Deer

River Hills

Fox Point

Glendale

Whitefish Bay

Shorewood

Milwaukee R.

Wauwatosa

Milwaukee

Lake
Michigan

West Allis

MILWAUKEE
CO.

Greenfield

St.
Francis

Cudahy

Greendale

Hales Corners

South
Milwaukee

Franklin

Oak Creek

Ethnic festivals, parades, church events, lectures, exhibitions, folk fairs, and a host of other events celebrate Milwaukee's dozens of nationalities. And it's a city of neighborhoods. Sherman Park, Merrill Park, Bay View, Walker's Point, Harambee, and the others have their different housing and lifestyle flavors. About 1.5 million persons live in the metropolitan area consisting of Milwaukee and its immediate suburbs.

You should start a jaunt at *Visit Milwaukee,* 648 N. Plankinton Ave. (414-273-3950 or 800-231-0903; www.visitmilwaukee.org), for the latest in brochures and information on attractions and events. Another visitor information center is located at General Mitchell Field, 5300 S. Howell Ave. (414-273-3950). The *Historic Third Ward,* a revitalized district just south of downtown, even has a web page. Check in with them at www.historicthirdward.org. The page tells what is happening in the warren of art galleries, eateries, ad agencies, and shops that have mostly taken over from the truckers and warehousemen of yore.

In fact, warehouses in the old produce market there are being turned into upscale shops and bars.

However, the *Milwaukee Public Market,* 400 N. Water St., which opened with much fanfare in 2005, keeps alive that tradition of peddling fresh fruits and vegetables. The facility is open from 10 a.m. to 8 p.m. Mon through Fri, 8 a.m. to 7 p.m. Sat, and 10 a.m. to 6 p,m. Sun. Cedarburg Coffee and C. Adams Bakery there opens at 7 a.m. Mon through Fri for any early birds needing a caffeine hit and a sweet-tooth fix. Thief Wine offers late hours on Thurs, Fri and Sat. It's best to call to confirm times: (414) 277-7707 (or www.thiefwine.com). In addition to

MILWAUKEE & ENVIRONS' TOP HITS

Art Smart's Dart Mart & Juggling Emporium	Milwaukee Art Museum
	Milwaukee County parks
Boerner Botanical Garden	Milwaukee Public Museum
Derry Hegarty's Pub	
	Sharon Lynne Wilson Center for the Arts
Havenwoods Environmental Awareness Center	
	Summerfest
Kehr's Kandy Kitchen	Usinger's Sausage
Lakefront Festival of the Arts	Woodland Pattern Books
Larry's Brown Deer Market	

Book It

The *Milwaukee Public Library* and the *University of Wisconsin–Madison libraries* are the state's largest, each holding more than two million volumes. The *Wisconsin Historical Society* in Madison has a vast collection of publications and books on US history, as well as that of Wisconsin. Many of the libraries have interesting special collections, such as one dealing with dogs and dog training donated to the University of Wisconsin–Milwaukee in 1997.

There also excellent locally owned bookshops, as well as the big box stores. Hosting numerous author appearances are *Boswell Book Company,* 2559 N. Downer Ave. (414-332-1181; www.boswell.indiebound.com); *Next Chapter Bookshop,* 10976 N. Port Washington Rd. (262-241-6220; www.nextchapterbookshop.com); and *Mystery One Bookstore,* 2109 N. Prospect Ave. (414-347-4077; www.mystery one.com).

the quality corn and apples, the market offers breads, cheese, meats, fish, and a host of specialty food items. Tables are available for anyone wishing to forage the stalls and then eat. Regular cooking classes are offered on the second mezzanine, so you can get an answer to "Is Chilean sea bass really bass?" In addition to street parking and 1-hour free parking in the market's adjoining lot under the I-794 freeway (with the entrance on Water Street), the Historic Third Ward operates nearby parking garages at 212 N. Milwaukee St. and 225 E. Chicago St. Contact the market at (414) 336-1111 or www.milwaukeepublicmarket.org.

From here, you should be able to strike out to see the city, which has been going through a downtown building boom that includes a major-league auditorium, a theater district, office towers, and hotels. Visitors who haven't been to Milwaukee in several years often find themselves turned around because the old landmarks have given way to the new.

You don't have to hit the shopping malls for interesting rummaging. There are favorite places where a shopper can count on excellent service, ease in access, unique items, and knowledgeable clerks. To find your way around this world, there's the *Milwaukee Map Service,* 959 N. Mayfair Rd. (414-774-1300 or 800-525-3822; www.milwaukeemap.com). The place is a magnet for geography buffs. Just the thing for *Wisconsin Off the Beaten Path* readers is the series of Wisconsin regional maps that show every road in the state, as well as city street and county maps. The map store is open 8 a.m. to 6 p.m. Mon through Fri and 9 a.m. to 4 p.m. Sat. You can e-mail the facility 24 hours a day at customerservice@milwaukeemap.com.

You won't need a map to find *Chez Jacques* at 1030 S. 1st St. (414-672-1040; www.chezjacques.com). Just follow your appetite into the heart of the Walker's Point neighborhood, south of the Milwaukee River. Owned by Jacques Chaumet, who hails from near Marseilles, the restaurant/bistro has the best French cooking in the city. Many of his serving and chef staff are also French natives, adding to the authentic touch. Mussels, beef bourguignonne, flank steak and *pomme frites,* and *canard roti à l'orange* are only a few of the menu items. Favorites are the bouillabaisse and crème brûlée. Chaumet regularly features entertainment, such as singer Kevin Soucie, whose French songs have roots deep in the Gallic cafe tradition, and Robin Pleur, whose winsome renditions remind listeners of the famed Édith Piaf.

For an eclectic mix of shopping and eating, Milwaukeeans usually head to **Brady Street,** a historic boulevard that has gone through numerous changes

Public Transportation

Wisconsin is still served by a number of motor-coach companies. One of the best is **Wisconsin Coach Lines,** 1520 Arcadian Ave., Waukesha 53186 (262-542-8861; www.wisconsincoach.com). There is no need to drive an auto to O'Hare International Airport in Chicago. Milwaukee and other communities in southeastern Wisconsin are served by United Limo motor coaches, which whisk passengers to the proper terminal. This certainly beats worrying about long-term parking or rental-car return when flying in or out of the Windy City. Call (800) 833-5555 for ticket prices and information.

On the national scene there's always **Greyhound.** For fare and schedule details, call (800) 661-TRIP (8747) or visit online at www.greyhound.ca/en/contactus.aspx. There also are charter firms in many major cities. Look in the local yellow pages for specifics.

Badger Coach Lines provides fast, frequent service between Milwaukee and Madison's downtown, as well as to the University of Wisconsin campus. Call (877) 292-8259 or (414) 276-7490 in Milwaukee; or use www.badgerbus.com for fares, departures, and arrivals. The route runs along I-94.

Most large cities also have excellent bus transportation along their streets, despite budget slashing. This is generally an inexpensive, eye-opening way to look over a town from the ground level. A local bus can get you into the most off-the-beaten-path locales, in addition to hitting all the high points. Even if you aren't familiar with bus riding, hop on board. Such a ride is generally cheaper than a cab, and you'll see plenty more. Some cities have buses with bike racks.

In Milwaukee, the **Intermodal Station** at 433 W. St. Paul Ave. hosts both buses and Amtrak. For train ticketing, call Amtrak at (414) 272-5841 or (800) 872-7245 (www .amtrak.com). Trains also stop at La Crosse, Tomah, Wisconsin Dells, Portage, and Columbus. The Wisconsin Department of Transportation website (www.dot.wisconsin .gov/travel/rail/amtrak.htm) provides detailed information on train and motor-coach links to numerous state cities.

Tread the Boards

Milwaukee's theater scene includes more than 20 drama, dance, and musical companies in town, including *First Stage* (414-267-2929; www.firststage.org), which gears its performances to children; the *Milwaukee Repertory Theater* (414-224-2490; www.milwaukeerep.com); *Theatre Gigante* (414-961-6119; www.theatre gigante.org); *Skylight Opera* (414-291-7800; www.skylightopera.com); *Milwaukee Chamber Theater* (414-276-8842; www.chamber-theatre.com); *Florentine Opera* (414-291-5700; www.florentineopera.org); *Milwaukee Ballet* (414-643-7677; www.milwaukeeballet.org); *Wild Space Dance Company* (414-271-0307; www.wildspacedance.org); *Ko-Thi Dance Company* (414-273-0676; www.ko-thi.org); *Boulevard Theater* (414-744-5757; www.boulevardtheatre.com); and the *Next Act Theater* (414-278-7780, www.nextact.org). Irish, Native American, and African-American theater companies, as well as those at area colleges and universities keep the ethnic performance-world vibrant and alive.

over the generations. It was reborn again in the late 1990s, and some of the trendiest restaurants and coffeehouses in the city can be found here. For the latest in customized beds, there's Brady Street Futons, 1200 E. Brady St. (414-277-8088; www.bradystreetfutons.com). If you just need nails, drop in at Brady True Value Hardware, 1234 E. Brady St. (414-272-9919. Foxy chicks make their way to **Miss Groove Intimate**, 1224 E. Brady St. (414-298-1694; www.miss groove.com). **Glorioso Brothers Grocery**, 1011 E. Brady St. (414-272-0540; www.gloriosoitalianmarket.com), and **Sciortino's Bakery**, 1101 E. Brady St. (414-272-4623; www.petersciortinosbakery.com), keep memories alive of what was once primarily a neighborhood of Italian émigrés.

Get plenty of laughs at the **Comedy Cafe**, 615 E. Brady St. (414-271-5653; milwaukeescomedycafe.com), then head for the **Hi Hat Garage**, 1701 N. Arlington St. (at the corner of Brady and Arlington; 414-225-9330; www.hihatgarage.com), where the mixologists know almost everyone by name by the second beverage. The **Nomad World Pub**, 1401 E. Brady (414-224-8111;

AUTHORS' FAVORITES

Ethnic festivals	Milwaukee Public Museum
Historic Third Ward	Wisconsin State Fair
Milwaukee lakefront	

www.nomadworldpub.com), has a great summer street scene and a cozy inside ambience for winter. ***Regano's Roman Coin,*** 1004 E. Brady St. (414-278-9334; www.facebook.com/romancoin), has been in the same family for more than 30 years. The quintessential Milwaukee tavern was built in 1890. Not far off Brady is another landmark bar, ***Wolski's Tavern,*** at 1936 N. Pulaski St. (414-276-8130; www.wolskis.com). Bumper stickers proclaiming I CLOSED WOLSKI'S show up around the world. Enter if you dare. In 2008, the bar celebrated its 100th birthday.

Whenever we think we have too many balls in the air, when the job seems overwhelming, when things start falling out of the sky, a quick fix comes at ***Art Smart's Dart Mart & Juggling Emporium,*** 1695 N. Humboldt St. (414-273-3278; www.jugglingsupplies.net). There's a psychological boost gained just by walking through the front door and knowing that many customers here drop a lot of things while perfecting their techniques. Glass cases are packed with Native American clubs, torches, beanbags, balls, and other similar tools. Hanging on the walls are darts, dart boards, wind-up airplanes, and a host of other geegaws. And kites! There are dragons, birds, and jets . . . red kites, yellow kites, blue kites, and rainbow kites. You can't beat it.

If you are into sausage in the wurst way, ***Usinger's*** in downtown Milwaukee (1030 Old World 3rd St.; 414-276-9100; www.usinger.com) has pounds and pounds of the stuff made the good, old-fashioned German way. Many of the clerks speak with a hint of a home-country accent. Hungry crowds pack the company's showroom on Saturday morning for their weekly purchases,

Everything in Sports

For sports fans, Milwaukee has the ***Brewers*** baseball club (414-902-4000; www.milwaukee.brewers.mlb.com), which plays at Miller Park (414-383-3787; www.milwaukee.brewers.mlb.com/mil/ballpark) and the ***Admirals*** for hockey (414-227-0550; www.milwaukeeadmirals.com). Soccer fans enjoy the ***Wave*** (414-224-9283; www.milwaukeewave.com) for pro indoor matches. Hoops fanatics love the ***Bucks*** (414-227-0500; www.nba.com/bucks) and Marquette and the University of Wisconsin basketball teams.

Indoor sporting events are generally held in the ***Bradley Center,*** 1001 N. 4th St., in downtown Milwaukee. The hall is big enough to hold a 747 jetliner. Even the nosebleed section provides great views. Television monitors mounted over the central floor help with close-up action.

Of course, the ***Green Bay Packers*** football champs are always a television draw, especially after their 2010 Super Bowl win.

flemishlook

Milwaukee's city hall is considered one of the world's best examples of Flemish-Renaissance design. The building celebrated its centennial in 1995. Extensive renovations in the early-to-mid-2000s brought extra sparkle back to the building.

so go midweek if you can to avoid the rush.

Woodland Pattern (720 E. Locust St.; 414-263-5001; www.woodlandpattern .org) presents an extensive selection of small-press and poetry books, feminist literature, international kids' books, and avant-garde music. A large hall doubles as an art/photo gallery, as well as a stage for a regularly scheduled calendar of poetry readers and musicians.

Easter means chocolate eggs, jelly beans, and fairy food at *Kehr's Kandy Kitchen* (3533 W. Lisbon Ave.; 414-344-4305). The weeks before the holiday, the tiny white building overflows with folks hunting for the perfect nest-filler for their kids, grandchildren, or themselves. Chocolate-covered cherries, white almond chocolate . . . ah, that list is tempting. It's great to see the staff carrying on the Kehr family's candy-making traditions. The company also has a convenient downtown outlet in the Milwaukee Public Market (www.milwaukee publicmarket.org/vendor_kehrs.php).

The *Burke Candy Company* is another confectionary lover's heaven, located at 3840 N. Fratney St. (414-964-7327 or 888-287-5350; www.burkecandy .com). Husband-wife team Julia and Tim Burke make the best toffee this side of, well, how about the moon. Their toffee and turtles and truffles could make a song. The products are certified kosher and can be purchased at an outlet attached to their production facility.

Frozen Custard

Milwaukee's frozen-custard shops are known for variety, delicious smoothness, and simply yum-yum ambience. Since the Hintz/Percy resistance is low when it comes to custard, our cars make their own way up to any one of a dozen stands in town. (Several look as if they date from the 1950s, which they do.)

Here are our top picks:

Gilles, 7515 W. Blue Mound Rd., (414) 453-4875, www.gillesfrozencustard.com.

Kopps, 7631 W. Layton Ave., (414) 282-4312; 18880 W. Bluemound Rd., Brookfield, (262) 789-1393; and 5373 N. Port Washington Rd., (414) 961-2006; (414) 282-4080 is the "flavor line"; www.kopps.com.

Leon's, 3131 S. 27th St., (414) 383-1784, www.leonsfrozencustard.us.

The nightclub/restaurant scene along the aptly named Milwaukee Street and environs downtown brings together trendies, including many visitors such as pro athletic teams and theatrical troupes who are in town and looking for fun after a game or show. The beautiful people can be found at more than a dozen hot spots in the neighborhood. Among the liveliest are *Carnivor Steak House,* 724 N. Milwaukee St. (414-223-2200); the Latin-influenced *Cubanitas,* 728 N. Milwaukee St. (414-225-1760); *Ouzo Cafe* for upscale Greek food, 776 N. Milwaukee St. (414-272-6896); and *Zarletti,* 741 N. Milwaukee St. (414-225-0000). Both the bustling street-level bar and cafe and the rooftop patio getaway, called Zen on 7, at the *Hotel Metro,* at the corner of Milwaukee and Mason Streets (414-272-1937), are among the best places to meet and greet.

If hunger strikes you, Downer Avenue is the place to be. *Cafe Hollander,* at 2608 N. Downer Ave. (414-963-6366; www.cafehollander.com), is a 2-story cafe with an impressive selection of Dutch and Belgian beers. The breeze off the lake can be enjoyed in the summer months on the patio with outdoor seating. Enjoy salads, sandwiches, and even pizza at Cafe Hollander. West Siders take in another Hollander at 7677 W. State St. in Wauwatosa (414-475-6771).

Dream Dance Steak is considered one of the city's best restaurants, located in the Potawatomi Bingo Casino, 1721 W. Canal St. (414-847-7883). The menu features items such as filets, bacon-wrapped venison Rossini, and award-winning Wisconsin cheese.

Tony Sendik's (2643 N. Downer Ave.; 414-962-1600; www.sendiks.com) is one of the largest fresh fruit and vegetable stores in the city. Ready-made bouquets are conveniently located by the front door, for shoppers and lovers in a hurry. Tony Sendik also runs a fresh fish shop in his store, where you can get hot carryouts of fish and chips.

In the 4600 and 4700 blocks of Burleigh Street on the near West Side, several kosher stores sell lox, bagels, and all the trimmings for a hearty breakfast.

The neighborhood around the intersection of W. Lisbon and W. North

firsttypewriter

The typewriter was invented in Milwaukee by Christopher Latham Sholes, with the help of Carlos Glidden and Samuel W. Soule. The device, the first practical machine of its kind, was developed in 1867. You can see a plaque dedicated to Sholes and his typewriter at the corner of W. State Street and N. 4th Street, behind the Milwaukee Arena and across the street from the *Milwaukee Journal-Sentinel* offices, 333 W. State St.

Avenues, where they connect diagonally, has an intercontinental flair, with an Indian grocery, two Greek and several Asian restaurants, a Greek gift shop, a Black Muslim mosque, and a Chicago-style hot dog stand.

Milwaukeeans, like the army, travel on their stomachs. There must be more high-quality eating places in this city than almost anywhere else, such as the **Mason Street Grill** in the Pfister Hotel, 424 E. Wisconsin Ave. (414-298-3131; www.masonstreetgrill.com). The best skyline view of Milwaukee is from the **Blu Bar,** at the top of the Pfister (414-273-8222; www.thepfisterhotel.com/blu).

What would Milwaukee be without its pubs? Some neighborhoods have a bar on each corner, plus an extra one in the middle, all of which have their regular clientele. Water Street downtown near City Hall has a "strip" of bars and restaurants that attracts the upwardly mobile set. But there are some special ones where neckties are certainly unnecessary and a down-home feel without pretension is prevalent.

An Irish touch can be found at **Mo's Irish Pub,** 142 W. Wisconsin Ave. (414-272-0721), featuring live entertainment, a good pouring of pints, and pub grub such as burgers. Try the Irish food, including stew and boxty, a potato griddle cake.

Derry Hegarty's Pub, 5328 W. Bluemound Rd. (414-453-6088), is located across the street from both a church and a cemetery—to ensure that any good Irishman has a direct, fast pipeline from the pub to heaven. Hegarty, originally of Cork, was a fixture on Milwaukee's pub scene for more than two decades. Many is the wake, wedding, and fancy ball we've attended there in the back room. Local politicos use this watering hole as a site for major fund-raisers. It serves exceptionally good pub grub, as well. For years the place has been the appropriate gathering spot for Irish groups. The Ancient Order of Hibernians and the Emerald Society hold regular meetings in one of the downstairs rooms, usually the snug one with the fireplace that is a favorite for winter sessions. Hegarty once had a great blustering Saint Bernard named Muldoon who loved beer. The dog has long since gone to its reward, yet Derry Hegarty's stays on and on and on. You just can't keep a good Corkman down. Hegarty himself died in 2011 and is buried across the street in Calvary Cemetery, final resting place of many of Milwaukee's-finest Irish, from the victims of the *Lady Elgin* sinking in pre–Civil War days.

Caroline's Jazz Club, 401 S. 2nd St., (414) 221-9444, located in the old warehouse district south of downtown across the Milwaukee River, presents some of the best sounds in town. Owner Caroline Rubitsky brings in top national talent, as well as provides a venue for local musicians. Beginning around 8 p.m. on Tues, Wed, and Thurs, smaller combos perform, while Fri and Sat nights are more wild with larger ensembles on stage. You can't beat Rubitsky's martini specials either. For more jazz, **The Estate,** 2423 N. Murray Ave. (414-964-9923; www.jazzestate.com), is a classic hideaway on Milwaukee's

Have a Sip

Visitors often work up a thirst when visiting Milwaukee. One of the first questions always asked is "where are the breweries?" The title of Beer City, bestowed on Milwaukee years ago, is still strong. However, only Miller remains as the last of the big breweries in town. Filling in are several smaller boutique breweries and brewpubs such as the St. Francis Brewery and Restaurant, the Horney Goat Hideway & Brewery, Big Bay Brewing Company, Stonefly Brewing, and the Water Street Brewery. The best tours are held at the following locations.

Miller Brewing Company's Visitor Center is located at 4251 W. State St.; (414) 931-2337 or (800) 944-5483 (LITE); www.millercoors.com. Call for updated tour information. The plant is located on the city's North Side.

Sprecher Brewing Co. can be found at 701 W. Glendale Ave., Glendale; (414) 964-2739; www.sprecherbrewery.com. Tours are at 4 p.m. Fri; 1, 2, and 3 p.m. Sat and Sun. In addition to its beer, Sprecher brews a mean root beer. It is so creamy and smooth that connoisseurs consider it a gourmet soda.

Lakefront Brewery is a small neighborhood brewery whose reputation for producing quality brew is growing. This is truly off the beaten path. You'll find Lakefront in the city's Riverwest neighborhood, just west of the Milwaukee River. The plant and tasting room is at 1872 N. Commerce (414-372-8800; www.lakefrontbrewery.com). The Friday fish fry, complete with live polka music, is a must.

The Milwaukee Ale House is a 1997 addition to the Historic Third Ward. An old warehouse was converted into the pub, which includes a restaurant. The elder Hintz likes Louie's Demise, a strong ale named after a long-ago relative of one of the owners. The fellow allegedly died in a barroom brawl. At least that's the family legend. Look for the big kettles in the alehouse windows at 233 N. Water St. (414-226-2337).

Water Street Brewery, 1101 N. Water St. (414-272-1195; www.ale-house.com), is comfortable, with great brew made on-site.

To see how to make excellent spirits, such as vodka, rum, gin, grappa, and absinthe, drop in at *Great Lakes Distillery,* 616 W. Virginia St. on Milwaukee's Near South Side (414-431-8683; www.greatlakesdistillery.com). This is the first distillery in the city since Prohibition.

East Side that presents smooth music almost every night of the week. Call or check the website to see who is performing.

Food for the cultural soul can be had at the small galleries dotting the Milwaukee landscape. *Dean Jensen Gallery* (759 N. Water St.; 414-278-7100; www.deanjensengallery.com) was opened by the former art critic for the old *Milwaukee Sentinel* newspaper. Wildlife art specialists are featured in the *Landmarks Gallery* at 231 N. 76th St. (414-453-1620). The *Tory Folliard Gallery* is at 233 N. Milwaukee St. (414-273-7311; www.toryfolliard.com).

Discover the Museum

Discover **Discovery World,** tucked inside the soaring Pier Wisconsin complex, at 500 N. Harbor Dr., overlooking Lake Michigan. The grounds are between the Milwaukee Art Museum and the Henry W. Maier Lakefront Festival Park, site of Summerfest and the city's many ethnic festivals. It features hands-on exhibits, labs, and workshops for making everything from birdhouses to water blasters. Tickets are $16.95 for adults, $14.95 for seniors 60-plus, $12.95 for kids 3 to7, $9.95 for college students, and free for youngsters under 3. Group rates and memberships are also available. A replica Lakes schooner, the *Denis Sullivan,* is also berthed at the pier and is available for tours, educational cruises, and party charters. For more details call (414) 765-9966 or visit www.discoveryworld.org.

Augmenting the gallery scene are the dozens of art fairs around the community, ranging from the nationally renowned Lakefront **Festival of the Arts** (http://lfoa.mam.org) in June, held on the grounds of the lakefront Milwaukee Art Center, to neighborhood and college fairs. The weather is often cold and rainy for at least one day out of the three for the lakefront fest. Keep an umbrella handy, just in case. But since the fest is now held under tents, the iffy weather is less of a challenge.

Milwaukee also is known as Cream City, a legacy of the 19th century when many homes were constructed from a creamy-colored brick. The houses are easily spotted around town, with large concentrations in the older neighborhoods on the near South Side and along the lakefront. For a time, more workers labored in the brickyards than in the breweries, producing millions of bricks a year. For a peek at how the other half lives, take a jaunt along Lake Shore Drive (Highway 32 of Red Arrow Division fame) past Milwaukee's Gold Coast mansions. Some are of the distinctive Cream City brick.

Even with the dense population, pockets of calm are easily found in a city that cherishes its parks and open spaces. **Havenwoods Environmental Awareness Center** (6141 N. Hopkins St.; 414-527-0232; www.dnr.wi.gov/org/land/parks/specific/havenwoods/center.html) has a 240-acre tract of fields and woodlots with 3 miles of marked trails. The center is a 20-minute drive from the central city. Many schools utilize the site for nature-study programs. Another getaway is the lakefront bike trail that wanders north from near the Henry W. Maier Lakefront Festival Park into the suburbs. The roadway is located on an abandoned railroad right-of-way, so the pedaling is smooth and easy. The three climate-controlled domes of the **Mitchell Park Horticultural Conservatory** (524 S. Layton Ave.; 414-649-9800; www.milwaukeedomes.org) are well-known Milwaukee landmarks. Their floral displays, rain forest, and desert area are always worth a stop. **Boerner Botanical Garden** in Whitnall Park (9400 Boerner Dr.; 414-525-5650; www.boernerbotanicalgardens.org) is another site where the bloom is always on the rose. Lakeshore State Park (www.dnr.wi .gov/org/land/parks/specific/lakeshore) is an urban oasis just off downtown on the Lake Michigan shore near the Henry W. Maier Festival Grounds. There are walking paths, boat docks, and fishing access. For more details call (414) 274-4281. The park's lakeside multiuse trail connects to the Hank Aaron State Trail and the Oak Leaf Trail, expanding the reach of cyclists into the far corners of the community.

Growing Power (5500 W. Silver Spring; 414-527-1546; www.growing power.org) is a great place to learn how to use worms in gardening. Owner Will Allen knows all the tricks. For observing an urban fish farm and the use of aquaponics, check out **Sweetwater Organics,** 2151 S. Robinson Ave.; (414) 489-0425; www.sweetwater-organic.com.

Historic Milwaukee, 828 N. Broadway #110, has devised several tours around Milwaukee, taking in the Historic Third Ward, Yankee Hill, Brady Street, East Town, and other neighborhoods. Be ready to stop in at any of the mom-and-pop groceries and restaurants found along the way (414-277-7795; www.historicmilwaukee.org). Daily tours from mid-June through mid-October kick off at 10 a.m., covering "Downtown thru the Eras," starting at the Plankinton Building and ending at the Milwaukee Art Museum. Meet in front of the statue at the street level lobby in the Plankinton Building (shops of Grand Avenue), 161 W. Wisconsin Ave.

Milwaukee is noted as the City of Festivals. Kicking off the year are the **Scottish Highland Games** in Hart Park, 7300 Chestnut St., Wauwatosa (414-422-9235; www.milwaukeescottishfest.com). The events are held in early June, with sheepherding demonstrations by border collies, bagpiping, and caber tossing. The latter is akin to throwing telephone poles end over end. For more kilts, the **Wisconsin Highland Games** are held the last weekend in August at the Waukesha County Expo Center in Waukesha (414-517-5163; www.wisconsinscottish.org).

June seems to be the heavy party month in Milwaukee, because **Polish Fest** also occurs at this time. So limber up your polka legs and prepare for munching pierogies and *smacznego.* The festival's offices are at 6941 S. 68th St. in suburban Franklin (414-529-2140; www.polishfest.org).

The Big Daddy of Milwaukee's festivals is **Summerfest,** a musical blowout that runs for 11 days—from the end of June through the Fourth of July weekend. Summerfest, one of North America's largest music events, brings a wide range of music to the 85-acre lakefront festival show grounds. Upward of a million people regularly attend each year to watch the world-famous talent and knosh their way around the vendor booths. The fest office is at 200 N. Harbor Dr. (414-273-2680; www.summerfest.com).

For the French connection, **Bastille Days** can-can do a Francophile fun-fun job. For details contact the East Towne Association, 770 N. Jefferson St. (414-271-1416; www.easttown.com). The city's French celebration is on Cathedral Square downtown. There's loads of ooh-la-la and dang good music, from Cajun to Breton to the music of chanteuse Édith Piaf.

We love fireworks, so **Festa Italiana** is on the top of our summertime calendar for pyrotechnics. Every night of the 4-day fest offers skybound starbursts that rival a Vesuvius eruption. Suggestion: Take a blanket and a cooler of lemonade and hunker down on the grounds of the Milwaukee Art Museum, across the still waters of the Summerfest lagoon. When the displays go pop, bang, and whistle, you'll get the best views of anywhere in town. The reflections on the water are not to be missed. For entertainer information contact Italian Community Center, 631 W. Chicago Ave.; (414) 223-2808; www.festaitaliana.com.

German Fest is oompah-rich in yodeling, lederhosen, tuba playing, and *spanferkel* sandwiches. With a name like ours, the Hintz's make this a must-see almost every year. There is plenty to see: marching bands, the Milwaukee symphony, and heritage displays. Dog lovers howl over the antics of the Badger Dachshund Club and its ground-hugging Dachshund Derby. You can reach the fest offices at 8229 W. Capitol Dr. (414-464-9444). The fest is held in July.

To understand the wonders of the Black cultural experience, take in the **African World Festival,** one of the more exotic of Milwaukee's lakefront

Munchies at the Fair

The **Wisconsin State Fair,** at 8600 W. Greenfield Ave., West Allis, is held at the end of July and early August. The fair is more than 100 years old, showcasing geese, horses, cheese, tractors, and geegaws. Son Dan says, "I have my plan. Always head straight for the Family Center, where the Wisconsin Potato and Vegetable Growers Association serves up huge baked spuds. Best ever!" Elder Hintz suggests, "Ask for the cherry toppings at the ice-cream booth run by the 4-H." We both agree that this is "eat on the cheap" and the way to go. After munching our way around the displays presented by the honey producers, pork farmers, and beef council, we roll out the door and head to the midway for carnival fun and to meet old friends. That's after a look at the rabbits, chickens, geese, pigs, horses, and Holsteins, of course. Call (800) 884-FAIR or check out www.wistatefair.com. In his callow youth, elder Hintz used to work for Royal American Shows, one of the country's major railroad carnivals, and played the Wisconsin fair venue. So a repeat visit to the show grounds brings back memories.

African Heritage

Take in an African and African-American museum experience while in Milwaukee. The **Milwaukee Public Museum** has an extensive Africa wing, with full-size dioramas of lion hunters and other displays. Early museum managers often made visits back to Africa to study cultures and bring back artifacts. We've always come away knowing more about life in rain forests and deserts than we ever thought possible. The museum is located at 800 W. Wells St.; (414) 278-2702; www.mpm.edu. The facility is open 9 a.m. to 5 p.m. Mon through Sun. Admission is $14 for adults, $11 for seniors (60-plus), $11 for kids ages13 to 17, $10 for children 3 to 12, and free for kids 3 and younger.

The **Wisconsin Black Historical Society Museum,** at 2620 W. Center St., highlights black contributions to the state. It provides an intimate glance at the African-American cultural experience. Call (414) 372-7677 for hours or check http://wbhsm .homestead.com.

events. The opening ceremonies highlight rich African traditions where native priests bless the water and earth. The prayers are accompanied by dancers, drummers, and singers. This authenticity continues throughout the festival, covering everything from foods to music to displays. High points are peanut soup, blues, and gospel. Contact the fest at 275 W. Wisconsin Ave. (414-291-7959; www.africanworldfestival-milwaukee.com). The fest is held in early August.

For the quarter Irish in the Hintz clan lineage, **Milwaukee Irish Fest** offers an obvious Gaelic fix. The fest is the world's largest Irish music and cultural event, held annually on the third weekend in August. Irish Fest was around well before *Riverdance* and *Lord of the Dance,* the two hit Irish musical extravaganzas of the late 1990s. The show laid the groundwork in developing a fan system for such productions. The festival's headquarters are at 1532 Wauwatosa Ave. (414-476-3378; www.irishfest.com).

Neither of us has entered the jalapeño-pepper-eating competition at **Mexican Fiesta,** but it is fun to watch. That is only one of the many activities as the Latino community struts its stuff on the lakefront. They have loads of great music and good food each August. For details you can reach the Mexican Fiesta at 1220 W. Windlake Ave.; (414) 383-7066; www.mexicanfiesta.org.

Colorfully costumed Native American dancers of all ages from around the country and Canada compete for top awards at **Indian Summer.** This fest holds its nationally recognized powwow in early September and is a major stop on the pro tour for the fancy, grass, and women's pro dance tour. Son Dan's grandfather used to teach Native American dancing way, way back in the 1930s. So we always go to see the latest versions of traditional steps. While there, the elder Hintz indulges in his fancy for buffalo burgers and Indian tacos. And there's more. Skilled native demonstrators share their handiwork. Observe them, then stroll through the four traditional tribal villages and look over the various types of huts and tepees. Dan is an Indian Summer music fan, soaking up its range of folk, country, and pop performers—all of whom are Native Americans. The fest headquarters is located at 10809 W. Lincoln Ave. (414-774-7119; www.indiansummer.org). *Arab World Fest* offers the food and entertainment of the Middle East (888-912-2722; www.arabworldfest.com).

Later in the year, all this ethnicity is summed up at *Holiday Folk Fair,* one of the major events presented by the International Institute of Milwaukee County (1110 N. Old World 3rd St.; 414-225-6225; www.folkfair.org). Held at the Wisconsin State Fair Park in mid-November, the Folk Fair is a rainbow mix of all the city's international traditions: from Latvian to Serb, Hungarian to Latino. The fair is the oldest in the country, having started in the 1940s.

But if you wish to travel around the world to see some "wild life" without really leaving Wisconsin, the *Milwaukee County Zoological Gardens* is a worthwhile stop. Among the 2,500 growling, barking, munching, humming, swimming, sniffing, and snuffling animals are leopard sharks, Chinese alligators, King penguins, ring-tailed lemurs, gorillas, snow leopards, Bactrian camels, and Thomson's gazelles, plus almost another 300 species. The sprawling park is located at 10001 W. Blue Mound Rd. For information call (414) 771-5500. Be aware that the animal buildings close 15 minutes prior to zoo-closing time. Admissions and hours vary throughout the year, so check the zoo website at www.milwaukeezoo.org.

OTHER ATTRACTIONS WORTH SEEING

Allen-Bradley clock tower

Annunciation Greek Orthodox Church

Bradley Center

Brady Street pubs, shops, and restaurants

Grand Avenue shopping mall

Irish Cultural & Heritage Center

Joan of Arc Chapel, Marquette University campus

Milwaukee Antique Center

Pabst Mansion

St. Josephat Basilica

Slim McGinn's Pub

University of Wisconsin union

Take a Cruise

The Milwaukee skyline looks very different when viewed from one of the city's cruise boats. All are kid-safe, but you should still keep an eye on the tykes. Each vessel offers onboard beverages, restrooms, and plenty of deck space. Their well-informed crews can answer questions about the height of the harbor's Daniel Webster Hoan Memorial Bridge and how many freighters visit during the city's shipping season.

Boats leave from one of several docks in the downtown area. Call to confirm schedules. Tours are generally Apr through Oct. The **Iroquois** (414-332-4194; www .mkeboat.com) docks downtown on the Milwaukee River between the Michigan and Clybourn Street bridges. The **Edelweiss** (414-276-7447; www.edelweissboats .com), departs from 1110 N. Old World 3rd St.. Reservations are required for this boat, which serves lunch, brunch, and dinner. Many have been the comfortable summer hours when we lazed away a Saturday afternoon aboard a harbor cruise on one of these vessels. Shades of Captain Ahab and pirates and the *Queen Mary* . . . the dreams of a relaxing off-the-beaten-waterway expedition!

To learn more about Wisconsin's ethnic community, read one of the several publications focusing on old-world heritages. You can easily pick up a copy of any of these Milwaukee-based newspapers or magazines.

For a calendar of Gaelic goings-on in Wisconsin (as well as throughout the Midwest), the **Irish American Post** has it all. The monthly online magazine goes one step further with reportage by top journalists in Ireland, Britain, and the United States. Contact the *Post* at 1815 W. Brown Deer Rd.; (414) 352-1868; e-mail: editor@irishamericanpost.com. You can check out the website at www .irishamericanpost.com.

The **Spanish Journal** gives the latest on the state's Hispanic community. The *Journal* is published at 611 W. National Ave. (414-643-5683). Subscriptions are $45 for 52 weeks. An online edition is found at www.spanishjournal.com. Individual copies are free. The free **Italian Times** can be found throughout the city at newsstands and at the Italian Community Center. Call (414) 223-2807 or log on to www.iccmilwaukee.com/italian-times.html. The Italian Community Center is located at 631 E. Chicago Ave. **The Vremia,** a national Russian newspaper, 11520 N. Port Washington Rd., Mequon, is also available (262-241-1655).

For African-American coverage, secure free copies of the **Milwaukee Courier** (6310 N. Port Washington Rd.; 414-449-4860; http://milwaukeecourieronline .com) at various locales around the city. Another weekly covering the African-American scene is the **Milwaukee Times** (1938 N. Martin Luther King Jr. Dr.; 414-263-5088). Individual copies are free. Copies of all these publications can usually be picked up at area newsstands.

Cross-Country Ski Fun

In many places, even in big cities like Madison and Milwaukee, skiers almost can ski out their front doors. Literally. When we lived only a few blocks from Milwaukee's Lake Michigan, it was simple to walk over to the parks rimming the shoreline. After strapping on our skis, we could cut along the top of the bluffs overlooking the lake or swoop down the slopes to the flatlands. It was then easy to cruise along the edge of the ice-packed lake. The ice, by the way, groans and sighs on a winter evening. This produces an eerie symphony, especially with the percussion of surf booming up from under the floes.

Personally, I dig nighttime skiing, with a hint of falling snow reflected in the street-lights. This makes for a truly amazing adventure. It is a bracing way to get ready to turn in for the evening . . . after a cup of hot chocolate (and marshmallows!), of course. Then snuggle under the quilts!

Milwaukee's East Side hotels—such as the Park East, County Clare, Knickerbocker, Pfister, and Astor—are close to these lakeside parks. So bring skis on your next winter visit to town.

For fabulous skiing near the city, trails abound in the north and south units of the Kettle Moraine State Forest, about a 45- to 60-minute drive from downtown Milwaukee (www.dnr.wi.gov/ORG/LAND/parks/specific/kms).

The Wisconsin Jewish Chronicle is located at 1360 N. Prospect Ave. (414-390-5738; www.jewishchronicle.org). The weekly newspaper covers Jewish activities throughout Wisconsin.

Milwaukee is an easy city in which to drive, even with the seemingly endless construction. Laid out by straight-thinking German engineers, most roads run east to the lake or due north and south. Seldom does an out-of-town driver get lost, except possibly while trying to find an on-ramp to I-94. If you spend too much time spinning around blocks, ask a patrol officer (yes, Milwaukee still has beat cops) or hole up in a Milwaukee hotel.

Lodgings range from the grande dames of Milwaukee's accommodations world at *The Pfister Hotel* (424 E. Wisconsin Ave.; 414-273-8222 or 800-558-8222; www.thepfisterhotel.com) and her sister, the former Marc Plaza, now the *Hilton Milwaukee City Center* (509 W. Wisconsin Ave.; 414-271-7250; www.hilton.com/Milwaukee-WI), to the usual collection of chain motels.

The Pfister, a AAA Four Diamond award winner and member of Preferred Hotels and Resorts Worldwide, was named Hotel of the Year in 1991 by the Wisconsin Innkeepers Association. The venerable hotel celebrated its 100th anniversary in 1993.

You'll need such a rest stop after galloping around town.

Places to Stay in Milwaukee & Environs

Aloft Milwaukee-Downtown
1230 N. Old World 3rd St.
(414) 226-0122
www.alofthotels.com/
Milwaukee
Moderate
Trendy, upscale on northern fringe of downtown; easy walking to sports arena and area restaurants.

Ambassador Hotel
2308 W. Wisconsin Ave.
(414) 347-8400
www.ambassador
milwaukee.com
Moderate
Renovated retro hotel with modern amenities, line of Aveda personal care products, and his/hers bathrobes and slippers; old fur storage vault now houses extensive wine selection.

County Clare
1234 N. Astor St.
(414) 27-CLARE (272-5273)
www.countyclare-inn.com
Moderate to expensive
Irish pub and inn offering whirlpool baths and a three-star restaurant with some of best stew this side of the Shannon; great place to stay during Milwaukee Irish Fest.

Hilton Milwaukee City Center
509 W. Wisconsin Ave.
(414) 271-7250
(800) 558-7708
www.hilton.com/
Milwaukee-WI
Moderate
Gracious updated property circa 1920s, located across Wisconsin Avenue from the Convention Center, with water slides for kids and adults who wish they were kids again; on-site Milwaukee Chophouse known for steaks.

Hotel Metro
411 E. Mason St.
(414) 272-1937
www.hotelmetro.com
Moderate to expensive
Luxury space in heart of nightclub district, fab martinis in personalized downstairs bar; constantly earns travelers' rave reviews.

Iron Horse Hotel
500 W. Florida St.
(414) 374-4766
www.theironhorsehotel
.com
Moderate to expensive
Old-time warehouse transformed into boutique hotel; sleek, modern-style conveniences; outdoor lounge, The Yard, is popular meeting place during the warmer months; geared toward business travelers and even motorcycle enthusiasts.

Park East Hotel
916 E. State St.
(414) 276-8800
(800) 328-7275
www.parkeasthotel.com
Moderate
On city's trendy East Side, a block from Lake Michigan and close to restaurants and shops downtowns,

Places to Eat in Milwaukee & Environs

Bacchus-Bartolotta Restaurant
925 E. Wells St. (Cudahy Towers)
(414) 765-1166
www.bacchusmke.com
Expensive
Marvelous, award-winning entrees, extensive wine cellar, and numerous special events highlighting foods from mushrooms to, well, whatever is delicious.

Beans & Barley
1901 E. North Ave.
(414) 278-7878
www.beansandbarley.com
Inexpensive to moderate
Legendary eatery for vegetarians, an attentive waitstaff and fast turnaround, fruit smoothies to die for.

FOR MORE INFORMATION

Visit Milwaukee
Greater Milwaukee Convention &
Visitors Bureau
648 N. Plankinton Ave.
Milwaukee 53203
(414) 273-7222
(800) 554-1448
www.visitmilwaukee.org

Blue's Egg
317 N. 76th St.
(414) 299-3180
www.bluesegg.com
Inexpensive to moderate
Open for breakfast/lunch
on Upper West Side with
hash galore and dynamite
pancakes; uses locally
grown produce.

Cafe Calatrava
Milwaukee Art Museum
700 N. Art Museum Dr.
(414) 224-3831
www.mam.org
Moderate
Located in the Milwaukee
Art Museum; overlooks
Lake Michigan; noontime
business and art crowd;
monster kids' menu
includes PB&J sandwich of
creamy peanut butter and
natural fruit preserves.

Cafe Lulu
2265 S. Howell Ave.
(414) 294-5858
www.lulubayview.com
Inexpensive to moderate
Eclectic neighborhood
eatery drawing from entire
community, funky bar, and
rocking staff; got to have
the hummus and pita.

Clifford's Fine Food
10418 W. Forest Home
Ave.
(414) 425-6226
www.cliffordsfinefood.com
Moderate
Features sliced roast
sirloin, ham steak (with a
pineapple ring, of course),
schnitzel, baked flounder
stuffed with crabmeat, and
a seafood platter.

Comet Cafe
1947 N. Farwell Ave.
(414) 273-7677
www.thecometcafe.com
Inexpensive
Hangover heaven for
Sunday breakfasts, perfect
cups of coffee; luckily
located in East Side club
district.

Coquette Cafe
316 N. Milwaukee St.
(414) 291-2655
www.coquettecafe.com
Moderate
In Third Ward's Landmark
Building, south of
downtown; dessert menu
to die for; cooking classes
for all ranges of skills.

Distil
722 N. Milwaukee St.
(414) 220-9411
http://distilmilwaukee.com
Moderate to expensive
Wide-ranging Scotch
selection; small plates
perfect for pre/post theater;
where trendies meet to talk
and be seen.

Five O'Clock Steakhouse
2416 W. State St.
(414) 342-3553
www.fiveoclocksteakhouse
.com
Moderate
Since 1948, this
steakhouse has been a
timely Milwaukee culinary
fixture; the name came
about years ago when an
alarm clock behind the bar
rang at 5 p.m., signaling a
free round for guests.

Horny Goat Hideaway
2011 S. 1st St.
(414) 482-4628
www.hghideaway.com
Inexpensive to moderate
Pool tables, dart boards,
various game machines, a
50-seat industrial outdoor-
bar facility, flat-screen
high-def TVs, 68 umbrella
patio tables; lots and lots of
in-house beers.

Karl Ratzch's
320 E. Mason St.
(414) 276-2720
Moderate
Old World Teutonic feel,
best strudel outside
Hamburg, large range of
beers to accompanying
traditional German dishes.

Mader's German Restaurant
1037 N. Old World 3rd St.
(414) 271-3377
www.madersrestaurant
.com
Moderate to expensive
Traditional German-style
downtown fixtures with
sauerbraten, goulash,
schnitzel, roast goose
breast, sausages, and
dumplings as menu
staples; lots of good beer.

Libby Montana Bar and Grill
5616 W. Donges Bay Rd.
(262) 242-2232
http://libby-montana.com
Inexpensive to moderate
Indoor sport facilities
are packaged in a
3,000-square-foot-plus
Volleydome, plus three

volleyball courts; hummus
platter, pub burgers,
cheese dogs.

Maxie's Southern Comfort
6732 W. Fairview St.
(414) 292-3936
www.maxies.com
Moderate
Cajun- and Low Country–
style foods, easy access
from freeway on west side
of town near Wisconsin
State Fair Park.

Mayura
1598 N. Farwell Ave.
(414) 271-8200
www.mayuramilwaukee
.com
Inexpensive
Indian cooking and Indo-
Chinese foods at their
finest, plus it delivers.

The Packing House
900 E. Layton Ave.
(414) 483-5054
Moderate
Iconic South Side supper
club founded in 1973;
grilled pork medallions,
sirloins, real meat loaf.

Pitch's Lounge and Restaurant
1801 N. Humboldt Ave.
(414) 272-9313
www.pitchsribs.com
Moderate
Since 1942, the meanest
highball on the Lower East
Side; ribs galore with sauce
to match.

Poco Loco
4134 W. River Ln.
(414) 355-9550
www.pocolococantina.com
Inexpensive
Only 20 stools, but
great summertime patio;
Hispanic-style high-end
dishes such as lobster
quesadillas, also hearty
beans and rice.

The Rumpus Room
1030 N. Water St.
(414) 258-7885
Moderate
www.rumpusroommke.com
Well-situated near the
sports complex, Milwaukee
Repertory Theater, and
other entertainment
venues; 62-page beverage
list; meat loaf almost as
good as grandma's.

Safe House
779 Front St.
(414) 271-2007
www.safe-house.com
Moderate
Secretive, fun; a Milwaukee
tradition adjacent to
Milwaukee Press Club's
Newsroom Pub; hearty
grub, steaks; open daily for
lunch and dinner.

SPiN Milwaukee
233 E. Chicago St.
(414) 831-7746
www.milwaukee.spin
galactic.com
Moderate
Has 16,500-square-foot
table-tennis space with
maestro-like courts, plus
bar and restaurant area;
co-owned by actress
Susan Sarandon.

Trocadero Gastro Bar
1758 N. Water St.
(414) 272-0205
http://ztrocadero.com
Moderate to expensive
Reminiscent of a French
tabac, East Side favorite
with wine specials; perfect
summertime patio and
yummy brunch.

Ward's House of Prime
540 E. Mason St.
(414) 223-0135
http://wardshouseofprime
.com
Moderate to expensive
Front room is a happening
club, with quiet dining in
rear; noted for steak and
veal Marsala.

Index

A

A-1 Cab Company, 32
A. C. Troyer Gallery, 154
Aerio Club, 115
African heritage, 183
African World Festival, 182
Albany Wildlife Refuge, 20
Albee's Yacht Club Bar &
    Grill, 116
Alford Park, 133
Al-Gen Dinner Club,
    The, 117
Algoma, 134
Algoma Chamber of
    Commerce, 162
Allyn Mansion Inn, 160
Aloft Milwaukee
    Downtown, 187
Aloha Beach, 75
Alpine Inn & Cottages,
    The, 160
Al Ringling Theater, 69
Ambassador Hotel, 187
American Club, The,
    149, 165
American Players
    Theater, 26
Americinn, 75
AmericInn of Green
    Bay, 160
Amnicon Falls State
    Park, 92
Anderson Park, 133
Angel Museum, 146
Angler's Bar & Grill, 116
Annie's Garden Bed &
    Breakfast, 75
Antoinette's, 166
Apostle Islands, 86
Apostle Islands Cruise
    Service, 87
Apostle Islands Lighthouse
    Celebration, 86
Apple Affair, 106
Apple Festival, 4
Apple River, 104
Apple River
    Hideaway, 104

Appleton, 139
Arab World Fest, 184
Arbor House, An
    Environmental Inn, 75
Arlington University of
    Wisconsin Agricultural
    Research Station, 45
Art Fair off the Square,
    52, 54
Art Fair on the Green, 30
Artrageous Weekend, 63
Art Smart's Dart
    Mart & Juggling
    Emporium, 175
Ashippun, 125
Ashland, 81
Ashland County, 81
Ashling on the Lough, 166
A's Restaurant & Music
    Cafe, 163
A&W Portage, 77
A&W Restaurant, 115
Aztalan State Park, 130

B

Babcock, 73
Babcock Hall, 57
Bacchus-Barlotta
    Restaurant, 187
Badger Coach Lines, 173
Badger Mine and
    Museum, 35
Bad River Chippewa
    Reservation, 83
Bad River Lodge and
    Casino, 88
Bagley Hotel, 41
Bailey's Harbor Yacht
    Club Resort, 159
Bald Eagle Days, 9
bands, Wisconsin blues &
    rock, 13
Baraboo, 68
Barker's Island Inn, 118
Barron County, 85
Bashaw Lake Resort, 113
Basswood Nature Trail, 21
Bastille Days, 182

Bayfield, 87
Bayfield County, 86
Bay Motel, 160
Bay Shore Inn, 127
Beans & Barley, 187
Beaver Dam, 125
Bee Cab Company, 32
Beef-O-Rama, 101
Beerntsen's
    Confectionary, 136
Belle Isle Sports Bar &
    Grille, The, 116
Belmont, 33
Beloit, 146
Beloit College, 146
Belts Soft Serve, 78
Bendsten's Bakery, 142
Bennett House, 68
Bergstrom-Mahler
    Museum, 158
Bernard's Country Inn, 78
Best Western–American
    Heritage Inn, 113
Best Western
    Janesville, 161
Best Western Lakefront
    Hotel, 135, 161
Best Western Riverfront
    Hotel, 41
Bevans Lead Mine, 17
Big Apple Bagels, 74
Big Fish Bash, 125
Bike Northwoods Tour, 52
Bike Wisconsin, 52
Birch Creek Inn, 161
Blackhawk Memorial
    County Park, 34
Black Hawk Unit (Lower
    Wisconsin State
    Riverway), 65
Black River, 31
Black & Tan Grille, 164
Blossom Day Festival, 4
Blu Bar, 178
Bluebird Springs
    Recreation Area, 30
Blue Heron Bicycle
    Works, 32

Blue Heron Landing, 123
Blue Hills, 85
Blue Mounds, 60
Blue Mounds State
 Park, 61
Blues Bash, 29
Blue's Egg, 188
Bluff Trail, 10
Boerner Botanical
 Garden, 181
Bong Recreation Area, 133
books about
 Wisconsin, 15
Bosacki's Boat House, 116
Boscobel, 11
Boscobel Hotel, 11
Boswell Book
 Company, 172
Boulevard Theater, 174
Bradley Center, 175
Brady Street, 173
Breakwater, 163
Breakwater Cafe, 82
Brekke's Fireside
 Resort, 113
breweries, 179
Brickhouse BBQ, 77
Bridgeport Resort, 163
Brisco County Wood
 Grill, 167
Bristol Renaissance
 Faire, 133
Brown County, 121
Browntown–Cadiz Springs
 State Recreation
 Area, 21
Bruce Mound Ski Hill
 Resort, 113
Brule River, 92
Budget Bicycle Center &
 Bicycle Rental, 51
Burke Candy
 Company, 176
Burlington Liars Club, 144

C
Cafe Calatrava, 188
Cafe Carpe, 131
Cafe Hollander, 177
Cafe Lulu, 188
Caldron Falls Flowage, 99
Camp Five Lumberjack
 Train, 93
Candlewood Inn, 159

Canterbury Garden Cafe,
 Fennimore Rose
 Garden Florist &
 Chocolate Shoppe Ice
 Cream, 43
Capital Brewery and Beer
 Garden, 59
Capitol Christmas
 Pageant, 54
Capitol Square, 52
Captain Bill's, 59
Caribbean Club Resort, 75
Carnivor Steak House, 177
Caroline's Jazz Club, 178
Cassville, 10
Catfish Days, 29
Cave of the Mounds, 60
Cedar Beach Inn, 159
Center Avenue Antique
 Mall, 19
Center Color Festival, 9
Chain O'Lakes, 157
Chalet Landhaus Inn, 41
Chanticleer Inn, 115
Charles Nash Park, 133
Chartroom Restaurant and
 Bar, 167
Chattermark Trail, 21
Chazen Museum of Art, 55
Cheese Country Trail, 20
Cheese Curd Festival, 9
Chef's Corner Bistro, 151
Chequamegon National
 Forest, 83
Chequamegon National
 Forest Headquarters,
 US Department of
 Agriculture, 114
Chez Jacques, 172
Chili John's, 123
Chocolate Fest, 144
Chocolate Shoppe Ice
 Cream Company, 77
Christmas in Torpy
 Park, 86
Christopher Columbus
 Museum, 49
Circus World Museum, 69
City Streets Riverside
 Restaurant, 167
Civilian Conservation
 Corps Museum, 101
Clark County, 90

Clasen's European
 Bakery, 59
Clausing Barn
 Restaurant, 154
Clifford's Fine Food, 188
Clintonville Motel, 159
Club 13 Restaurant &
 Lounge, 117
Cohorama, 132
Columbia County, 45
Comedy Cafe, 174
Comet Cafe, 188
Comfort Inn
 (Minocqua), 112
Comfort Suites/Comfort
 Dome (Appleton), 159
Community Soup, 93
Cookery, The, 164
Cooksville, 146
Coon Creek, 31
Copa Cabana, 76
Copper Culture State
 Park, 100
Copperleaf Boutique
 Hotel, 159
Coquette Cafe, 188
Cork Restaurant & Pub,
 The, 165
Cottage Baker, the, 42
Council Grounds State
 Park, 96
Country Garden
 Restaurant, 5
Country House Motel &
 RV Park, 113
Country Inn & Suites by
 Carlson, 159
County Clare, 187
County House Resort, 162
Courthouse Pub, 165
Covered Bridge County
 Park, 140
Cranberry Festival, 9
Cranberry Highway, 73
Cravings Coffee & Ice
 Cream Co., 74
Crawford County, 4
Crex Meadows Wildlife
 Area, 90
Crivitz, 99
Cronometro, 51
cross-country skiing, 186
C-Side Inn, 88
Cubanitas, 177

Culver's, 44
Curley's Restaurant, 141
Czech-Slovak Community
    Festival, The, 40

D
dairy industry, 30
Dalles Restaurant &
    Lounge, 117
Dana's Beer Cheese Bar &
    Grill, 117
Dane County, 49
Dane County Farmers'
    Market, 52
Darlington Golf and
    Country Club Bar &
    Grill, 42
Dave's Falls, 99
Dean Jensen Gallery, 179
Delavan, 150
Del-Bar, The, 78
Dell Creek Wildlife
    Area, 67
Dells Boat Tours, 67
Denniston House, 10
De Pere, 121
Depot Bar & Grill, 7
DeRango's Pizza
    Palace, 167
Derry Hegarty's Pub, 178
Devil's Lake State Park, 64
Dickeyville Grotto, 17
Discovery World, 180
Distil, 188
Dockside Deli, 140
Dodge County, 123
Dodge County
    Fairgrounds, 125
Dodgeville, 23
Don Q Inn, 23
Doolittle's Pub &
    Eatery, 43
Door County, 126
Door County Chamber of
    Commerce, 162
Doty Cabin, 158
Doubletree by Hilton, 75
Douglas County, 90
Dream Dance Steak, 177
Driftless Area Art
    Festival, 9

E
Eagle Cave, 37

Eagle River, 107
Eagle River Chamber of
    Commerce Information
    Center, 114
Eagle River Guides
    Association, 107
Edelweiss, The, 185
Edgewater Hotel, The, 75
Edgewater Resort, 160
Eichelman Beach, 133
Eleven Gables Inn, 151
Ella's Deli & Ice Cream
    Parlor, 77
Ella's Restaurant, 78
Elroy-Sparta Trail, 36
Elvehjem, 55
Emma Carlin Hiking
    Trail, 129
Emy J's, 64
End of the Line
    Caboose, 151
Erin, 153
Essen Haus un Trinken
    Halle, 53
Estate, The, 178
Evansville, 146
Experimental Aircraft
    Association Air
    Venture, 125
Experimental Aircraft
    Association (EAA)
    AirVenture, 158

F
Fabric Gallery of
    Wisconsin, 154
Fairlawn Mansion and
    Museum, 91
Fall Polka Fest, 54
Fargo Mansion Inn, 129
Fawn Doe Rosa Park, 102
Fenmore Hills Motel, 13
Fennimore, 12
Fennimore Doll & Toy
    Museum, 13
Fennimore Railroad
    Historical Society
    Museum, 12
Festa Italiana, 182
Festival of the Arts, 180
Festival of the Trees, 125
Fiberglass Animals, Shapes
    & Trademarks, 37
Field to Fork, 167

52 Stafford, An Irish
    Inn, 166
Fireside Dinner
    Theatre, 131
First Capitol State Park
    and Museum, 33
Fischer Creek State
    Recreation Area, 137
fish boil, 127
Five O'Clock
    Steakhouse, 188
Flannery's Wilhelm Tell
    Bar & Restaurant, 43
Flint Ledge Trail, 10
Florentine Opera, 174
Folk Festival, 86
Folklore Village, 23
Fond du Lac, 129
Fond du Lac Convention
    & Visitors Bureau, 162
Fond du Lac County, 129
Forest County, 92
Forsyth Sunlite Resort, 113
Fort Atkinson, 130
Forward Janesville, 162
Fox Cities of Wisconsin
    Convention & Visitors
    Bureau, 162
Frank's Diner, 166
Freight House, The, 43
French Country Inn, 127
Friederick's Family
    Restaurant, 43
From the Ground Up
    Coffee House, 74
Frontier Bar, 93
frozen custard, 176
Fullers Family
    Restaurant, 118
Fun 'n the Sun Houseboat
    Rentals, 29

G
Galesville Public
    Library, 106
Geneva Inn, 151
Genoa National Fish
    Hatchery, 38
Geology Museum, 56
George W. Mead Wildlife
    Area, 64
German Fest, 182
giant concrete penny, 111
Gilles, 176

Gillett's Golden Oldies
    Restaurant, 43
Glacial Lake
    Cranberries, 73
Glarnerladen Antiques &
    Collectibles, 19
Glas, 167
Glidden, 85
Glidden District, 84
Glorioso Brothers
    Grocery, 174
Golden Eagle
    Restaurant, 115
Golden Inn, 118
Golden Mast Inn, 155
Golden Rondelle, 143
Goodman Park, 99
Goose Island
    Campground, 30
Governor Dodge State
    Park, 24
Governor, Office of
    the, 42
Granary Restaurant,
    The, 166
Grandad's Bluff, 27
Grand Army of the
    Republic (GAR)
    Hall, 11
Grand Army of the
    Republic Memorial
    Hall, 53
Grant County
    Courthouse, 13
Great Annual Bike
    Adventure Along the
    Wisconsin River, 52
Great Dane Pub &
    Brewing Company, 77
Greater Madison
    Convention & Visitors
    Bureau, 51, 76
Greater Milwaukee
    Convention & Visitors
    Bureau, 188
Great Lakes Distillery, 179
Great Lakes
    Dragaway, 145
Great Oak Trail, 21
Great River Roadhouse, 42
Great River State Trail, 32
Great Wolf Lodge, 68
Grecco's, 117

Green Bay Botanical
    Garden, 123
Green Bay Convention &
    Visitors Bureau, 162
Green Bay Packers Hall of
    Fame, 122
Green County, 18
Green County tours, 19
Green Fountain Inn, 163
Greunke's Restaurant, 115
Greyhound, 173
Growing Power, 181

H
Hampton Inn
    (Appleton), 159
Hampton Inn
    (Janesville), 161
Hanchett-Bartlett
    Homestead, 146
Harborside Inn & Kenosha
    Conference Center, 161
Harbor View
    Restaurant, 117
Harry's Restaurant, 140
Hartman Creek State
    Park, 157
Haunted Mansion, 68
Havenridge Nature
    Trail, 21
Havenwoods
    Environmental
    Awareness Center, 180
Hawk's Inn, 156
Hayward, 104
Hayward Area Chamber of
    Commerce, 114
Heartland Motel, The, 113
Henry S. Reuss Ice Age
    Visitor Center, 148
Henry Vilas Zoo Run
    Run, 54
Herschleb's Restaurant and
    Ice Cream Co., 74
Hiawatha State Park
    Trail, 88
Hiawatha Trailer
    Resort, 114
Hideout, The, 104
High Falls Dam, 98
HighGround Veterans
    Memorial Park, 90
Hi Hat Garage, 174
hiking snacks, 98

Hillside Home School, 25
Hilton Madison Monona
    Terrace, 75
Hilton Milwaukee City
    Center, 186, 187
Hintz's North Star
    Lodge, 109
Historic Arnold
    House, 106
Historic Cheesemaking
    Center, 19
Historic Indian Agency
    House, 47
Historic Milwaukee, 181
Historic Third Ward, 171
Hixon Forest Nature
    Center, 31
Hmong New Year
    Festival, 9
Hoard Historical Museum
    and Dairy Exhibit, 130
HoBo's Korner
    Kitchen, 141
hodag, 101
Holiday Acres, 113
Holiday Folk Fair, 184
Holiday Folk Fair, A, 30
Holiday Inn (Stevens
    Point), 75
Holy Hill, 152
Honey of a Museum, 125
Hoofbeat Ridge, 62
Horicon Marsh Days, 124
Horicon National Wildlife
    Refuge, 123
Horny Goat
    Hideaway, 189
Horse & Colt Show, 9
Hotel Chequamegon, 82
Hotel Mead, 76
Hotel Metro, 177, 187
Houdini Historical
    Center, 138
Houdini Plaza, 139
House of Embers, 78
House on the Rock, 24
House on the Rock
    Resort, 27
Hudson, 103

I
Ice Age Interpretive
    Center, 102

Ice Age National Scenic Trail, 20
Ice Rally Cross, 9
Indian Shores/Shoreline Inn, 114
Indian Summer, 183
Indian Trail, 10
Inn at Cedar Crossing, 127
Inn at Lonesome Hollow, 5
Inn at Pine Terrace, 156
Inn on Maple, 127
Inn the Kettles, 159
Inn Town Motel, 113
Intermodal Station (Milwaukee), 173
International Crane Foundation, 69
International Snowmobile Hall of Fame, 108
Iola, 157
Iowa County, 22
Irish American Post, 185
Iron County, 93
Iron Horse Hotel, 187
Iroquois, The, 185
Isthmus, The, 51
Italian Times, 185
Ivanhoe Pub & Eatery, 167

J
James Sheeley House Restaurant, 115
Jeffer's Black Angus, 44
Jefferson County, 129
Jim & Susan Bakke Art Studio, 56
John Michael Kohler Arts Center, 150
Journeys Marathon, 86
J. W. Jung Seed Company, 124

K
Kalahari, 68
Karibalis Restaurant, 116
Karl Ratzch's, 189
Kehr's Kandy Kitchen, 176
Kemper Center, 132
Kennedy Park, 134
Kenosha, 132
Kenosha Area Convention & Visitors Bureau, 162
Kenosha County, 132

Kenosha County History Center, 132
Keshena, 100
Kettle Moraine glacial areas, 155
Kettle Moraine State Forest—Northern Unit, 148
Kewaunee County, 134
Kewpee, 167
Key Magazine, 97
Kirsch's, 151
Kitchen at Arcadia Books, The, 44
Klondike Days, 86
Kohler, 149
Kohler Design Center, 148
Kopps, 176
Kreher Park and Beach, 81
Kress Inn, 160

L
La Crosse, 27
La Crosse Clock Company, 30
La Crosse Convention and Visitors Bureau, 44
La Crosse County, 27
La Crosse Queen, 28
La Crosse River, 31
La Crosse River Bicycle Trail, 32
La Crosse River Marsh, 31
Lafayette County, 33
Lafayette County Courthouse, 33
Lakefront Brewery, 179
Lake Geneva, 150
Lake Geneva Cruise Line, 152
Lake Mills, 129
Lake Mills–Aztalan Historical Society Museum, 130
Lake Superior Big Top Chautauqua, 89
Lakeview Restaurant, 43
Lancaster, 13
Landmark Motel, 160
Landmarks Gallery, 179
Langlade County, 94
Laona, 92
Larry the Logroller, 92
Larsen Bakery, 142

Laura Ingalls Wilder Children's Day, 125
Lawler Park, 7
Law Park, 50
Lazy L Tack & Trailers, 89
L. C. Wilmarth's Deep Water Grille & South Shore Brewery, 82
Legend Larry's, 165
Lehmann's Bakery, 142
Lehman's Supper Club, 117
Leon's, 176
Leopold Memorial Reserve, 48
L'Etoile Restaurant, 77
Libby Montana Bar and Grill, 189
Life O'Riley Farm & Guesthouse, 12
Lighthouse Inn Hotel & Restaurant, 165
Lincoln County, 96
Lincoln Park, 134
Lincoln-Tallman House, 147
Little Bohemia Resort, 110
Little Norway, 61
Little Quinness Falls Dam, 98
Little White Schoolhouse, 129
Lock and Dam No. 6, 105
Lock and Dam No. 8, 38
Logan Museum of Anthropology, 146
Log Cabin Family Restaurant, 76
Logger's Bar & Grill, 117
Lola's on the Lake, 164
loons, 108
Lumberjack World Championships, 105
lutfisk suppers, 103

M
Machinery Row Bicycles, 51
Machut's Supper Club, 166
MacKenzie Environmental Center, 47
Mad City Marathon, 53
Mad-City Ski Team, 50

Madeline Island Ferry
Line, 87
Madeline Lake Resort, 115
Mader's German
Restaurant, 189
Madison, 49
Madison Art Fair, 52
Madison Children's
Museum, 56
Madison Civic Center and
Gallery, 54
Madison Magazine, 51
Madison Mallards, 58
Madison Museum of
Contemporary Art, 57
Madison Parks
Department, 51
Madison's lakes, 50
Maggie's Restaurant, 115
Main Entrance, 44
Mama's Supper Club, 116
Mangia Restaurant, 166
Manitowish Waters, 110
Manitowoc, 135
Manitowoc County, 135
Mansion Hill Inn, 55, 75
Marathon County, 63
Mardi Gras, 29
Marinette County, 96
Mario's Pizza, 77
*Marquette University
Tribune,* 97
Marshfield, 71
Mason Street Grill, 178
Maxie's Southern
Comfort, 189
Mayura, 189
Mazomanie, 62
McClintock Park, 99
Menominee Camp Logging
Museum, 100
Menominee County, 100
Menominee Indian
Reservation, 100
Mercer, 94
Merrill, 96
Merrimac ferryboat, 66
Mexican Fiesta, 183
Mid-Continent Railway
Museum, 69
Midwest Horse Fair, 54
Milaeger's Inc.'s
greenhouses, 142
Milio's, 77

Miller Brewing Company's
Visitor Center, 179
Milwaukee, 169
Milwaukee Admirals, 175
Milwaukee Ale House,
The, 179
Milwaukee Ballet, 174
Milwaukee Brewers, 175
Milwaukee Bucks, 175
Milwaukee Chamber
Theater, 174
Milwaukee County
Zoological
Gardens, 184
Milwaukee Courier, 185
Milwaukee Irish Fest, 183
Milwaukee Map
Service, 172
Milwaukee Public
Library, 172
Milwaukee Public
Market, 171
Milwaukee Public
Museum, 183
Milwaukee Repertory
Theater, 174
Milwaukee Times, 185
Milwaukee Wave, 175
Mineral Point, 22
Minhas Craft Brewery, 18
Mining Museum, 17
Minocqua–Arbor Vitae–
Woodruff Chamber of
Commerce, 114
Miss Groove Intimate, 174
Mississippi Ridge Trail, 10
Mississippi Valley
Partners, 114
Mitchell Park Horticultural
Conservatory, 180
Mitchell's Hilltop Pub &
Grill, 78
Monk's Bar & Grill, 78
Monroe, 18
Monroe County, 36
Monticello, 19
Mo's Irish Pub, 178
mounds, Indian, 60
Mount Horeb, 60
Mount La Crosse, 30
Mullen's Dairy Bar and
Eatery, 131, 168
Mystery One
Bookstore, 172

N
Nashotah House, 156
National Fresh Water
Fishing Hall of
Fame, 104
National Mustard
Museum, 59
National Railroad
Museum, 122
National Society of the
Colonial Dames of
America, The, 48
Natural Bridge State
Park, 70
Neenah, 158
Nelson Dewey State
Park, 8
New Concord Inn of
Minocqua, 112
New Diggings, 35
New Glarus, 20
New Glarus Hotel, 42
New Glarus Hotel
Restaurant, 43
New Glarus Tourism
Bureau and Chamber
of Commerce, 44
New Glarus Woods, 20
Newport State Park, 128
Next Act Theater, 174
Next Chapter
Bookshop, 172
Nicolet National Forest, 92
Nine-Mile Recreation
Area, 63
Noah's Ark, 68
Nomad World Pub, 174
Nor Door Sport and
Cyclery, 110
Norman Rockwell
Exhibit, 71
Norskedalen, 41
Norske Nook, 116
North Country Trail, 84
Northern Great Lakes
Visitor Center, 85
North Freedom, 69
Northland College, 83
North Shore Recreation
Area, 100

O
Oconomowoc, 154

Oconomowoc Gallery, Ltd., 154
Oconto, 100
Oconto County, 100
Octagon House, 103
Octagon House Museum, 131
O&H Danish Bakery, 142
Oktoberfest, 9, 29
Oktoberfest Car Races, 9
Old Car Show and Swap Meet, 157
Olde Stage Station Restaurant, 163
Old Feed Mill, The, 77
Old Firehouse and Police Museum, 91
Old Immigrant Trail, 10
Old Middleton Centre, 59
Old Post Office Restaurant, 164
Old Rittenhouse Inn, 88
Old Wagon Road Trail, 10
Old World Wisconsin, 153
Olympia Resort & Conference Center, 155
Oneida County, 101
Oneida Nation Museum, 121
Open House Imports, 61
Ott To Recover, 19
Outagamie County, 137
Outagamie Museum and Houdini Historical Center, 138
Ouzo Cafe, 177
Over Our Head Players, 143
Overture Center for the Arts, 57
Owl Cafe, 43
Ozaukee County, 139

P
Packing House, The, 189
Pardeeville Watermelon Festival, 48
Park East Hotel, 187
Parkwood Lodge, 160
Pasquale's International Cafe, 163
Paul Bunyan's Northwoods Cook Shanty, 78, 116

Pea Patch Motel & Saloon, 116
Pebble House, 140
Pecatonica Trail, 33
Pelletier's Rest & Fish Boil, Fish Creek, 163
Pendarvis, 22
Peninsula Park View Resort, 160
Pennoyer Park, 133
Penny Parade, 111
Perrot State Park, 106
Perry's Cherry Diner, 167
Persen's Dunn Lake Resort, 114
Peshtigo, 96
Peshtigo Fire Museum, 96
Pfister Hotel, The, 186
Phillips, 102
Pier Natural Bridge Park, 37
Pine Hill Resort, 112
Pink Poodle, The, 55
Pioneer Village, 71, 139
Pitch's Lounge and Restaurant, 189
Platteville Chamber of Commerce, 44
Poco Loco, 189
Point Beach State Forest, 137
Pointe Resort & Club, 112
Point of Beginnings Heritage Area, 35
Polish Fest, 181
Polk County, 102
Polynesian Resort, 76
Popeye's Galley and Grog, 151
Popeye's Restaurant, 151
Portage, 47
Porte des Morts Passage, 127
"Port, the," 140
Port Washington, 139
Potosi, 15
Prairie du Chien, 5
Prairie du Chien Chamber of Commerce and Tourism Council, 44
Prairie du Chien Museum at Fort Crawford, 7
Prairie Performing Arts Center, 143

Prairie Villa Rendezvous, 6
Prentice Park and Campground, 81
Presque Isle Heritage Society Museum, 108
Price County, 102
Prime Quarter Steak House, 165
public libraries, 91

Q
Quality Inn & Suites (Green Bay), 161

R
Racine, 141
Racine Art Museum, 143
Racine County, 141
Racine County Convention and Visitors Bureau, 162
Racine Marriott, 162
Racine Theater Guild, 143
Radisson Hotel (La Crosse), 41
Ray Radigan's, 166
Recovery, The, 19
Red Rooster Cafe, 23
Regano's Roman Coin, 175
Reggae Sunsplash, 29
Residence Inn, 159
Rhinelander, 101
Rhinelander Cafe & Pub, 117
Rhinelander Logging Museum, 101
Rib Mountain, 63
Richland County, 37
Ripon, 129
River Edge Galleries, 137
Riveredge Nature Center, 138
Riverfest, 29
Riverside USA, 27
Riverstone Restaurant, 116
Riverview Terrace Cafe, 26
Road America, 148
Robbins Restaurant, 166
Robot World, 67
Rock Aqua Jays, 147
Rockbridge, 37
Rock County, 146
Rock Island, 128

Rock River Archaeological Society, 126
Rolling Meadows Sorghum Mill, 147
Rollo Jamison Museum, 17
Ron's Place, 132
Rotary Riverview Boardwalk, 148
Round Barn Restaurant & Lodge, 44
Rowe Pottery, 62
Rumpus Room, The, 189
Rusk County Information Center, 114
Rustic Roads, 95
Rustic Woods Campground, 163
Rutabaga Festival, 85

S
Safe House, 189
Sal's Elkhart Inn, 164
Sand Cave Trail, 10
Sandhill Outdoors Skills Center, 74
Sandhill State Wildlife Area, 73
Sauk County, 64
Sauk-Prairie Chamber of Commerce, 76
Sawdust Days, 125
Sawyer County, 104
Sayner, 109
Scaturo's Baking Company & Cafe, 167
Scheer's Lumberjack Show, 111
Schramm's Annual Great Bicycle Ride Across Wisconsin, 52
Sciortino's Bakery, 174
Scofield House, 127
Scottish Highland Games, 181
Scuttlebutts, 151
Sentinel Ridge Trail, 8, 10
Seven Mile Fair & Market Square, 143
Shack Smokehouse & Grill, the, 118
Shawano Area Chamber of Commerce, 114

Sheboygan Area Convention and Visitors Bureau, 162
Sheboygan County, 147
Sherry-Bett Historic Civil War Museum, 40
Shihata Orchard Fest, 9
Shopko Americafest, 125
Shoreline Restaurant, 164
Shotgun Eddy's Rafting, 95
Sideline Sports Bar & Grill, 164
Simmons Island Marina, 134
Simmons Island Park, 133
Simpson's Restaurant, 168
Sixth Street Theater, 143
Skylight Opera, 174
Sledfest Grass Drag Racing, 9
Smokeys, 116
Snowflake Annual Ski Jumping Tournament, 39
Snowflake Ski Club, 39
snowmobiling, 87
snowshoeing, 110
Snowshoe Weekend, 86
Snowshoe Workshop at Retzer Nature Center, 125
Soda Pops, 107
Solar Town Pharmacy, 5
Soldiers Grove, 4
Southern Kettle Moraine Forest, 154
Southport Marina, 134
Southport Park, 133
Spanish Journal, 185
Speakeasy Lounge and Restaurant, 165
SPiN Milwaukee, 189
Sprecher Brewing Co., 179
Spring Green Chamber of Commerce, 76
Spring Green General Store & Cafe, 44
Spurgeon Vineyards and Winery, 12
Square Rigger Galley at Square Rigger Lodge, 165
SS *Edmund Fitzgerald,* 89
SS *Meteor,* 91

St. Brendan's, 161
St. Charles Borromeo Church, 11
St. Croix County, 103
St. Croix Railroad, 103
Stevens Point Area Convention & Visitors Bureau, 76
Steve's Pizza Palace, 43
St. Feriole Island, 7
St. John Mine, 16
Stockyard H&L Cattle Co., 89
Stonefield Village, 8
Stora Enso, 71
St. Patrick's Day Parade, 153
Sturgeon Bay, 126
Sugar River Trail, 20
Summerfest, 181
Sun Prairie, 63
Sun Prairie Library and Museum, 63
Sunset Riding Stables, 31
Superior, 90
Svoboda Industries, 135
Swanberg's Bavarian Inn, 116
Sweetwater Organics, 181
Swiss Aire Motel, 42
Swiss historical village, 22

T
Taliesin, 25
Tall Timbers Resort, 114
Taste of Madison, 53
Taste of the Dells, 54
Ten Chimneys, 154
Tendick Nature Park, 141
Tenuta's Delicatessen and Liquors, 134
theater (Milwaukee), 174
Theatre Gigante, 174
Thirsty Pagan Brewing Company, 118
Three G's Resort, 113
Three Rivers Lodge, Radisson Hotel, 43
Timbavati Wildlife Park, 68
Timm's Hill, 102
Titletown Brewery, 165
Tony Sendik's, 177
Tory Folliard Gallery, 179

Town & Country
Jamboree, 9
Towne House
Restaurant, 42
Trattoria Stefano, 167
Traxler Park, 147
Trempealeau County, 105
Trempealeau Hotel, 105
Trempealeau National
Wildlife Refuge, 106
Trillium, 38
Trocadero Gastro Bar, 190
Turtle-Flambeau
Flowage, 94
Twelve Foot Falls, 99
Twin Bridge Park, 98
Twin Bridge Resort and
Supper Club, 99
Tyrol Ski Basin, 61

U
Union Star Cheese
Factory, 158
University of Wisconsin–
Madison libraries, 172
*University of Wisconsin–
Milwaukee Post,* 97
Upper Mississippi Wildlife
and Fish Refuge, 8
Usinger's, 175
US Watermelon
Speed-Eating
and Seed-Spitting
Championships, 48

V
Valhalla Recreation
Area, 88
Value Inn, 161
Vernon County, 38
Veterans' Memorial
Park, 98
Victorian Swan on Water,
A, 75
Vilas County, 107
Vilas County Historical
Museum, 109
Village Inn–Waupaca, 163
Village Pizzeria of
Amery, 115
Villa Louis, 5
Viola Horse and Colt
Show, 40
Visit Milwaukee, 171

Von Stiehl Winery, 134
Voyageur Inn, 71
Vremia, The, 185

W
Walleye Weekend,
125, 129
Walnut Springs Trail, 10
Walnut Trail, 21
Walworth County, 150
Ward's House of
Prime, 190
Warren J. Taylor Sunken
Garden, 134
Washburn County, 112
Washington County, 152
Washington Island, 128
Water Street Brewery, 179
Waukesha, 156
Waukesha County, 153
Waukesha County
Historical Museum, 156
Waupaca, 157
Waupaca Area Chamber
of Commerce, 114
Waupaca County, 157
Waupaca Woods
Restaurant, 168
Wausau, 63
Wausau/Central Wisconsin
Convention & Visitors
Council, 76
Wax World of the
Stars, 68
Weber's Farm Store, 72
Wedges, 165
Wedl's Hamburger and Ice
Cream Parlor, 132
Wehmhoff Woodland
Preserve, 145
Westby House Inn and
Restaurant, 39
Westby House Victorian
Inn & Restaurant, 42
West Salem, 32
Whistling Straits, 150
White Gull Inn, 127, 164
White Lace Inn, 127
White Pillars, 122
Whitewater Lake
Recreation Area, 150
WI Futurity Saddlebred
Horse Festival, 54

Wildcat Mountain State
Park, 39
Wilderness Waterpark
Resort, 68
Wild Rice Restaurant, 115
Wild Space Dance
Company, 174
Wild Tomato Wood-fired
Pizza and Grille, 164
Wilhelm Tell Supper
Club, 22
William D. Hoard, 30
Willy Street Co-op, 55
Wilson Schoolhouse
Inn, 41
Wind Point
Lighthouse, 142
Windsor Food &
Spirits, 44
Wine Knot Bar & Bistro,
the, 166
Wingate Inn, 161
Wingspread, 144
Winnebago County, 158
Wisconsin Badger, 97
Wisconsin Black Historical
Society Museum, 183
Wisconsin Capitol
building, 53
Wisconsin Chamber
Orchestra, 52
Wisconsin Cheese Makers
Association, 58
Wisconsin Coach
Lines, 173
Wisconsin Concrete
Park, 102
Wisconsin curiosities, 111
Wisconsin Dells, 66
Wisconsin Dells Visitor &
Convention Bureau, 68
Wisconsin Department of
Agriculture, 58
Wisconsin Department of
Tourism, 42
*Wisconsin Heritage
Traveler, The,* 28
Wisconsin Highland
Games, 181
Wisconsin High School
Rodeo Association
Championships, 37
Wisconsin Historical
Museum, 56

Wisconsin Historical
Society, 172
*Wisconsin Jewish
Chronicle, The,* 186
Wisconsin Maritime
Museum, 135
Wisconsin Public
Radio, 58
Wisconsin Rapids, 71
Wisconsin Rapids
Convention & Visitors
Bureau, 76
Wisconsin Restaurant
Association, 57
Wisconsin State Fair, 182
Wisconsin Trails, 97
Wisconsin Veterans
Museum, 56
Wolff's Log Cabin, 117
Wolf River Lodge, 95

Wollersheim Winery, 61
Wollersheim Winery Open
House, 54
Wollers Shoreview Supper
Club, 115
Wolski's Tavern, 175
Wood County, 71
Wood County Park
System, 74
Woodland Pattern, 176
Woodruff, 110
World Championship
Snowmobile
Derby, 109
World Dairy Expo, 54
World's Largest
Grandfather Clock, 134
World's Largest One-Day
Outdoor Fish Fry, 140

World's Largest
Warm-Water Fish
Hatchery, 112
Wright, Frank Lloyd,
25, 26
Wyalusing State Park,
8, 10
Wyoming Valley
School, 26

Y
Yellowstone Lake State
Park, 34

Z
Zarletti, 177
Zippy's Brass Rail, 43